Public and Private in Natural
Resource Governance

To young scholars in Germany – may they
eventually get the independence they deserve.

Public and Private in Natural Resource Governance

A False Dichotomy?

Edited by Thomas Sikor

from Routledge

First published by Earthscan in the UK and USA in 2008

For a full list of publications please contact:
Earthscan
2 Park Square, Milton Park, Abingdon, Oxfordshire OX14 4RN
711 Third Avenue, New York, NY 10017

First issued in paperback 2016

Earthscan is an imprint of the Taylor & Francis Group, an informa business

Notices
Practitioners and researchers must always rely on their own experience and knowledge in evaluating and using any information, methods, compounds, or experiments described herein. In using such information or methods they should be mindful of their own safety and the safety of others, including parties for whom they have a professional responsibility.

Product or corporate names may be trademarks or registered trademarks, and are used only for identification and explanation without intent to infringe.

Typeset by Domex e-Data Pvt. Ltd, India
Cover design by Susanne Harris

A catalogue record for this book is available from the British Library

Library of Congress Cataloging-in-Publication Data

Public and private in natural resource governance : a false dichotomy? / edited by Thomas Sikor.
   p. cm.
  Includes index.
  ISBN-13: 978-1-84407-525-6 (hbk.)
  1. Natural resources–Co-management. I. Sikor, Thomas.
  HC85.P83 2008
  333.7–dc22   2008001738

ISBN 13 : 978-1-138-99696-0 (pbk)
ISBN 13 : 978-1-84407-525-6 (hbk)

Contents

PART I – PUBLICS

PART II – PUBLIC–PRIVATE HYBRIDS

PART III – 'PRIVATES'

PART IV – VISIONS FOR A SUSTAINABLE FUTURE

List of Figures and Tables

FIGURES

TABLES

List of Contributors

Eva Barlösius is professor of sociology at the Institute for Sociology and Social Psychology of Leibniz University, Hannover in Germany. She works in the fields of rural sociology, sociology of food and sociological theory.
Email: eva.barloesius@uni-due.de

Oliver Bens is a geopedologist and head of the Staff Scientific Executive Board of GeoForschungsZentrum Potsdam in Germany. His research focuses on the development and properties of soils in the context of landscape formation processes.
Email: bens@gfz-potsdam.de

Reinhard F. Hüttl is professor of soil protection and recultivation at Brandenburg University of Technology, Cottbus, and Chair of the Executive Board of GeoForschungsZentrum Potsdam, both in Germany.
Email: huettl@gfz-potsdam.de

Ramses Iwan has been a field researcher at the Center for International Forestry Research (CIFOR) since 2001. He is a member of Setulang Village in Malinau, East Kalimantan, Indonesia.
Email: r.iwan@cgiar.org

Daniela Kleinschmit conducts research on resource governance at Göttingen University, Germany. She coordinates a group of young scientists, supervises PhD students and teaches students in MSc programmes.
Email: dkrumla@gwdg.de

Max Krott holds a chair for forest and nature conservation policy at Göttingen University, Germany. He sits on the executive board of the International Union of Forest Research Organizations and is editor-in-chief of *Forest Policy and Economics*.
Email: mkrott@gwdg.de

Godwin Limberg has been a researcher at CIFOR since 2001. He has worked with forest communities in Malinau, East Kalimantan (Indonesia) on participatory processes in decision making.
Email: g.limberg@cgiar.org

Moira Moeliono has been a researcher at CIFOR since 2001. She looks at national–local policy linkages, policy learning at the local level and community natural resource management.
Email: m.moeliono@cgiar.org

Tim O'Riordan is emeritus professor of environmental sciences at the University of East Anglia, UK. He is a member of the UK Sustainable Development Commission, and is active in designing river catchments and coastal areas for sustainability.
Email: t.riordan@uea.ac.uk

Marianne Penker is professor for sustainable economic development at the University of Natural Resources and Applied Life Sciences Vienna, Austria. Her interests include rural development, rural governance, ageing societies and food.
Email: marianne.penker@boku.ac.at

Tobias Plieninger is a forest and environmental scientist at the Rural Land Uses Group of the Berlin-Brandenburg Academy of Sciences and Humanities. His research focuses on the history, ecology and management of cultural landscapes.
Email: plieninger@bbaw.de

Ortwin Renn is professor of environmental sociology at Stuttgart University and directs the Research Unit for Interdisciplinary Risk Analysis and Sustainable Technology Development. His research focuses on risk governance, communication, technology assessment and citizen participation.
Email: ortwin.renn@soz.uni-stuttgart.de

Irene Ring is head of the social sciences working group on the conservation of nature and biodiversity at the Helmholtz Centre for Environmental Research – UFZ in Leipzig, Germany. Her research deals with conservation economics, fiscal instruments for biodiversity conservation and biodiversity conflict management.
Email: irene.ring@ufz.de

Jutta Roosen is professor for marketing and consumer research at Technische Universität München in Germany. Her research primarily treats questions of consumer evaluation of food safety and the effects of information on consumers' demand for food. *Email*: jroosen@tum.de

Waltina Scheumann recently joined the German Development Institute. Her publications are on institutional aspects of water management in developing countries and cooperation on trans-boundary water bodies in the Middle East and Africa.
Email: waltina.scheumann@die-gdi.de

Thomas Sikor works at the School of Development Studies of the University of East Anglia, UK. His research examines changes in rural governance, institutions and property with a particular interest in postsocialist transformations.
Email: t.sikor@uea.ac.uk

Insa Theesfeld holds a doctoral degree from Humboldt University, Berlin in Germany and specializes in institutional and resource economics. She works on methodological interest in institutional analysis and water resource management in Eastern Europe.
Email: theesfeld@iamo.de

Andreas Thiel is research and teaching fellow at Humboldt University, Berlin (Germany) and holds a PhD from Oxford Brookes University. His research interest is institutional change in land and water governance in the context of Europeanization.
Email: andreas.thiel.1@rz.hu-berlin.de

Eva Wollenberg was a scientist at CIFOR, where she worked on local forest governance, participatory decision making and adaptive management. In January 2007 she became the director of the Center for Sustainable Agriculture at the University of Vermont.
Email: lini.wollenberg@uvm.edu

Foreword

In a sustainable world, public and private property rights and responsibilities merge. All actors should share common values and common purposes. Maintaining ecological life support functions requires a robust and secure humanity that cares for its neighbours and its descendants. This is the routeway to a humanity that also cares for its planet.

This excellent volume explains clearly, and with much case study support, that public and private sectors increasingly are becoming blurred. What is slightly disturbing is that this blurring may not result in a clear purpose or a shared endeavour. Indeed, if anything, the contributions reveal that, while public and private are becoming more companionable, the outcome is neither consistent nor predictable.

The volume itself is a fine example of a process that brought together a variety of scholars with both theoretical and practical experiences in the public–private management front. What emerges from this fine collection of essays, together with the two binding synthesis chapters by Thomas Sikor, is that there is a long history of public–private association, yet little that bears any effective impact on a successful conversion to sustainability.

So we are witnessing a fascinating transition. There is a real requirement for effective cooperation between the two approaches. The earlier distractions between them, based on a highly misunderstood separation of 'public' and 'private' interest, is beginning, thankfully, to disintegrate. Indeed, one can think of many public bureaucratic examples where self-serving organizational interests are more akin to the 'private' mode. This is happening in the so-called 'outsourcing' of many aspects of public service from healthcare to prison management. And one can equally recall private philanthropy, which extends a private investment to a long-term public value. The Victorian architects and engineers readily spring to mind, as do many businesses, especially in the US, which fund art centres and school computers in hundreds of communities across the land.

But the real value of this collection lies in its prognosis of greater fusion to come. I like to promote the notion of companionship rather than partnership for this approach. Partnerships can, and do, freeze in mutual misunderstanding and incapacity to see a common journey. Companionships are designed to travel and to learn from each other. The truly successful transition to sustainability will require new, highly creative, companionships that breach our comfort zones of familiar ways of measuring and working.

This is the message of this book. Public and private are beginning to engage in a new set of companionships that can truly breach the conventional and the anticipated, and reach out for new approaches for measuring, learning and communicating. The best part of this book lies in its carry-through of case work into a wide range of examples: the modulation of property rights, regulatory sharing, new learning and fresh ways of communicating that encompass a whole new set of companionships.

Waiting in the wings is yet another volume. For surely the ultimate prize is a single sustainable 'sector' where citizen, civic, corporate and public all fuse into new ways of creating sustainable livelihoods. Without that fusion, I cannot see any meaningful sustainable future.

Already, a number of 'private' companies are tackling public purposes. Novo Nordisk, a Danish pharmaceutical firm making insulin for diabetics, is spending as much on research and development in its cooperation with health authorities and clinics to avoid the number of diabetics actually increasing, as it is on its medicinal products. A number of 'private' water companies in the UK are cooperating via a range of regulatory bodies and custodial agencies to manage water as a utility, not as a commodity. This will mean funding catchment care soil erosion reduction and biodiversity for public recreational value, as much as funding pollution research.

And so on. We are beginning to witness a quiet revolution the world over of companionship fusion for sustainable futures. Long may it flourish. This book certainly helps to pave the way.

Tim O'Riordan
November 2007

Acknowledgements

I would like to thank the Cooperation Fund of Berlin, Germany for its financial support. The Cooperation Fund funded the 5th Blankensee-Colloquium held in Potsdam, Germany on 13–15 January 2006, which offered a wonderful forum for exploring the ideas that have informed the thematic orientation of this book and for discussing first versions of the contributions to the book. The Cooperation Fund has also contributed financial support to the production of this book.

Blankensee-Colloquia are funded by the Cooperation Fund with the approval of the Senate of Berlin. The presidents and rectors of the Freie Universität Berlin, Humboldt-Universität zu Berlin, Technische Universität Berlin, Berlin-Brandenburg Academy of Sciences, Social Science Research Centre Berlin and Institute for Advanced Study Berlin oversee the Colloquia. They select the themes of the colloquia through an annual competition that invites proposals examining issues of cultural and social change, and include contributions by international scholars from the social sciences and humanities.

The goal of the Blankensee-Colloquia is to support young scholars in Berlin and Brandenburg through offering them the opportunity to introduce or develop an innovative field of research by way of an international workshop. The Colloquia are thereby expected to strengthen academic scholarship in Berlin and Brandenburg, support innovative research approaches and help foster institutional collaborations in the region.

The 5th Blankensee-Colloquium provided my coorganizers, Eva Barlösius and Waltina Scheumann, and me with a wonderful opportunity to explore our shared interest in natural resource governance. I thank Eva and Waltina for their many contributions to the Colloquium and the present book. I also appreciate the support of the staff of the Institute for Advanced Study, in particular Joachim Nettelbeck and Martin Garstecki.

There are many people who have made important contributions to this volume. David Baldock, Franz von Benda-Beckmann, Kerstin Dressel, Rainer Müssner and Jeff Romm helped the lively exchange at the Colloquium as discussants. Johannes Stahl, Rebeccah Blum and Sally Sutton assisted with the production of the volume by making sure that the individual contributions complied with not only English language rules but also the publisher's format requirements. At Earthscan my gratitude goes to Mike Fell, Alison Kuznets and two anonymous referees.

Above all, though, I thank the contributors to this volume. Their enthusiasm provided the foundations for an exciting intellectual endeavour that began with the Blankensee-Colloquium, produced this volume and has hopefully not come to an end yet.

Wissenschaftskolleg zu Berlin

INSTITUTE FOR ADVANCED STUDY

KOOPERATIONSFONDS

List of Acronyms and Abbreviations

AdB	Águas do Barlavento
AdS	Águas do Sotavento
APA	environmental protection area
BSE	bovine spongiform encephalopathy
BtL	Biomass-to-Liquid
CEBra	Centre for Energy Technology
CHP	combined heat and power
CIFOR	Center for International Forestry Research
CIPRA	Commission Internationale pour la Protection des Alpes
CU	conservation unit
EC	European Commission
ENOB	Energie Nord-Ost-Brandenburg
ESA	environmentally sensitive area
GHG	greenhouse gas
GMO	genetically modified organism
ICMS-E	Imposto sobre Circulação de Mercadorias e Serviços-Ecológico
ISC	Irrigation System Company
MAF	Ministry of Agriculture and Forestry (Bulgaria)
MEW	Ministry of Environment and Water (Bulgaria)
RPPN	private natural heritage reserve
SAC	special area for conservation
SARS	Severe Acute Respiratory Syndrome
UNESCO	United Nations Educational, Scientific and Cultural Organization
WTO	World Trade Organization
WUA	water user association
WUO	water user organization

Introduction: Public–Private Relations and Key Policy Issues in Natural Resource Governance[1]

Thomas Sikor, Eva Barlösius and Waltina Scheumann

This book addresses a great dichotomy in thought regarding resource governance: the distinction between public and private. In common thinking, we tend to sort social phenomena according to the categories *public* and *private*. We regard something as private if it only pertains to individuals. It is public if it affects the concerns of a community, such as a national society. In addition, we presume that something cannot be public and private at the same time. The categories demarcate two clearly separate spheres without any overlaps or ambiguities. We consider actors, actions, resources and property rights to be *either* public *or* private.

Yet, practice in resource governance has gone ahead of our thinking. The state, civil society and various kinds of communities establish diverse forms of *publics*; one example of these is the countless village communities around the world asserting their claims to local forests against state forest departments. Alternatively, private actors and actions display different forms of autonomy, indicating the existence of many different kinds of *privates*. Just compare the numerous restrictions imposed on landowners in the European Union (EU) for the sake of broader interests with the relative autonomy enjoyed by the food processing industry. There are as many privates as there are publics. Publics and privates demonstrate that it is not useful to think of public and private as singular entities. There are multiple publics and numerous privates, thus blurring their respective definitions.

In addition, public and private may not be as separate as we like to think. We are witnessing the emergence of various kinds of hybrid institutions running through the public/private divide. Throughout the world, for example, governments have promoted associations in agricultural water management, endowing groups of private actors with public powers. Likewise, we see so-called public–private partnerships mushroom all around us, such as when international pharmaceutical companies join forces with government agencies and local communities for the sustainable management of biodiversity. These *public–private hybrids* indicate that there may be things that are simultaneously public and private – or, to complicate matters, are neither public nor private. They obscure the supposedly sharp division between public and private.

This book takes a closer look at publics, privates and public–private hybrids in resource governance. It traces the definitions of public and private – actors, actions, resources and property rights – in actual cases of resource governance from around the world, cases that originate from Western Europe, developing countries and the postcommunist world. In this way, the book intends to help us update our understanding of public and private in reaction to actual developments on the ground. It is a book about publics, privates and public–private hybrids in practice, and what they mean for our thoughts about resource governance. It is about the blurring of the sharp dichotomy between public and private in practice.

The book challenges the dichotomy between public and private in thought regarding natural resource governance. Yet it does not stop here. It develops new concepts of public and private to make sense of current changes in resource governance. In a nutshell, the book demonstrates that we can discern three distinctions between private and public: between state and market, between political community and the more particularistic spheres of social life and between the socially visible and the personal. Therefore, we should think of *distinctions* between public and private instead of a single grand dichotomy. Distinctions between public and private occur along these three dimensions, taking place concurrently and overlapping with each other, as this introduction elaborates later.

The book brings together contributions by experts from six policy fields: agri-environmental stewardship, biodiversity conservation, bioenergy management, the protection of food quality and safety, forestry and rural water management. This is a daring enterprise considering the different customs that these fields have developed with regard to the concrete uses of the terms public and private. It is even more adventurous taking into account that the cases originate from highly diverse settings with varying traditions in thought and practice of public and private. Yet, once we consider these categories as analytical concepts, we recognize that public and private lie at the heart of contemporary debates in all these fields and across settings, notwithstanding the entrenched divisions and deep ditches separating them. Consequently, the analyses, as disparate as they may appear to us at first sight, demonstrate a remarkable degree of convergence around the premise of the book. This convergence tells us that something big is taking place in resource governance practices: a radical transformation in the relationship between public and private.

The book attests to the gains from research that crosses the boundaries we have built around individual policy fields. As we have gained specialist skills, we have lost sight of changes taking place in other fields. When we look at issues in a particular policy field, we often tend to miss that other fields are dealing with the very same issues. For this reason, the Introduction looks at key issues in current policy debates common to many policy fields. It reviews crosscutting policy issues, illustrates them with examples from the six policy fields covered in this volume, and explores their implications for our understanding of public/private relations in resource governance. Yet before it does so, it goes back to the intellectual tradition that has exerted strong influence on our thinking about public and private: the liberal-economistic model.

PUBLIC AND PRIVATE IN THE LIBERAL-ECONOMISTIC MODEL

In the liberal-economistic model, the public/private dichotomy is typically seen in terms of the distinction between state administration and market economy (Weintraub, 1997). The model portrays the state as the location of the public, as being responsible for the general interests of society. It leaves private matters to the self-regulating market, in which private agents engage with each other in voluntary transactions. State and market, therefore, take on the roles of public and private. This liberal-economistic model has become a dominant interpretation of the public/private distinction, extending from its original application in economic affairs to many other fields, such as education, health and – our primary concern – natural resources.

The liberal-economistic model has long ruled how we think about resource governance (see for example, Tietenberg, 2004). We consider the state to represent the public, and the market to be the forum for private interaction. This becomes evident when we talk about the state being the public sector and market actors representing the private sector. Consequently, much of the debate in resource governance is about the boundaries and relations between state and market. What actions should the state undertake? What resources should be the concern of the state? What kinds of social interaction should take place in the market? Under what conditions and how should the state 'intervene' in the market? What are appropriate roles for the state and market in resource governance? Where should we draw the boundary between state and market?

The boundaries and relations between state and market are at the core of much debate on resource governance. This becomes clear, for example, in the perennial discussions about market solutions versus state hierarchies (e.g. see Hartwick and Olewiler, 1998, especially chapter 6). In virtually every resource problem we can identify full-blooded free market advocates and others who argue for hierarchical approaches implemented by the state. The two are usually at loggerheads, as both sides tend to exhibit the same fervour. In irrigation, for example, we can find some of the most powerful state agencies in the world administering water allocation to thousands of farmers across expansive areas. At the same time, free marketeers promote the assignment of property rights to private users and the development of water markets.

We have also become accustomed to classifying resources as either private or public goods. Resources are private goods if individual private actors can appropriate them. They are public goods if they are essentially collective. Take, for example, grass and orchids growing in a meadow: we think of the grass as a private good because a farmer can come, cut the grass, transport it home and feed it to her livestock. The orchids, in contrast, may be public goods if they belong to an endangered species. The orchids provide a value to society that cannot be divvied up or appropriated by individual actors. In more technical terms, their enjoyment is non-rival, as opposed to the rival use of grass.

Ownership is another important field in which we have come to distinguish between public and private. Things are either in public or private ownership. Something is in private ownership if an individual actor can use it, dispose of it, and exclude others from its use. It is in public ownership if the state decides on usage, disposal and exclusion. In this way, we tend to believe that agricultural land is in private ownership – as compared with forests, which are often in public ownership.

Finally, we have commonly distinguished between private and public preferences. Preferences are either public or private. They are private if they are individual and expressed in markets, public if they are collective and dealt with in political processes. This means, for example, that we have to express private preferences for organic food by purchasing such food. In contrast, we believe that the formation and expression of public preferences for organic food production as an alternative to conventional agriculture fall within the domain of the state.

Yet we have also come to recognize that the dichotomy between state and market is no longer present, if it ever was. A second look at the above examples illustrates major discrepancies between thought and practice. First, state agencies and markets are not the only spheres of social action in irrigation management. By now thousands of village communities and local associations have assumed public powers and formed 'local publics' or, in the words of Wade (1994), 'village republics' located between state and market. Second, agricultural environments not only contain private and public goods, but also a whole range of goods located between the two extremes, making agriculture multifunctional (OECD, 2001). Third, property rights to agricultural and forestland are not simply private or public, demonstrating the presence of 'alternatives to public and private ownership' (Geisler and Danecker, 2000). Preferences, finally, are not simply private or public, as consumer boycotts indicate the possibility of presumably private actions generating public effects (see Hirschman, 1974).

Nevertheless, public and private remain prominent concepts in our thinking about resource governance. We continue to operate with these concepts even though we recognize that the distinction between state and market no longer matches resource governance on the ground. We speak of public–private hybrids when the contradictions between actual governance relations and our liberal-economistic model become too stark. In this way, public and private have become black boxes in our thinking, as they conceal more than they clarify. It is time to open them up and take a fresh look at public and private in practice.

CURRENT ISSUES IN RESOURCE GOVERNANCE

A look at current debates in resource governance demonstrates the benefits of such an undertaking. Public and private lie at the core of key issues we discuss. Our debates on these issues attest to fundamental changes in public and private practices making up resource governance. The changes in practice are fundamental in the sense that they not only involve new approaches and instruments to order the relations between public and private but also modify the very nature of public and private in the process. How these changes in governance practices redefine public–private relations is the subject of this section. The section reviews crosscutting issues in debates about resource governance and illustrates those with brief references to the six policy fields covered in the book.[2]

Regulation

Regulation is perhaps the most classical means by which public actors aim to influence private action for the sake of public interests. Public actors try to sway private actors by imposing restrictions on their actions. Public actors use their coercive capacity to confine the range of actions available to private actors. At the same time, the latter retain the possibility of engaging in voluntary interactions in markets. Regulation, therefore, affects the relations between public and private. Nevertheless, the logic of regulation presumes that public and private are two separate spheres of state and market.

Regulation is at the centre of current debates in European food policy (see also Chapter 8). The regulation of food safety and quality was previously left to national governments. In addition, many matters had remained in the hands of food producers and traders, on the one side, and consumers, on the other. Yet now, in the aftermath of bovine spongiform encephalopathy (BSE) and other food crises, consumers call upon the European Commission (EC) to control food quality and safety by way of regulation. They also demand new regulatory institutions for effective control and for the creation of new expertise about how to monitor and evaluate food. These demands have led to a flurry of new legislation at the European level, culminating in the General Food Law Regulation in 2002 and the establishment of the European Food Safety Authority.

Regulation has also been the primary means by which the German state has supported the development of the bioenergy sector (see also Chapter 7). A law requires the private utilities operating in Germany to purchase electricity from bioenergy production at a set price. The price is fixed by the state and thus independent of the ups and downs in the electricity market. In addition, the German parliament has recently abolished the exemption from petroleum taxes previously granted to the use of transport biofuels. It has replaced the subsidy with a regulation that defines a minimum quota on the use of biofuels by the oil and gas industry. In other words, the new law requires the industry to blend conventional gasoline and diesel with biofuel at a set quota. These regulations are considered the foundations of the rapid growth observed in the German bioenergy sector over recent years and are expected to continue into the coming ones.

Regulation is a common feature in numerous policy fields. The EU, for example, influences agricultural producers by way of mandatory restrictions on allowable farming practices and codes of good agricultural practice. Regulation is also one of the mainstays of biodiversity conservation, as illustrated by the various restrictions on resource use connected with the establishment of parks and other protected areas. Foresters, in turn, use regulatory approaches to affect the management and exploitation of forests, as indicated by the common distinction between production and protection forests. In the water sector, finally, states have instituted detailed regulation of water prices and for the protection of water supplied to households.

Subsidies

The agri-environmental schemes in the EU are one well-known example of the use of subsidies in resource governance. Under these schemes, agricultural producers receive significant payments aimed at the protection of Europe's cultural landscapes and water bodies. The payments are tied to restrictions on allowable farming practices, such as the use of chemical fertilizers and heavy machinery. Their rationale is that many producers would either give up farming altogether or move to environmentally less desirable farming practices in the absence of these payments. The payments enable them to preserve cultural landscapes considered valuable to greater society and to protect water bodies from pollution by chemical inputs used in agriculture.

Agri-environmental schemes in the EU are but one example of the use of subsidies in resource governance. Subsidies are a common instrument in natural resource policy. International biodiversity conservation programmes often pay local people living in and around protected areas for environmentally desirable practices. In forestry, there is currently a great deal of interest in the potential of payments for environmental services to safeguard the environmental functions of forests. In the bioenergy sector, the German government has subsidized the production and use of biofuels. In the food sector, governments subsidize organic food producers under the assumption that they provide broader social benefits in the form of better food quality and environmental protection. In addition, consumer interest groups have called for the integration of health concerns in the design of agricultural subsidies in the EU.

In this way, subsidies are another instrument to arrange the relations between public and private. In contrast to regulation, public actors do not try to influence private actors by imposing restrictions on their actions but by offering monetary payments. As with regulation, however, subsidies derive their justification from a clear separation between public and private. The rationale underlying subsidies presumes that private actors engage in voluntary interaction in markets. The state may institute financial incentives on the basis of its coercive capacity, but private actors retain the freedom to decide whether or not to engage in market transactions.

Decentralization

Decentralization is a primary issue in current resource policy in all fields.[3] Numerous countries, ranging from Brazil in Latin America to Poland in Central and Eastern Europe, have decentralized procedures for designating and administering protected areas. In the agricultural water sector, public authority has shifted from centralized agencies to regional and local units. In agri-environmental policy, however, programme design and implementation have rested in the hands of sub-national authorities since the beginning, as has quality and safety control in the food sector. Nevertheless, the latter has witnessed calls for centralizing some control functions in the aftermath of BSE and other food scandals.

With regard to forestry, decentralization has become a primary issue in international debates and actual policies (see also Chapter 1). Governments all over the world are in the process of shifting selected powers over forests from centralized forest departments to local state authorities. Concurrently, they are seeking to strengthen the accountability of local authorities to their populations. Decentralization thus implies a radical break with the nature of state power over forests in the past. Not only are powers moved downward, but they are also shifted from forest departments to integrative political units. Local state authorities are integrative in the sense that the scope of their authority is much broader than that of specialized state units organized around particular functions.

Decentralization is concerned with the nature of public. Effecting shifts from the central government to lower-level authorities, decentralization recognizes the concurrent existence of multiple publics. In addition, decentralization attests to the diverse nature of public, as it involves different combinations of powers and accountabilities that are moved downward. Therefore, decentralization involves moves toward multiple publics, multiple in number and kind. Yet, as with regulation and subsidies, decentralization maintains the clear distinction between public and private and leaves the public firmly rooted in the state. It does not imply any changes in the nature of the private sphere, nor does it modify the boundary between public and private.

Privatization

Privatization is an issue in contemporary resource policy that is as significant as decentralization. Over the past two decades, governments around the globe have privatized rights to natural resources. Large-scale privatization has taken place in previously socialist countries, where governments have transferred rights to agricultural land, forest and water to private actors. Privatization has also shaped the global food sector, albeit in a different process. In the food sector, global producers and large retailers first shaped the production of conventional food by way of quality controls and standards imposed by them and are now setting out to do the same with organic food.

Privatization has been a major trend in agricultural water management (see also Chapter 3). In the past, enormous state bureaucracies used to allocate water to farmers and manage irrigation systems. They received large sums for investing in new irrigation and drainage structures and for handling their subsequent operation from state budgets. Over the past two decades, however, governments in developing and postsocialist countries have reconsidered their direct involvement in agricultural water management in reaction to fiscal crises, the declining importance of agriculture and other reasons. They have changed the legal status of the irrigation agencies, the rules governing revenue generation and budgeting procedures in an attempt to convert the centrally financed state agencies to financially autonomous service providers. In this way, they expected the irrigation agencies to improve their operations by subjecting them to the laws of the market.

Privatization involves movements from the public to the private sphere by shifting actions and/or resource rights across the boundary between public and private. As with the previous policies, it maintains the separation between public and private. Things are either public or private, and the state and the market are the real-world incarnations of public and private, respectively. Nevertheless, privatization contributes to the creation of diverse private actors. These *privates* possess diverse bundles of property rights and face different sets of obligations. Some of them have the mandate to serve particular public interests and remain under the direct oversight of the state. In this way, privatization leads to many privates – not only in numbers but also in kinds – just as decentralization promotes the recognition of multiple publics.

Participation

Participation has become a trademark of debates on resource governance in all policy fields. In the food sector, for example, there are increasingly forceful calls for public access to information as a precondition for enhanced citizen participation in decisions about food quality and safety. In agricultural water management, irrigation agencies in some countries have begun to include citizen representatives in their governing boards and management units. In biodiversity conservation, programme managers seek ways to involve local people in decisions about the design and day-to-day management of protected areas. Similarly, government officials supervising agri-environmental schemes hold hearings and consultations with farmers about programme targeting and specifications.

Participation has been the subject of extensive debate in international forestry, too (see also Chapter 1). Starting in the late 1970s, government foresters experimented with approaches that involved local people in forest management. Under various comanagement arrangements, such as India's Joint Forest Management Program, forest departments granted villagers selected rights to forests from which they had legally been excluded in the past. Villagers could collect firewood and other nontimber forest products from forests in return for contributions to the management and protection of forests. The underlying rationale was that villagers not only benefited from enhanced access to forests but could also make important contributions to sustainable forest management. Now, 30 years later, experience has demonstrated that people's participation in forest management can take many forms. In some forms, villagers' participation has been rather nominal, improving information flows from the state to people but leaving most of the decisions about forest management in the hands of the state. In other forms, villagers have come to participate in decisions on forest management and the distribution of benefits from the use of forest.

Therefore, participation may concern the relations between public and private (see also Chapter 9). In its more restricted forms, participation is similar to subsidies and regulation by serving as a means by which public actors seek to influence private action. Yet, in its more empowering forms, participation goes beyond subsidies and regulations by opening up new avenues for private actors to become involved in public affairs. Empowering participation alters the nature of public actors, softening the separation between public and private. The underlying idea is that the broader political community – and not the state alone – should be responsible for public concerns. All citizens have equal rights to participate in public affairs, including the state and other actors constituting the political community. As a result, nonstate actors are not confined to the private realm of the market but may also take on public roles as a part of the broader political community.

Devolution

Devolution goes even further than participation in its more empowering forms. Devolution shifts public powers from the state to an institution outside the state. In this way, the rationale underlying devolution no longer follows the distinction between state and market as public and private. The logic driving devolution dissolves the equation of the public with the state. It broadens the notion of public to include a wide array of institutions outside the state – that is, those institutions that are constituent elements of the broader political community. Devolution thus recognizes the concurrent existence of diverse publics inside and outside the state. Although these publics may not be part of the state, they are not private.

Along with privatization, devolution has been a key trend in the agricultural water sector (see also Chapter 2). While numerous governments in developing and postsocialist countries changed their involvement in agricultural water management, in most cases they sought to devolve some authority to local-level organizations. In reaction, a great variety of water user organizations and irrigation associations were spawned across rural areas. These organizations received diverse kinds of public powers over water management, such as the power to set water charges, enforce sanctions and decide on budget allocations. National laws also made them subject to diverse mechanisms of accountability towards the state and local populations. Hence, devolution has resulted in a wide array of organizations in rural water management today.

The influence of devolution extends far beyond rural water management. In forestry, governments have also begun to devolve some authority over forests to various kinds of local organizations. In the food sector, agricultural producers have long established organizations that promote regional labels to outsiders and monitor compliance with the associated regulations among their members. In the agri-environmental field, farmers organize themselves in cooperatives to coordinate and jointly perform environmental services to greater society.

Public–private partnerships

Public–private partnerships receive much attention in broader debates about governance, but they have yet to gain significance in practices of resource governance. Nevertheless, there is significant interest in the potential of public–private partnerships as part of natural resource governance. In forestry, international health and beauty companies enter into contracts with local communities in the Amazon for the harvesting of raw products. Farmers, the processing industry and local state authorities of the agri-environmental field cooperate to develop new markets for agricultural crops as a way to preserve agricultural uses of the land. In contrast, public–private partnerships have yet to generate significant interest in debates about the governance of food and water.

International efforts to conserve biodiversity offer perhaps some of the most indicative cases of public–private partnerships (see also Chapter 5). These include international drug companies who have signed agreements with state research organizations to collaborate in the prospecting for new pharmaceutical substances. Drug companies and research institutes enter into cooperation because they expect mutual benefits. The drug companies hope to benefit from the expertise, access and legitimacy attributed to national research institutes. The research institutions, in turn, seek to enlarge their operations by gaining additional financial resources. Another example is a protected area managed by private companies and international conservation organizations, such as The Nature Conservancy. In this case, private actors take over the day-to-day management of protected areas from state agencies. They even gain the authority to monitor and enforce the regulations on land use set by the state's environmental agency. In return, they receive significant leverage from the state in the actual management and use of the protected area (see also Chapter 10).

Public–private partnerships cut across the presumably clear separation between state and market. State and nonstate actors not only cooperate but also form new institutions that are neither solely state nor entirely market. Public–private partnerships thus contradict the separation between public and private as state versus market. Of course, the partnerships may act like private actors when they engage in voluntary interactions with other actors on markets. Nevertheless, the partnerships are not purely private in the sense of the market. They also imply that the state and nonstate actors join forces for the sake of public concerns. Obviously, those public concerns are no longer the same as those of the state. Instead, the partnerships may bring together state and nonstate actors to pursue particular interests of the broader political community. In this way, public–private partnerships have a similar effect on public/private relations as devolution. The partnerships contribute and respond to the formation of new publics – publics not in the sense of the state but in the sense of the political community.

Labelling

Labels are another example of the emergence of new kinds of publics that are different from the state. This becomes especially clear if one ignores for the moment labels administered by state agencies and focuses on those promoted by industry. The striking observation is that market-based actors influence public concerns by way of labelling. These concerns simultaneously reflect consumers' market choices. In this way, private actions – industry initiatives and consumers' choices – constitute new publics, publics not in the sense of the state but of what is socially visible. All the same, labels also generate new social visibilities if they are promoted by state agencies or political organizations. In these cases, the public generated by labelling coincides with the publics associated with the state and constituted by the political community. This does not change the observation, however, that labels work due to the emergence of new public concerns and may involve the formation of new kinds of publics different from the state and political community.

Labels have mushroomed in the food sector (see also Chapter 8). Until a few years ago, it was mostly regulatory state agencies, producer associations and consumer groups that used labels to signal particular food attributes. They promoted the labels to publicize a wide variety of attributes, such as organic production, regional origin, motivation by a particular lifestyle, and commitment to particular production conditions (fair trade). In recent years, however, labels promoted by producers and retailers have proliferated. In many cases, retail chains have introduced their own labels to make consumers aware of certain food attributes. These labels have intersected with labels promoted by groups of food producers. In the EU, retail and producer labels are joined by different labels promoted by the EC and member states. The result of this is a confusing diversity of labels that often intend to indicate similar food attributes.

Labels have also become a common feature in forestry and agri-environmental management. In forestry, the nongovernmental Forest Stewardship Council has successfully promoted a label certifying sustainable timber harvests (see page iv). In agri-environmental management, agricultural producers increasingly form organizations promoting special regional labels for their products. Just consider the countless bottles of Chianti wine you see in supermarkets across Europe and North America.

What does this brief overview show us? First of all, we detect striking similarities in policy issues among the six fields covered in this book. Not a single issue finds attention in only one field. In contrast, some issues are present in all six fields at the same time. It is quite common for researchers, policy experts and practitioners in a particular field to discuss the pros and cons of an issue that is also the subject of debate in at least two or three other fields. Second, public and private are at the core of the major debates on resource governance. Key issues in contemporary policy debates all deal with public and private in one form or another.

Most importantly, these debates are evidence that public–private relations are undergoing radical changes in resource governance. We find that these changes not only lead to new combinations of state and market actors but also challenge the very notions of public and private in our thinking. The changes are radical in at least three ways. First, they involve major transformation of resource governance in each policy field. Second, changes in public–private relations take place in all policy fields at the same time. And third, they challenge the most basic tenets of the liberal-economistic model. What is at stake is no less than our understanding of public and private in resource governance.

CHANGES IN PUBLIC/PRIVATE RELATIONS

Some of the policy issues, we note, match the presumptions of the liberal-economistic model, as they take place within the confines of the dichotomy between state and market. Regulation and subsidies are classical means available to the state to influence the interactions of private actors on markets. They rearrange the relations between public and private but do not modify the very nature of public and private actors themselves, challenge the clear separation between public and private nor alter the distinction between them as state versus market.

Publics, privates and public–private hybrids

Yet we also observe that the remaining policy issues contradict the presumptions underlying the liberal-economistic model. It is no longer useful that we think of public and private as a clear dichotomy between state and market. The public is not necessarily the state. Nor is the private realm epitomized by the market. Similarly, we need to abandon the idea that public and private are separate entities divided by a clearly demarcated boundary. Public and private are not singular entities, we find, and they may show many more overlaps than we tend to believe.

We find that there are multiple *publics* and many *privates*. Decentralization takes place on the assumption that the state does not represent a singular public but actually represents multiple publics. These publics are not just many in number but are also of a different nature, as they possess diverse powers and are accountable to their populations by various means. Similarly, privatization seeks to create new privates – new not only in the sense of specific private actors that did not exist before but also with the implication that the new actors constitute different kinds of privates. These privates differ in the nature of the rights available to them and obligations imposed on them.

Next to publics and privates, we identify a general phenomenon that many call *public–private hybrids*. We see public and private actors cooperate in a variety of ways, thereby blurring the supposedly clear division between public and private in the liberal-economistic model. Participation, devolution, public–private partnerships and labelling all bring together state and nonstate actors in one form or another. In this sense, they establish public–private hybrids according to the presumptions of the liberal-economistic model. They may be simple in practice but become hybrids in our thinking because they do not fit the neat delineations of the dichotomy between state and market in the traditional model.

Publics, privates and public–private hybrids obscure the public/private dichotomy in the liberal-economistic model. This demonstrates that we cannot retain the premise of a single grand dichotomy, as it no longer corresponds to the changes in actual governance practices. Moreover, it would be unsatisfactory to stop at this observation; diagnosing the blurring is not enough. If practice differs from thought in such a radical manner, then we ought to develop new models to think about public and private in resource governance. We need new concepts to make sense of the changes that have taken place in practice.

New models of public and private in resource governance

We may consider that distinctions between public and private have multiple dimensions. As the American political scientist Jeff Weintraub (1997) has shown, political thinkers have used the notions of public and private in different ways. Public and private have always been seen in paired opposition, making it impossible to isolate public from private in our thinking. Yet the underlying distinctions between public and private have been different in political theory.

For our interest in resource governance, we can discern three distinctions between private and public.[4] The liberal-economistic distinction between state and market is only one of them. There are at least two further distinctions that have emerged in actual practices of resource governance. The three can be briefly characterized as follows:

(a) The distinction between the state as the public sphere and the private sphere of voluntary interaction epitomized by the market.
(b) The distinction between the political community as the public realm and the private as the more particularistic spheres of social life. The public here is different from the liberal-economistic model, because the political community extends beyond the confines of the state. The political community may be based on principles of citizenship or social belonging, granting people various opportunities to participate in public life. This distinction is somewhat familiar to us, as we have moved our focus from government to governance. Village communities and nongovernmental organizations (NGOs) are good examples of public actors in this sense. Participation, devolution and public–private partnerships are policies that seek to share public powers with public actors located outside the state.
(c) The final distinction is made between the socially visible and the personal. This is the notion of public we commonly use when we speak about making something public or going public with an issue. The public here is different from (a) and (b) because some aspects of the state or the political community are not socially visible. Conversely, the socially visible may include aspects that do not belong to the state or the political community. The media is a good example, as it helps create publics that are neither the state nor political communities (see also Chapter 6). The media is a primary actor developing public spheres in the sense of (c), but it also acts on markets as a private actor in the sense of (a) and is concerned with issues from the more particularistic spheres of social life in the sense of (b), such as fashion clothes. Among the key policy issues discussed above, labelling is a good example of policies that seek to create publics in the sense of socially visible spaces.

Therefore, we should think of *distinctions* between public and private instead of a single grand dichotomy between state and market. Distinctions between public and private occur along multiple dimensions, the public sphere comprising the state, political community and the socially visible, and the private sphere constituting the market, the particularistic spheres of social life and personal life. These distinctions take place concurrently, leading to multiple publics and privates and blurring the boundaries between public and private. The distinctions are clearly related, as the state may act publicly in all three senses at the same time. Yet the various divisions between public and private are not mutually reducible, as the underlying distinctions are different.

The overlapping nature of these three public/private distinctions also explains why some forms of governance look like public–private hybrids to us.

We see them as hybrids from the viewpoint of the liberal-economistic model, as they cross the separation between public and private. In this model, public–private partnerships are neither solely private nor entirely public. Yet once we shift our lens, such hybrids may well make sense according to another public/private distinction. State actors may no longer appear public to us but act in rather particularistic or personal ways. Conversely, market actors may no longer be private in their actions as members of the broader political community or in the limelight of the socially visible.

These insights demonstrate that publics and privates are relative in a very fundamental manner. This implies, as Franz von Benda-Beckmann (2000) has noted, that all publics are relative, because they are only considered to constitute a form of public if set in relation to a particular form of private. They are also relative, as we have noted above, because publics are multiple in number and kind. In addition, publics are relative because different forms of public emerge simultaneously from various underlying distinctions between public and private. A particular village association, for example, may form a kind of public – in the sense of political community – in relation to its individual members. Nevertheless, the very same association may engage in transactions on markets for natural resources and thus act as a private actor according to the distinction between state and market. Therefore, privates are as relative as publics.

THE BOOK: A BRIEF OVERVIEW OF THE PARTS AND CHAPTERS

The book examines the relations between public and private in resource governance by way of ten empirical analyses. Each analysis traces the definitions of public and private in a particular case. The cases come from the six policy fields covered in this book: agri-environmental stewardship, biodiversity conservation, bioenergy management, the protection of food quality and safety, forestry, and rural water management. The analyses look at public and private actors, action, resources and resource rights in each case. Many include comparisons between different kinds of publics or privates.

The empirical analyses are grouped around four themes. Part I of the book looks at the publics in resource governance associated with states and political communities. This part resonates closely with the literature on the move from government to governance, as discussed in the introduction to Part I. In Chapter 1 Wollenberg et al discuss how decentralization in Indonesia's forest sector leads to the emergence of new public institutions that are more firmly lodged in political communities. Theesfeld examines in Chapter 2 how state actors undermine efforts to promote new public institutions rooted in political communities in Bulgaria's water sector. Thiel analyses the move from public institutions grounded in local political communities to centralized state agencies in Portugal's water sector in Chapter 3.

Part II focuses on public–private hybrids and expands the scope of analysis to all three distinctions between public and private. The analysis thereby moves beyond the literature on government versus governance, as discussed in the introduction to Part II. Three case studies indicate how some public–private hybrids combine elements of state and market in new forms of collectivities rooted in political communities and social visibilities. In Chapter 4 Penker shows how various types of hybrid organizations have developed on the foundations of political communities formed around the notion of cultural landscapes in Austria. Ring analyses in Chapter 5 how the introduction of ecological transfers between state and local governments has created opportunities for local political communities to overcome the classic divide between state and market in Brazilian biodiversity conservation. Kleinschmit and Krott demonstrate in Chapter 6 how the media, being located between market and state, creates new publics in the sense of socially visible spaces in its reports about national and international forestry issues.

Part III brings together two case studies of private actors in resource governance. These actors are private in the sense that they operate in markets or engage in other forms of voluntary interaction. Yet some of these actors simultaneously act publicly as participants in political communities and creators of social visibility. In Chapter 7 Plieninger et al identify the role of pioneering individuals as setting apart developments in two bioenergy clusters in Austria and Germany; pioneers who see themselves as avant-garde for the benefit of the larger political community. In Chapter 8 Roosen looks at the rapid growth of labels in markets for safe food in Germany and France, including labels introduced by market actors who create new areas of social visibility.

Part IV presents visualizations of sustainable resource governance. The scenarios are based on various dimensions of public–private relations. Renn develops varieties of risk governance associated with diverse forms of publics rooted in political communities in Chapter 9. In Chapter 10 O'Riordan proposes the principle of ecosystem services to bring together state and market as parts of the broader political community.

Sikor concludes the book with an outlook on property rights to natural resources set in relation to the three kinds of publics identified in the book, drawing on the empirical analyses presented in the preceding chapters.

WHY SHOULD WE CARE ABOUT THE RELATIONS BETWEEN PUBLIC AND PRIVATE?

This book deals with publics, privates and public–private hybrids. It develops new models with which to consider public–private relations in resource governance. It contains ten empirical analyses that document the emergence of new kinds of publics and privates in specific cases of resource governance from around the world. Yet, why should we care about abstract concepts? Why do we need a new understanding of publics and privates in resource governance?

The answer is probably evident to the scholars among us. Public and private are fundamental categories of thought regarding resource governance. We need to make sure that our thinking keeps up with developments on the ground. Nevertheless, why should the achievers and implementers among us care about abstract categories? What will we gain from a new understanding of the relations between public and private in resource governance? The reasons are clear and compelling.

First, our analyses and actions need to look beyond individual policies at the greater picture. We need to examine how individual policies and actions merge, thereby altering the relations between public and private in resource governance. These relations are one of the chief levers for resource use, and hence for their economic efficiency, social equity and ecological sustainability. Moreover, they are a factor that can be influenced by purposeful action. There is nothing natural to the natures and roles of public and private in resource governance. Public and private are constantly in the making.

Second, improved models of public/private relations will help us better understand what is going on in practice. Once we can make sense of what is happening on the ground, we are in a better position to formulate policies and strategies in support of sustainable resource governance. Improved understanding is particularly crucial at this point, as not only the roles of public and private are changing but also their very nature. It will help us avoid endless debates due to confusion in our perception of such topics as the differences and similarities between devolution and privatization. The new models will also offer us a better grasp of practical questions, such as the potentials of decentralization versus devolution as strategies to promote sustainable resource governance under different circumstances.

Third, the notion of private retains a mythical status in our thinking about resource governance. In practice, however, we observe a wide range of privates enjoying diverse bundles of rights and facing various sets of obligations. It is time to debunk the myths of unlimited rights and absence of obligations long nurtured by the liberal-economistic model. In this way, opening up the black box of 'private' creates new possibilities not only for the scholars and thinkers among us to envision new forms of private but also for policy experts and practitioners to design and implement governance based on new privates.

Finally, the concept of public continues to endow actors and their actions with substantial normative weight. Just consider the legitimacy gained by an advocacy group if it allegedly represents the public interest. Consequently, much of our advocacy and advice follows the objective of promoting new publics or modifying existing publics in natural resource governance. Researchers develop models of and analyse experience with public actors contributing to sustainable resource governance. Policy experts discuss suitable functions for public actors to promote sustainable resource use in the various policy fields. Activists lobby for changes to public concerns, as well as modifications to the powers and accountabilities of public actors. We all seek to influence resource publics in one way or another. Much of our work is about the creation of new publics.

NOTES

1   The authors thank Tobias Plieninger, Ortwin Renn and Jutta Roosen for valuable comments.
2   What follows is, of course, a very stylized discussion of crosscutting issues. This discussion does not intend to deny the variation in public/private relations over time and space or to hide the different traditions surrounding the concrete uses of the terms public and private. Its aim is to illustrate how public and private, understood as analytical concepts, lie at the core of numerous policy debates.
3   As important as decentralization is, there is significant confusion about the (theoretical) definition of decentralization, i.e. which changes in governance powers constitute decentralization and which do not. Moreover, the differences between decentralization, devolution and participation are often not clear. The definitions used in this book, therefore, differ from other definitions used in the literature (e.g. Ribot and Larson, 2005).
4   The three distinctions are slightly different from the four identified by Jeff Weintraub. The difference may be due to differences in scope between Weintraub and this book. Weintraub reviews general political theory while we look at actual practices in resource governance.

REFERENCES

Benda-Beckmann, F von (2000) 'Relative publics and property rights: A cross-cultural perspective' in Geisler, C and Danecker, G (eds) (2000) *Property and Values: Alternatives to Public and Private Ownership*, Island Press, Washington, DC, pp151–174

Geisler, C and Danecker, G (eds) (2000) *Property and Values: Alternatives to Public and Private Ownership*, Island Press, Washington, DC

Hartwick, J and Olewiler, N (1998) *The Economics of Natural Resource Use*, Addison-Wesley, Reading, MA

Hirschman, A (1974) *Exit, Voice, and Loyalty: Responses to Decline in Firms, Organizations, and States*, Harvard University Press, Cambridge, MA

OECD (Organisation for Economic Co-operation and Development) (2001) *Multifunctionality: Towards an Analytical Framework*, OECD, Paris

Ribot, J and Larson, A (eds) (2005) *Democratic Decentralization through a Natural Resource Lens*, Routledge, London

Tietenberg, T (2004) *Environmental Economics and Policy*, Pearson Education, Boston

Wade, R (1994) *Village Republics: Economic Conditions for Collective Action in South India*, ICS Press, Oakland, CA

Weintraub, J (1997) 'The theory and politics of the public/private distinction' in Weintraub, J and Kumar, K (eds) *Public and Private in Thought and Practice: Perspectives on a Grand Dichotomy*, The University of Chicago Press, Chicago, IL, pp1–42

PART I – PUBLICS

Introduction to Part I

There is a need, as we have come to recognize in the Introduction, to take a fresh look at the relations between public and private. We begin our inquiry by considering publics in natural resource governance; that is, those spheres of social life that affect our collective concerns. Part I presents three empirical investigations of publics in natural resource governance. The analyses deal with rural water management and forestry, and draw on cases from a developing, a postcommunist and an industrialized country – Indonesia, Bulgaria and Portugal. Their relevance, however, goes far beyond the two policy fields and the three cases, as they speak to some of the key policy debates surveyed in the Introduction: decentralization, participation and devolution.

Chapter 1 looks at publics in forest comanagement and local governance, thereby addressing a contemporary debate in international forest policy. Drawing on long-term research in Borneo, Indonesia, Wollenberg and her co-authors examine the effects of comanagement and local governance on how social groups define public interests and make public decisions. They refer to comanagement as a form of forest governance that involves the participation of local people in decisions about forest use and forest management. Well known examples include Joint Forest Management in India, Community Forestry in Cameroon and indigenous forestry concessions in Bolivia. Under such programmes, forest departments typically retain control over forest management (Ribot and Larson, 2005). Local governance, in contrast, involves decentralizing powers from central to local governments in multiple sectors, not only forestry. Such a downward transfer of powers has taken place in Indonesia, India, Bolivia and Uganda, among other countries (Colfer and Capistrano, 2005).

Wollenberg et al find that comanagement and local governance affect the publics present in forest governance. Comanagement grants central government actors and larger scale social forces direct leverage in public decisions and the definition of public interests, as it leaves control over forests at the central level, in particular in the hands of centralized forest departments. As a result, comanagement constitutes the public in ways that emphasize national interests and forestry concerns, firmly rooting the public in the state. Local governance, in turn, results in public decisions and interests that reflect the power structures and preferences of local society to a larger extent. The influence of local society on public decision making is much higher under local governance than under comanagement. Local governance, therefore, shifts forest publics not only from the central to the local level but also strengthens their integration with local political communities.

Chapter 2 examines publics in natural resource governance by taking on another important policy issue of current relevance: devolution. Theesfeld analyses attempts in Bulgaria to promote water user associations for rural water management. Bulgarian legislation has sought to shift the control of rural water management from the state administration to water user associations formed by people in a particular locality. If people organize themselves, they can gain ownership rights to internal canal systems. The idea and associated policy are, as we know, not particular to Bulgaria. Water user associations have been a key element of water policy in many countries in South and Southeast Asia, postcommunist Central Asia, West Africa, Latin America and even the US (Roth et al, 2005; Perret et al, 2006).

Theesfeld argues that water user associations imply a radical redefinition of publics in rural water governance. They exemplify a form of water publics rooted in local political communities. These publics are radically different from the publics constituted in state centred water management that dominated Bulgarian water management under communism. As a result, Bulgarian state actors are resisting the new policy of devolution. They are slowing down policy implementation and successfully lobbying for a change in legislation that strengthens the powers of the state in water governance. Bulgaria's rural publics, therefore, are the site of heavy political contestation, caught in a limbo between state agencies and local political communities.

Chapter 3 maintains the concern with water publics, but shifts to a different context with different policy issues at stake. Thiel examines shifts in the governance of water provision and sanitation in the Algarve, Portugal from the 1980s to the early 2000s. These shifts took place in the context of two large-scale changes: the Algarve became a major destination for international tourists, and Portugal joined the EU in 1986. The changes in the governance of water in the Algarve, therefore, connect with much broader transformations of Europe's water policy (Hassan, 1996) and the Europeanization of environmental policy (Jordan and Liefferink, 2005; Wurzel, 2006).

Thiel suggests that the Algarve's water publics have undergone a fundamental reconstitution over the past three decades due to water shortages associated with tourism development and Portugal's integration into the EU. Integrative water publics centred in local political communities have given way to sectoral, state centred publics associated with the national government and EU. In the 1980s, municipalities used to claim broad authority over economic and social development in their jurisdiction, control over water being only one aspect of their powers. By the early 2000s, however, the national government had taken over much of the control of water provision, exercising this by way of regional agencies and so-called multimunicipal systems in line with the water regulations of the EU. In addition, the shift to the national and European levels granted national level NGOs and business associations unprecedented influence in collective decision making. We recognize that Chapter 3 describes a trajectory that is opposite to the current emphasis on decentralization (see Introduction) and the argument made in Chapter 1.

Looking at all three chapters together, we find that they attest to the presence of multiple publics in natural resource governance. They may be coexisting in a particular setting at the same time, as highlighted by Chapters 1 and 2. Alternatively, publics may change over time, affecting the ways collective decisions are made and collective differences are defined, as illustrated in Chapter 3. Yet overall, they support the argument of the Introduction that we should stop thinking about the public in the singular. There are many publics in natural resource governance.

We also realize that the state assumes a central role in resource governance. The state has been and remains one of the primary contenders for the location of publics. It continues to claim much control over natural resource management, as indicated by the large administrative structures set up by governments around the world for the management of water and forest. The Indonesian state claims control of forests. Bulgarian state actors assert their powers over irrigation management. And Portugal's national government has brought the provisioning of water in the Algarve under its authority.

Nevertheless, the chapters also demonstrate that resource publics are located at different points *within* the state. In other words, control over collective decisions and the definition of collective interests lie at multiple points. A common distinction is between local and central levels of the state, as reflected in the analyses of Chapters 1 and 3. As Indonesia decentralizes government powers, its central government and local authorities compete over public powers. Similarly, as water became scarce in the Algarve and Portugal joined the EU, the national government gained a large share of the public powers previously held by local governments. Another important distinction is between the legislative and more specialized administrative sections of the state, as illustrated in all three chapters. The two branches of the state possess different powers and are accountable to their populations by different means. In Indonesia, the central forest department is much more isolated from societal forces than governmental legislatures. In Bulgaria, the national parliament enacts far-reaching legislation on the devolution of water governance, which the water administration is not ready to support. In the Algarve, the decision making over water provision in the early 2000s dominated by national and regional water agencies was different from that under the local governments in the 1980s.

Yet we also find plenty of evidence in the chapters that the state is not the sole contender for the location of resource publics. Various kinds of local political communities assert claims to represent public interests or be involved in public decisions. These communities may include state actors, but they go significantly beyond the confines of the state. They are more inclusive than the state, as nicely illustrated by Chapter 1. In Borneo, ethnic identities and kinship relations have emerged as 'key organizing principles' of local publics in the wake of decentralization, replacing the dividing line between state and nonstate. Similarly, the rationale underlying the promotion of water user associations presumes the existence of local communities including state actors, such as mayors, and nonstate actors, such as regular villagers. Even in Portugal, where the national government has gained much control over rural water provision, NGOs and business associations demand a say in collective decision making.

The distinction between the state and the broader political community is, of course, not new to us. We have become familiar with it through the debate about government versus governance. For almost two decades now, we have concerned ourselves with shifting from state centred natural resource management to forms of governance that recognize multiple forms of making collective decisions and defining collective interests. These efforts have resulted in an abundant literature on new forms of governance that give local people, local communities and civil society actors a greater role in natural resource governance, including work on commons (e.g. Baden and Noonan, 1998; Dolsak and Ostrom, 2003), community based natural resource management (e.g. Baland and Platteau, 1996; Agrawal and Gibson, 2001), comanagement (e.g. Poffenberger and McGean, 1996; Borrini-Feyerabend and Taghi, 2000), adaptive collaborative management (e.g. Colfer and Byron, 2001), and decentralized governance (e.g. Agrawal, 2005; Ribot and Larson, 2005).

The three analyses presented in Part I support this attention to multiple publics in natural resource governance. Moreover, we recognize, they highlight specific features of the move from government to governance. First, state agents remain important actors in resource governance, as they are members of the political community. In consequence, we should not think about states and political communities as binary opposites in resource governance, as if governance rests with *either* state *or* political community. Second, the move from government to governance adds a new quality to resource governance; it is not just about adding new actors. And third, even though states remain important actors in resource governance, they are no longer the same when we move from government to governance. The state operates through coercion in the liberal-economistic model, limiting the range of action available to market based actors. As members of the political community, however, states interact with other actors in a very different manner: that is, through negotiations and other forms of participation in political affairs. This motivates a shift from the classical policy instruments of the state to new ones (cf Jordan et al, 2003).

REFERENCES

Agrawal, A (2005) *Environmentality: Technologies of Government and the Making of Subjects*, Duke University Press, Durham, NC

Agrawal, A and Gibson, C C (eds) (2001) *Communities and the Environment: Ethnicity, Gender, and the State in Community-Based Conservation*, Rutgers University Press, New Brunswick, NJ

Baden, J A and Noonan, D S (eds) (1998) *Managing the Commons*, Indiana University Press, Bloomington, IN

Baland, J-M and Platteau, J-P (1996) *Halting Degradation of Natural Resources: Is there a Role for Rural Communities?*, Clarendon Press, Oxford

Borrini-Feyerabend, G and Taghi, F M (2000) *Co-management of Natural Resources: Organising, Negotiating and Learning-by-Doing*, Kasparek, Heidelberg

Colfer, C J and Byron, Y (eds) (2001) *People Managing Forests: The Links between Human Well-Being and Sustainability*, Resources for the Future, Washington, DC

Colfer, C J and Capistrano, D (eds) (2005) *The Politics of Decentralization: Forests, Power and People*, Earthscan, London

Dolsak, N and Ostrom, E (eds) (2003) *The Commons in the New Millennium: Challenges and Adaptation*, MIT Press, Cambridge, MA

Hassan, J (ed) (1996) *The European Water Environment in a Period of Transformation*, Manchester University Press, Manchester

Jordan, A and Liefferink, D (eds) (2005) *Environmental Policy in Europe: The Europeanization of National Environmental Policy*, Routledge, London

Jordan, A, Wurzel, R K W and Zito, A R (eds) (2003) *New Instruments of Environmental Governance? National Experiences and Prospects*, Frank Cass, London

Perret, S, Farolfi, S and Hassan, R (2006) *Water Governance for Sustainable Development: Approaches and Lessons from Developing and Transitional Countries*, Earthscan, London

Poffenberger, M and McGean, B (eds) (1996) *Village Voices, Forest Choices: Joint Forest Management in India*, Oxford University Press, Oxford

Ribot, J and Larson, A (eds) (2005) *Democratic Decentralization through a Natural Resource Lens*, Routledge, London

Roth, D, Boelens, R and Zwarteveen, M (2005) *Liquid Relations: Contested Water Rights and Legal Complexity*, Rutgers University Press, New Brunswick, NJ

Wurzel, R K W (2006) *Environmental Policy-Making in Britain, Germany and the European Union: The Europeanization of Air and Water Pollution Control*, Manchester University Press, Manchester

1

Locating Social Choice in Forest Comanagement and Local Governance: The Politics of Public Decision Making and Interests

Eva Wollenberg, Ramses Iwan, Godwin Limberg and Moira Moeliono

INTRODUCTION

Living far from centres of power, the estimated 600 million people living in tropical forest areas rarely have formal influence on decisions about their natural resources or about public investments that might improve their well-being. Yet policies that decentralize control over natural resource management and governance have enormous potential to give local people more influence.

Decentralization is now widespread. Eighty per cent of all developing countries or countries in transition are engaged in some form of decentralization (Gregersen et al, 2005, citing Manor, 1999). More than 60 countries have decentralized some aspect of natural resource management (Larson, 2005, citing Agrawal, 2001).

Decentralization has taken two forms that each has a distinctive impact on local people, yet the forms are often conflated. The impacts derive from differences in the kinds of public governance institutions leading them and the levels of social choice that these enable.

We use public in the sense of relating to a group of people that form a generalized political community.[1] According to this definition, there can be many publics based on who has authority and the power to make decisions. The nationstate is only one public actor among many, including local communities. Private refers to entities acting on more specialized interests, especially at the individual or household level.

The first common form of decentralization is *centrally driven forest comanagement*, the granting of formal rights from central or meso-level forestry agencies to community-level groups to conduct forestry or agroforestry. Examples include Joint Forest Management in India, Integrated Social Forestry in the Philippines, Community Forestry in Cameroon and indigenous forestry concessions in Bolivia. The state institution is usually a central forestry department, hence a body that is national, sectoral and technocratic. Social choice, the collective decision making of a group, occurs at the national level through elections and parliaments that only have indirect leverage on technical departments. According to the framework for this volume, comanagement reflects a neoliberal, economic view of *public* (see the Introduction), according to which forest governance is driven primarily by the state. Ribot and Larson (2005) describe this as administrative decentralization.

The second form is *local governance*, the granting of formal control from central to local governments for administration and decisions in multiple sectors. Local governments receive powers and authority previously held by the centre, as well as financial allocations from the centre or from locally generated taxes, fees and royalties. The degree of power, responsibility and finances in each sector has varied from country to country. Forest management is often not fully granted to local government units. The administrative level at which decentralization occurs is usually one or two levels above communities. Examples include decentralization in Indonesia to *kabupatens*, in India to *panchayats*, in Bolivia to *municipios* and in Uganda to districts. Local governance assigns forest decisions to a local political community, which includes local government and other local authorities, rather than exclusively to the state. Ribot and Larson (2005) describe this as political or democratic decentralization.

In this chapter we contrast the impacts of increased local governance in Indonesia with the general trends in the impacts of centrally driven forestry. We analyse the implications of these two models and their corresponding public–private relations in terms of the levels of social choice they enable. The chapter shows the importance of understanding public decisions in terms of the kinds of private social influence they allow. The public–private divide becomes much less clear as social choice becomes more localized. Community, ethnic and kinship relations have stronger impacts on how decisions are made.

DECENTRALIZATION AND SOCIAL CHOICE

Decentralization's impacts (Fisher, 1999; Blaser et al, 2005) are usually linked to:

- types of powers decentralized (fiscal, administrative, affected sectors);
- amount of control devolved (deconcentration or decentralization,[2] devolution);
- the level to which control is given (household, community, local government, province or state).

In recent years, people have given more attention to decentralization's governance functions, especially to the downward accountability and representative function of administrative units to their constituency, or what has been called democratic decentralization (Ribot, 2003; Ribot and Larson, 2005). A focus on governance functions better captures the relations of influence between the governed and the people that make public decisions. The result is that it can explain convincingly, for instance, why local administrators of colonial forestry in Africa who were upwardly accountable had little incentive to meet local people's needs and delivered forestry profits primarily back to colonial authorities (Ribot, 2003).

In this chapter, we expand on the notion of democratic decentralization by examining social choice. Social choice has conventionally referred to the problem of how to best aggregate choices among individuals in a group (Arrow, 1951; Kangas et al, 2006). Analysis of social choice has focused on modelling and evaluating voting behaviour (Kant and Lee, 2004; Nurmi, 1995; Martin et al, 1996). We use social choice here in a broader sense to refer to the institutions that allow groups to collectively make public decisions. Our analysis focuses on the spectrum of ways in which a society and its components interact with a state apparatus to produce public decisions.

Social choice thereby provides an analytical framework that captures the multiple ways in which private interests translate into public interests. Understanding the extent of social influence on the state enables a more complete understanding of the nature of public interests: their lack of neutrality, varying authority and partisan interests (see Introduction; Baviskar, 2001). It underscores the *social* nature of public decisions.

As social choice can occur at multiple levels of society and the state, it defines a public interest specific to a given level or unit of decision making (cf the notion of multiple publics described by Schlossberg and Shuford, 2005; Aggens, 1983).[3] Decentralization policies can redefine the meaning of public interest by changing the level at which social choices are driven. Decentralization may devolve social choice, for example, from national to provincial, district, watershed or village levels. Where social choice is more localized, society can have new types of influence because the state is physically closer, fragmented (and hence often weaker) and enmeshed in local social obligations (Wollenberg et al, 2006). The power the state retained by trying to be neutral and impersonal is severely diminished. Its actions are more transparent to the people it is serving, who can make more direct demands. Understanding government becomes less important than understanding governance, as nonstate actors and institutions take on more influential roles.

The decisions and expressions of public interest that accompany social choice also reflect the tensions and struggles that exist at that level. The influences will vary at different levels in terms of ethnic and economic divides, public sector capabilities and incentives, private sector opportunities and interests, institutions for decision making and conflict management, available knowledge, cultural meanings and felt symptoms of environmental degradation. As social choice becomes more localized, people marginalized at the national level can have more influence, and knowledge of the biophysical environment increases, but capabilities and access to resources may decline.

Thus the *level and scope of the social choice* that drives a policy and the *interactions between social or state forces at this level* are necessary to distinguish among different kinds of decentralization and their impacts. Such information can show which kinds of decentralization are likely to give local people more influence.

In the examples examined in this chapter, comanagement does not change the level of social choice, while decentralization to local governments does. Comanagement devolves only technical powers of forest practice to the local level, while retaining social choice and the broader powers of governance at the central level. We expect that decentralization to local government would result in choices that better reflect the power structures and preferences of local society. By extension, more centralized programmes would reflect the interests of the central government and the larger scale social forces (commercial interests, donors, national and international NGOs and social movements) affecting them, with a potential for a higher divergence with local interests. We examine these propositions below.

DECENTRALIZING FORESTRY VERSUS GOVERNANCE: COMPARING EXPERIENCES

We contrast decentralization in which decision making is driven by central government with decentralization driven by local government. Much has been written about experiences with centrally driven comanagement programmes for forests (Fisher, 1999; Shackleton et al, 2002; Edmunds et al, 2003a, 2003b). We briefly summarize the nature of these programmes, observations about their impacts and their causes. This information provides a backdrop for and a contrast to the analysis of local governance in Malinau District, Indonesia. We conclude with a comparison and some questions about the interactions between the two types of decentralization.

Comanagement of forests: Centrally driven forestry

Comanagement policies have become a widespread form of decentralization in the last three decades. Eight per cent of forestland worldwide is estimated to be under these arrangements (White and Martin, 2002).[4] The policies are most common in countries that have a large proportion of state forestland (Gregerson et al, 2005). In India alone, 27 per cent of India's 65 million hectares of state forest is under comanagement, affecting almost ten million people in 84,632 user committees across 27 states (World Bank, 2006).

These decentralized approaches to forest management have provided large numbers of local communities or individuals with legal access to state land or forests in exchange for forest stewardship. Local people receive a formal acknowledgement from the state regarding their right to practice agriculture, use selected forest products (usually limited to those of low commercial value) or share benefits from sales of timber or other valuable forest products. As a result of these rights and their increased legal status, local people have become more politically visible and inclined to speak out. Many programmes have provided special support to women or minority groups to have a voice in local organizations and a share in forest benefits. The programmes have been implemented relatively quickly, a great deal of information has been conveyed to forest users, and land tenure and roles are clear. They have successfully rehabilitated large areas of degraded lands and significantly expanded forest cover in a number of countries (Edmunds et al, 2003b).

Although touted as devolution and promoted as increasing benefits to and the participation of local people, for the most part comanagement has merely promoted a limited set of economic rights that have expanded forested areas. It has only marginally supported local control and self-determination. By using the policies to control 'management decisions related to tree resources, work plans, budgets, market outlets and local organizations' as 'strategic points of intervention', this form of decentralization has left the state in control of major decisions and only changed how that control was exercised (Edmunds and Wollenberg, 2003).

Thus while local people have control over many implementation decisions, the general framework is predetermined by the national programme. Government units at the district, state or provincial levels set objectives, administer the programmes and retain key roles (see Table 1.1). Programme objectives reflect forest departments' priorities, such as the production of commercial timber and other forest products, biodiversity conservation and maintenance of ecological services. Enhancing local people's livelihoods is only a secondary objective, if one at all (Sarin et al, 2003).

In terms of social choice, decisions about comanagement policies are driven by central technical forestry agencies and made into law through central decree or national law. Local people have little direct input into this level of social choice. Local institutions provide a means for making collective decisions about management decisions, but even these are upwardly accountable to the forestry agency, not to forest users. Pre-existing local organizations that did have some local accountability were often incorporated into the national programme (Sarin et al, 2003). Forestry units rarely coincide with administrative units and tend to act independently of local governments (Shackleton et al, 2002). The state has invoked the 'public interest' (Lynch, 1998) and scientific management (Guha, 2001) to legitimize this control.

Comanagement programmes have consequently been criticized for not promoting the democratic devolution of forestry and even undermining the possibilities for local democratic decision making (Sundar, 2001; Sarin et al, 2003). Over time the divergence in local inhabitants' priorities and the benefits

Table 1.1   *The role of the central state in comanagement*

The role of the central state
Protecting wider 'public goods' (watersheds, biodiversity, carbon sinks and other ecological services)
Determining forest boundaries
Determining the eligibility of individuals and communities to forests
Deciding which rights and benefits should be devolved to communities
Determining acceptable forms of local organizations and institutions to conduct forestry
Setting the terms of agreements with local organizations
Retaining the right to cancel agreements with communities and withdraw rights to forests and forestland
Collecting taxes, fees and royalties
Distribution of forest benefits to communities
Regulating forest product markets
Mediating conflict
Providing legal recourse and helping local organizations enforce regulations and sanctions
Providing technical assistance
Providing or subsidizing labour and equipment for nurseries, regeneration, harvesting, transport and processing
Addressing local inequality and ensuring representation of marginal groups in forest decisions
Helping communities to defend their rights, including protection against powerful external groups such as mining and timber companies and organized traders
Supporting local capacity building

Source: Adapted from Shackleton et al (2002)

of these programmes have only increased, as local people demand more benefits and seek more self-determination (Edmunds et al, 2003b). Sectoral assistance through forestry departments alone is also unlikely to have a significant impact on the lives of local residents, as they do not have the expertise or mandate to assist in other important aspects of people's lives such as health, infrastructure or education. Local people continue to participate in them, however, for the legal recognition, development assistance and incremental benefits they receive. For most they are an improvement over previously centralized forest practices.

As long as forestry departments can exercise control to acquire the timber or other forest goods and services they need, they will have little interest in closing this gap. Forestry departments maintain control through the force of their association with the central government and their option to resort to military tactics and assistance. The departments have few social links with local society, other than through their field officers, who often make concessions to local interests in the implementation of policies. Forest communities' capacity to mobilize resistance has varied with their access to information and resources, although generally weak communication and transportation infrastructures make organizing mobilization difficult in most places.

Social choice under comanagement policies is thus driven by forest departments' interests and the national and international forces with which they contend. Local social choice is severely constrained.

Local governance

By contrast, decentralization to local government creates new governance opportunities that potentially offer more real control and benefits to local groups. Local governance offers not only a narrower constituency where the public interest is at a level closer to the people, but also the 'potential for greater coincidence between local traditions and informal rights... and formal norms imposed by government' (Gregerson et al, 2005). What are the implications of this potential social influence? We draw from our decade of work in the district of Malinau, Indonesia, to examine what happened.

Malinau's experience

Malinau is a district of 42,000 hectares with a population of about 45,000 on the island of Borneo. Residents are primarily indigenous Dayak groups, who belong to about 18 ethnic groups. The district is one of the few remaining forested areas of Borneo and has designated 90 per cent of its area as state forestland. It has one of the highest levels of biodiversity in Southeast Asia (Meijaard et al, 2005).

Decentralization in Indonesia began formally in January 2001, although local governments had begun seizing control one to two years earlier during the political reforms that followed Soeharto's resignation in 1998. District governments received the right to retain a proportion of the benefits from their natural resources and to generate income in their jurisdictions. In return, they are expected to administer development in their areas. District governments continue to receive the bulk of their funds from the central government. In addition, district leaders and local assemblies are now required to be elected directly by local people, rather than by their parties, or to be appointed by the provincial leader.

The forestry sector was only partly decentralized. Districts have the responsibility to manage protected and plantation areas but not production forests. Districts can only authorize small-scale concessions of 50,000 hectares or less. The centre retained ownership over forestland. An initial rush by districts, including

Malinau, to facilitate small-scale timber harvesting (not management) in their areas was stopped in 2003 by central government decrees and lobbying. Economic incentives cause the districts to continue to try to cash in on the value of their forests. The Malinau district has made persistent efforts to convert forestland into more lucrative oil palm plantations. There has never been any comanagement scheme in Malinau, as is the case for most of Indonesia's Outer Islands.[5]

Meanwhile, decentralization has coupled the state and local social forces in important ways. Before reforms, 'government' was a distant, unknown, inaccessible entity to most residents of Malinau and other remote forest areas. Residents were familiar with the local, unofficial politics of customary leaders, ethnic relationships and local bosses. Reforms have since brought the government closer to the people and, in doing so, merged the two domains of authority.

Government is more familiar because government offices are physically more accessible and staffed by local residents. Previous ethnic minorities at the national level now lead local government. Communication between government and nongovernment entities is more practical, response times are faster and the state authorities that are accessible have more decision making influence. Nearly all of the new local government is from the local population, so officials are more familiar with traditional values and lifestyles. The informal, personal and ethnic sphere of politics has intermingled with the formal, impersonal and anonymous state.

District politics has thus required balancing adherence to the informal claims to resources, reciprocity and personalized relationships of traditional community life with the bureaucratic, patronizing, money-politics culture of the state.

The most powerful politicians and local people have been those who have maintained influence in both domains and used that influence to bridge domains in specific initiatives. Consequently, small-scale timber harvesting was a partnership of the district leader's office, the District Forest Service, local timber bosses and the heads of specific *adat* (traditional customary) communities. For villages, it represented their first significant receipt of cash from timber. The plans to develop oil palm have built upon similar alliances. In contrast, Inhutani II – the large, centralized, parastatal forestry company – withdrew from the area once it no longer had the support of local communities.

Building influence across these two domains has shifted people's attention to exercising power through local alliances, rather than through top-down decrees or alliances upward in the hierarchy of the state. In doing so, no one entity has held the ultimate base of power. Entities within government have been more interdependent, as has been district government with local communities. As attention has shifted to these local alliances, initiatives have been formed through a mix of formal and informal agreements that have allowed district officials to dodge the attention of central authorities and be less than fully transparent to communities. The resulting collusive behaviour has created huge benefits for some. It has also prevented people from building trust in the government or their village leaders.

Ethnic groups have acted as the common social foundation of the informal and formal political spheres. Reforms have enabled ethnicity to take on elevated importance. Ethnic groupings, in the form of villages, have been the basis for claims to districts for land and forest resources. Often descended from traditional customary authorities, ethnic authorities represent villages, although not always very democratically. Ethnic groups have also been the basic building blocks of social capital and political alliances, albeit repressed during the state building efforts of the Soeharto regime. Local people use ethnic identity to 'place' others as family, community, ally, rival or unknown outsider and indicate social position. The organization of local ethnic associations – usually invoking the informal authority of customary institutions – has blossomed with decentralization. The district government tried to maintain its support and legitimacy through balanced representation of powerful ethnic groups such as the Kenyah, Lundaye and Tidung. They have made increased use of and appealed to cultural symbols and events, such as the forest and harvest festivals, to gain popular support. They have taken the new ethnic associations seriously, inviting their representatives to district events and participating in events of the associations.

General political reforms gave local people more freedom of speech, which has encouraged outspokenness about district government and demands for transparency. Protest and outright conflict increased dramatically in the early years of the transition but seem to have declined since the district government established a more weighty presence.

As a result, patterns of who holds power and how it is exercised are changing in Malinau. These changes are by no means unproblematic. The substance of governance – as measured by responsiveness, efficient allocation of resources, transparency, accountability and justice – has been weak. Local governance has been constrained by its unclear roles, low capacities, an unorganized civil society and strong self-interest. As in other parts of Indonesia and countries with local government (Gregerson et al, 2005; Larson, 2005), roles have been unclear, and local government in Malinau has pursued economic development and financial priorities at the cost of long-term environmental goals. Development of unified, enforceable institutions for defining and distributing property, managing natural resources, handling conflict or promoting participation has been uneven, unclear and slow. Agreements have been weak, unenforceable and unstable. Most officials have not had adequate exposure, training or experience in their areas of responsibility, let alone in democratic local government. Local people have remained relatively unorganized and uninformed. Officials have found many demands of local people exorbitant or difficult to respond to. Demands on government have often been more for material gain than for the promotion of self-determination and the improvement of collective institutions.

The handing over of power to local officials has accelerated the possibilities for collusion, corruption and the promotion of self-interest (Smith et al, 2003).

As the financial and political stakes have risen, so has the internal deal making and haggling. Higher-level officials have pursued lucrative profits, including those from timber and mining, justified under the cover of producing income from the district. Lower officials have concerned themselves with their own cut from projects, opportunities to travel and earn per diems, and trivial power struggles. The result has been a preoccupation with personal gain and petty politicking within the bureaucracy.

Central government has reacted to what it sees as local government's excessive self-interest by trying to reestablish control, especially in forestry. The Ministry of Forestry established district offices accountable to the centre (*Unit Pelaksanaan Technis Daerah*, UPTD), which have been ineffectual. The Ministry passed Government Regulation 34 in 2002, reestablishing the Ministry's authority over nearly all commercial forestry. Nevertheless, most control from the centre is now informal or through party connections.

The new structures of local government thus provided a vast potential for change, but the factors described above have slowed the development of democratic reforms. Local decision makers seem to be retreating towards old patterns of control and politicking for personal gain, with forests and their conversion as the centrepiece of attention. Nationally, coordination of forest management has become difficult and there are no clear mechanisms for planning on a larger scale.

While we have presented a case study of only one site, the opportunities and problems faced in Malinau are similar to what has been experienced with local governance elsewhere (Capistrano and Colfer, 2005; Gregerson et al, 2005; Larson, 2005; Ribot and Larson, 2005). These other experiences demonstrate the need to balance the tendency for elite capture, excessive self-interest and low capacities of local governments with stronger controls through measures such as overriding regulations, minimum environmental standards, multistakeholder processes, stronger will and ideology, and subsidies to build capacities and encourage interest in public goods and services (Gregerson et al, 2005; Larson, 2005; Ribot, 2005). While some think democratic local governance is only a pipedream (Capistrano and Colfer, 2005), others see it as a necessary goal to work towards, even if democracy can only be partial (Ribot, 2005).

DISCUSSION

The patterns of comanagement and local governance that we have presented represent two types of decentralization that have had major impacts on people living in forest areas over the last several decades. The patterns are distinct in their structure, processes and outcomes. They should not be conflated if we want to understand decentralization's effects.

Table 1.2 highlights the differences between the two types of decentralization. It shows that social choice under comanagement forestry is controlled by the central legislature and forest department and restricted to forest management. At this central level, there is little influence of local society on the

Table 1.2   *Comparison of social choice available under comanagement and local governance policies*

Aspect	Comanagement	Local governance
Level of social choice driving decisions	Central legislature, forest departments	Local government
Scope of social choice	Forest management	Local administration, multisectoral
Accountability and responsiveness of decision makers to local communities	Low; local organizations upwardly accountable	High potential
Source of legitimacy of decision makers	Scientific management, national law, national public interest, donor endorsements	Elections, local origins, local government law, local communities of public interest
Capacities	Good technical forestry information; poor in rural development	Good local knowledge; mixed in other regards
Other important decision makers	Local communities and third parties (e.g. NGOs) who implement policies	National government that determines policies and funding; forestry departments retain some control over forests
Role of communities	Instrument for forest management	Constituency, political support
Accessibility of state officials that can influence decisions	Low	High
Social and economic interdependence of state and local society	Low: – Focused on forest product protection and extraction – Employment, labour	High, multidimensional: – Geographic space – Ethnic affiliations – Family connections – Employment, labour – Collusion for private gain
Neutrality of state	Highly impersonal	Mixture of personal and impersonal
Social mobilization and protest	No clear mechanism	Potentially possible through local democratic procedures

state. On the contrary, the state controls local society through upwardly accountable organizations and contracts to meet its own forestry aims. The bureaucracy is efficient in distributing information and implementing programmes widely. It cannot meet the high priority demands of local people such as health, roads or education, as these fall outside its mandate. State concerns are often quite divergent from those of local communities.

In contrast, social choice under local governance is controlled by local governments and covers more sectors, although the forest sector may remain dominated by the centre. At this level the influence of local society on the state is much higher. Local officials are from the local society and so are more acquainted with and tied to it. For the first time, minority groups have a dominant role in government. Officials are accountable to a constituency and more physically accessible to them. Politics is more personalized and likely to integrate traditional authorities and decision making. Communities have added means of directly expressing and leveraging their dissent.

Neither type of decentralization, however, is absolute in the level of social choice at which it operates. Both involve a blend of decisions and authorities from the community to the national level, and with third party actors such as NGOs. In this way, they serve to link multiple publics and levels of public interest. Under relatively centralized comanagement, local communities implement forest management. Under local governance, central government often provides discretionary funding to local governments. In both cases, the strengthening of these other roles can widen the span of publics served. As forests often serve multiple public and private needs, governance that meets the concerns of diverse publics has an advantage.

What are the implications of the two patterns of decentralization for local people's well-being? More localized social choice should be a positive impact in its own right if it gives local people more say over their lives. It is also an institution that can lead to further benefits such as better services or an improved economy. Comanagement has provided a limited package of economic rights and benefits directly to communities, including less advantaged groups who would not have otherwise been able to compete with the local elite (see Table 1.3). Local people have little influence on the programme, other than in how they implement it. They do, however, have clear roles, clear tenure and access to some forest resources and better information. It is a management model driven by top-down bureaucratic objectives and controls. Forests have tended to increase under comanagement, although not always with the species or in the places community members would like.

Local governance has provided a more open-ended and comprehensive right to decision making and authority that is closer to communities, albeit not at the community level. Local groups have potentially much more influence on local governance, especially more powerful elites. Minority groups appear to be less well protected by local governments; information is poor and roles are murky.

Table 1.3   *Outcomes of comanagement and local governance for communities*

Aspect	Comanagement	Local governance
Main positive outcomes for communities	Increased forest cover (for biodiversity and timber) Economic rights and benefits to communities Clear tenure More nominal local opportunities for women and minorities	Increased funding available for local development Minorities and disadvantaged groups on a national scale now empowered decision makers
Main negative outcomes for communities	Limits to options available Use rights rather than ownership Little influence on forestry department Elite capture	Excessive self-interest and corruption Incompetence Environmental degradation Elite capture Minorities with lowest influence benefit least

Some officials are incompetent. It is a political model driven by more messy democratic objectives and controls. Forests have tended to decrease under local governance. Local governments have less interest in guarding long-term public interests at the level national and international interests of a larger scale would have them do.

While both policies present trade-offs to local people, we suggest that the potential gains of decentralization to local government are likely to be greater over time, as long as mechanisms are in place to build capacities and guard against self-interest that is detrimental to disadvantaged groups, neighbours and environmental sustainability. There is more room for political negotiation and local mobilization under local governance (Bauman and Farrington, 2003). As others have noted, the lower the level of organization, the better they worked to meet local communities' interests (Shackleton et al, 2002). The opportunity for marginalized ethnic groups to participate meaningfully in formal politics is already a significant gain and may indeed transform local political orders (Wollenberg et al, 2006).

Different types of decentralization are not necessarily exclusive, however. It may be desirable to have options for both comanagement and local governance to best meet the needs of different publics and their underlying social interests. This combination of decentralization policies is increasingly common in many countries. The challenge here seems to be in linking community organizations effectively with local government and its planning and budgeting processes (Shackleton et al, 2002). Otherwise, Shackleton et al explain, local government councils and forest user groups tend to compete for resources and income, as was the case in the Philippines, Zimbabwe and Zambia. In other cases, such as

Botswana, user groups operating in isolation from local government miss opportunities for additional benefits and local support.

These experiences raise fundamental questions about the linkages among plural systems of authority and how local people negotiate their interests among them. In addition to the formal policies we have examined here, authorities can include customary and civil society organizations. How can decentralization be more inclusive of these forms of authority and not give exclusive authority to the state (Sikor and Tran, 2007)? Neat links among all of these are rare. Are they necessary? Or do the overlaps reflect the necessary social tensions that exist among different levels of the 'public'?

CONCLUSIONS

Decentralization policies distribute decision making authority in different ways. In this chapter we have reviewed how the decentralization policies of comanagement and local governance differ. We have highlighted the importance of the level and scope of social choice and the influence of society on the state as key determinants of decentralization policies' impacts.

Although decentralization inherently involves a blend of authorities at different levels, our analysis has emphasized the importance of distinguishing which level of social choice drives decisions and the role of local people in this process.

We have tried to show that the social forces acting at each level of decision making affect how the public interest is defined as well as the ability of private interests to access the policy making process and exercise their own influence. Local governance has given people, particularly people living in forest areas, multilayered opportunities to influence government and to work from inside the system, sometimes with few checks. It has changed the very nature of how the state functions locally, combining customary and more personal forms of politics with the conventional impersonal politics of the state. The identity of local government, its authority and its style are more intermingled with customary political communities.

The notion of public under such circumstances becomes quite complex. Public decisions reflect negotiated agreements between local political communities and the state. The state itself is multilayered and represented by multiple, often competing or uncoordinated entities. Local political communities represent a new kind of more pluralistic, public institution that depends more on local social structures and power relations. Within them it is often difficult to distinguish between private and public interests. Ethnic identities, community identities or family identities can take on more political importance. Public interests at the local level can be surprisingly unpublic in the interests they promote.

Local governance thus offers more scope for meeting some local people's immediate interests because it allows social choice to be more embedded in local politics. This helps those who are already influential at the cost of further marginalizing the weak. It also can exacerbate undesirable trends that locally influential people may choose to pursue, such as excessive forest exploitation. In forest areas, meeting the long-term interests of publics at different levels can be critical as well. Checks and balances across different levels of social choice and civil society are needed to balance these different interests. Agendas for poverty alleviation or environmental protection will be best met where local governments are accountable to broader principles and provided incentives. In this way, local people should be able to have a greater measure of self-determination and their forests too.

ACKNOWLEDGEMENTS

The authors are grateful for the insights and assistance provided by Thomas Sikor, Tobias Plieninger, Jeff Romm, Elinor Ostrom, Dina Hubudin, Made Sudana, David Edmunds, Peter Wilshusen, and the people and district government of Malinau.

NOTES

1   This definition stems from the common current usage and the word's etymological roots in old French (public) and older Latin (poplicus) of 'pertaining to the people' (cf 'of, pertaining to or in the service of a community or nation' in *Webster's Encyclopedic Unabridged Dictionary of the English Language*, 2001, p1562). We have added an explicitly political dimension for the purpose of this chapter.

2   It is confusing that decentralization has been used both as the generic term for all shifts from the centre to local authorities as well as to the specific case of the delegation of powers to the local level where power is retained by the centre.

3   As per our definition of public, the public interest in this sense does not have an exclusive association with government or the state.

4   Decentralization of management to communities is related to but distinct from decentralization policies that provide tenure rights over forestland to local or indigenous groups or provide communities opportunities to participate in logging concessions and their benefits.

5   In contrast, social forestry schemes in Java promoted agroforestry and local employment in government-run teak plantations and did represent a weak form of comanagement.

REFERENCES

Aggens, L (1983) *Identifying Different Levels of Public Interest in Participation*, The Institute for Water Resources, US Army Corps of Engineers, Fort Belvoir, VA

Arrow, K (1951) *Social Choice and Individual Values*, Wiley, New York

Bauman, P and Farrington, J (2003) 'Decentralising natural resource management: Lessons from local government reform in India', *Natural Resources Perspective*, no 86, Overseas Development Institute, London

Baviskar, A (2001) 'The politics of accommodating multiple interests in local forest management: The Indian experience', *International Journal of Agricultural Resources, Governance and Ecology*, vol 1, no 3/4, pp243–263

Blaser, J, Küchli, C, Colfer, C J P and Capistrano, D (2005) 'Introduction' in Colfer, C J P and Capistrano, D (eds) *The Politics of Decentralization: Forests, Power and People*, Earthscan, London, pp1–9

Capistrano, D and Colfer, C J P (2005) 'Decentralization: Issues, lessons and reflections' in Colfer, C J P and Capistrano, D (eds) *The Politics of Decentralization: Forests, Power and People*, Earthscan, London, pp296–313

Edmunds, D and Wollenberg, E (2003) 'Whose devolution is it anyway? Divergent constructs, interests and capacities between the poorest forest users and states' in Edmunds, D and Wollenberg, E (eds) *Local Forest Management: The Impacts of Devolution Policies*, Earthscan, London, pp150–165

Edmunds, D, Wollenberg, E, Contreras, A, Dachang, L, Kelkar, G, Nathan, D, Sarin, M and Singh, N (2003a) 'Introduction' in Edmunds, D and Wollenberg, E (eds) *Local Forest Management: The Impacts of Devolution Policies*, Earthscan, London, pp1–19

Edmunds, D, Wollenberg, E, Contreras, A, Dachang, L, Kelkar, G, Nathan, D, Sarin, M and Singh, N (2003b) 'Conclusion' in Edmunds, D and Wollenberg, E (eds) *Local Forest Management: The Impacts of Devolution Policies*, Earthscan, London, pp166–181

Fisher, R (1999) 'Devolution and decentralization of forest management in Asia and the Pacific', *Unasylva*, vol 50, no 4, pp3–5

Gregersen, H M, Contreras-Hermosilla, A, White, A and Phillips, L (2005) 'Forest governance in federal systems: An overview of experiences and implications for decentralization' in Colfer, C J and Capistrano, D (eds) *The Politics of Decentralization: Forests, Power and People*, Earthscan, London, pp13–31

Guha, Ramachandra (2001) 'The prehistory of community forestry in India', *Environmental History*, vol 6, no 2, pp213–238

Kangas, A, Laukkanen S, Kangas, J (2006) 'Social choice theory and its applications in sustainable forest management – a review', *Forest Policy and Economics*, vol 9, no 1, pp77–92

Kant, S and Lee, S (2004) 'A social choice approach to sustainable forest management: An analysis of multiple forest values in Northwestern Ontario', *Forest Policy and Economics*, vol 6, no 3–4, pp215–227

Larson, A M (2005) 'Democratic decentralization in the forestry sector: Lessons learned from Africa, Asia and Latin America' in Colfer, C J and Capistrano, D (eds) *The Politics of Decentralization: Forests, Power and People*, Earthscan, London, pp32–62

Lynch, O (1998) 'Law, pluralism and the promotion of sustainable community-based forest management', *Unasylva*, vol 49, no 194, pp52–56

Martin, W E, Schields, D J, Tolwinski, B and Kent, B (1996) 'An application of social choice theory to USDA. Forest Service decision making', *Journal of Policy Modeling*, vol 18, no 6, pp603–621

Meijaard, E, Sheil, D, Nasi, R, Augeri, D, Rosenbaum, B, Iskandar, D, Setyawati, T, Lammertink, M, Rachmatika, I, Wong, A, Soerhartono, T, Stanley, S and O'Brian, T (2005) *Life after Logging, Reconciling Wildlife Conservation and Production Forestry in Indonesian Borneo*, CIFOR and UNESCO, Jakarta

Nurmi, H (1995) 'On the difficulty of making social choices', *Theory and Decision*, vol 38, no 1, pp99–119

Ribot, J C (2003) 'Democratic decentralization of natural resources: Institutional choice and discretionary power transfers in sub-Saharan Africa', *Public Administration and Development*, vol 23, no 1, pp53–65

Ribot, J C (2005) 'Choosing representation: Institutions and powers for decentralized natural resources management' in Colfer, C J P and Capistrano, D (eds) *The Politics of Decentralization: Forests, Power and People*, Earthscan, London, pp86–106

Ribot, J C and Larson, A (2005) *Democratic Decentralization through a Natural Resource Lens*, Routledge, London

Sarin, M, Singh, N, Sundar, N and Bhogal, R (2003) 'Devolution as a threat to democratic decision making in three states in India' in Edmunds, D and Wollenberg, E (eds) *Local Forest Management: The Impacts of Devolution Policies*, Earthscan, London, pp55–120

Schlossberg, M and Shuford, E (2005) 'Delineating "public" and "participation" in PPGIS (Public Participation Geographic Information Systems)', *Urban and Regional Information Systems Association (URISA) Journal*, vol 16, no 2, pp15–26

Shackleton, S, Campbell, B M, Wollenberg, E and Edmunds, D (2002) 'Devolution and community-based natural resource management: Creating space for local people to participate and benefit?', *Natural Resources Perspectives* vol 76, Overseas Development Institute, London

Sikor, T and Tran Ngoc Thanh (2007) 'Exclusive versus inclusive devolution in forest management: Insights from forestland allocation in Vietnam's Central Highlands', *Land Use Policy*, vol 24, no 4, pp644–653

Smith, J, Obidzinski, K, Subarudi, I and Suramenggala, I (2003) 'Illegal logging, collusive corruption and fragmented governments in Kalimantan, Indonesia', *International Forestry Review*, vol 5, pp293–302

Sundar, N (2001) 'Is devolution democratization?', *World Development*, vol 29, no 12, pp2007–2023

Webster's Encyclopedic Unabridged Dictionary of the English Language (2001) Thunder Bay Press, San Diego

White, A and Martin, A (2002) *Who Owns the World's Forests? Forest Tenure and Public Forests in Transition*, Forest Trends and the Center for International Environmental Law, Washington, DC

Wollenberg, E, Moeliono, M, Limberg, G, Iwan, R, Rhee, S and Sudana, M (2006) 'Between state and society: Local governance of forests in Malinau, Indonesia', *Forest Policy and Economics*, vol 8, no 4, pp421–433

World Bank (2006) *India Unlocking Opportunities for Forest-Dependent People: Agriculture and Rural Development Sector Unit South Asia Region*, Oxford University Press, New Delhi

2

Devolution in Bulgaria's Irrigation System: Contesting the Public

Insa Theesfeld

INTRODUCTION

Theories of collective action are generally pessimistic about the chances that resource users would organize to supply a public good, even if they benefited from joint provision. Similarly, the so-called tragedy of the commons (Hardin, 1968) has become a widely used metaphor to denote the over-exploitation of subtractable resources by greater numbers of individuals in the absence of an effective property rights regime. Nevertheless, the logic underlying Hardin's model has also provoked extensive research into common property regimes, attesting to the ability of (mostly small) groups to organize joint provision (e.g. Bromley and Cernea, 1989; Wade, 1994; Bromley, 1998; Grafton, 2000; Dietz et al, 2003). This latter research suggests the potential of common property regimes for the management of natural resources as alternatives to state intervention and privatization.

More broadly, ample empirical evidence demonstrates that there is no clear dichotomy between private and public. At the two polar ends of the spectrum, governance is enacted by a single central authority, on the one hand, and a fully decentralized system of individual decision making, on the other (Ostrom, 1999). Yet between these two extremes is a range of options that may be described as polycentric governance systems involving higher levels of government as well as local systems. In a polycentric system, citizens are able to organize not just one but multiple governing authorities at various levels of scale.[1] Similarly, Ostrom (1999) has shown that complex polycentric governance systems are able to cope more effectively with tragedies of the commons.

This chapter looks at institutional changes in Bulgaria's irrigation sector as a particular case of a tragedy of the commons. It examines attempts in Bulgaria by the national government and the World Bank to promote water user associations for rural water management. It discusses the failure of these attempts, as indicated by contradictory policy decisions and implementation delays. Drawing upon the notions of public and private discussed in the Introduction to this volume, the chapter argues that water user associations exemplify a form of public institution rooted in local political communities. This follows the second distinction between public and private identified in the Introduction – understanding the political community as the public realm and the private as the more particularistic spheres of social life. The associations are radically different from the state-centred organizations that have dominated Bulgaria's irrigation sector. Consequently, the water user associations do not work because the underlying notion of a political community conflicts with efforts by the Bulgarian state to consolidate its control over rural society.

The chapter starts with a discussion of the redistribution of management responsibilities assigned to the agricultural producer cooperatives during the socialist era to the irrigation system state firm during the postsocialist period, which was accompanied by policies redistributing property rights to land and irrigation infrastructure. It then provides evidence for pseudodevolution due to the actual implementation process of Bulgaria's recent legislation in the irrigation sector, which results in a concentration of property rights on the side of state authorities. The evidence shows that what gives the impression of being a devolution-oriented reform that hands over decision power in resource management to local communities is in fact a further concentration of power in the irrigation sector.[2] Finally, the chapter concludes with an analysis of the empirical evidence in the light of two distinctions between private and public.

NEW FORMS OF IRRIGATION GOVERNANCE

Bulgaria's economy experienced a political and economic transition from a centrally planned to a market-oriented economy, with a strong impact on the agricultural sector.

Two policy styles have a major influence on the irrigation sector during this transition process: first, privatization and land restitution policies that are closely linked to questions of redistribution of property rights to irrigation infrastructure; and second, policies encouraging community based self-organization in the irrigation sector that frequently impose the institutional blueprint of water user associations (WUAs) on the local level.

Socialist irrigation governance

At the beginning of the socialist period, in the mid-1950s, the existing water syndicates were regarded as inconsistent with communist ideology. Although their degree of self-administration was limited in practice, they symbolized local self-governance of communities before collectivization. The individual water syndicates were liquidated and their association was dissolved (Theesfeld and Boevsky, 2005). Collectivization of agricultural land resulted in the socialist collective farms, the so-called agricultural producer cooperatives.[3] During the

1960s, the socialist government started new programs and initiatives to promote irrigated agriculture under these agricultural producer cooperatives. All over the country the agricultural producer cooperatives began building small water dams and canal systems with financial support from the state. The agricultural producer cooperatives, and later the even larger production units of agri-industrial complexes, were dominant throughout the socialist period. Hence, the irrigation infrastructure was built to serve their needs. Large-capacity canal systems were constructed. The water outlets were located at great distance from one another and did not allow for extensive regulation. Water metering was only necessary at the main water outlets, as the whole command area of irrigation belonged to one client – the agricultural producer cooperative.

Private farming on small plots (0.1 hectare) has been allowed since the mid-1980s, when nearly all producer cooperatives provided workers with a small plot of land to cultivate for household consumption. Transition experts agree (Davidova, 1994) that those small-scale producers secured the food supply in rural areas. Nevertheless, they relied on the producer cooperatives for input and technological supply (Penov, 2002). These subsistence plots were mostly planted with vegetables and forage crops and were located in close vicinity to the canals. Approximately 1.6 million micro-scale farmers thus became familiar with irrigation practices.

At first sight, the socialist agricultural system represents a very centralized one. The producer cooperatives and later the agri-industrial complexes held most of the property rights and obligation in the irrigation sector, such as the operation and maintenance on the midsized infrastructure or construction works. In fact, decisions were taken at the community level – at the producer cooperative – yet the small-scale producers had no voice in the decision processes. With the termination of the socialist era, the clear assignment of responsibility and the decision making power of the producer cooperative management were lost. The result has been open-access resource and infrastructure.

Reorganization of the state and privatization

The transition period saw a redefinition of the state's responsibilities as well as the privatization and redistribution of property rights. Two ministries are currently at the head of Bulgaria's hierarchical structure of the irrigation sector. The Ministry of Environment and Water (MEW) is responsible for Bulgaria's water sector, including the environmental supervision of the country's natural water resources and the coordination of the overall water balance. MEW coordinates water supply and demand for the various sectoral components: power, industry, municipality and agriculture. Water consumption in agriculture comprises crop irrigation, livestock breeding and fish farming. For the irrigation sector in particular, the Irrigation Office, which is affiliated with the Plant Growing Directorate of the Ministry of Agriculture and Forestry (MAF), is in charge.

The Irrigation Office can be considered the coordination unit implementing state irrigation policy.

MAF delegates the management of the irrigation sector to the Irrigation System Company (ISC) state firm. ISC is registered under commercial law as a stock-holding company with the state as the sole owner. It has a monopoly on irrigation water supply. Irrigation systems based on market coordination such as trading water rights or quotas do not exist. Irrigation sector management is centralized. Decisions are implemented top-down, and currently there are no opportunities for the agricultural water users to participate. No organization besides ISC plays a major role in the irrigation sector. ISC is responsible for the management, operation and maintenance of all state-owned irrigation and drainage systems in Bulgaria. Twenty-three regional branches operate semi-autonomously but answer to the head office in Sofia, especially for financial control (World Bank Office Sofia, 1999).

Figure 2.1 illustrates the hierarchical structure of the state-managed irrigation sector in Bulgaria and portrays the leading role of MEW and MAF. The figure also depicts the umbrella structure of the ISC from the head office to the regional branches and on to the employees working in the villages – the water technicians and the water guards.

Bulgaria experienced agrarian privatization reform and land restitution policies after 1989, impacting on the current agricultural sector (Davidova et al, 1997;

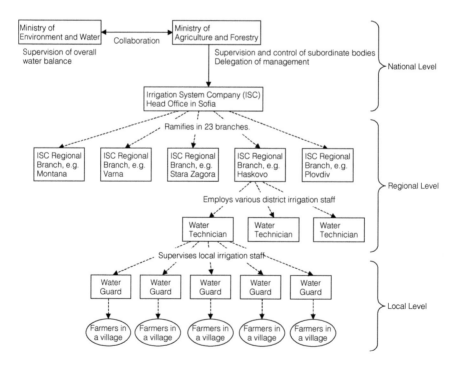

Figure 2.1 *Hierarchical structure of Bulgaria's irrigation sector*

Swinnen, 1997; Hanisch and Boevsky, 1999). The resulting design and implemention of the land restitution process is largely responsible for the poor condition of the current irrigation system. In many respects, changes in the irrigation sector are not only strongly connected with but also the result of changes in the ownership and property rights structure of land. At the end of the privatization process, land plot ownership within real (physical) boundaries was finally restored to previous owners or their heirs. Land ownership in Bulgaria prior to collectivization had already been highly fragmented (Hanisch, 2003). The postsocialist restitution process only served to intensify the fragmentation of the land (Yovchevska, 2002; Hanisch and Boevsky, 1999). As a result of the completed restitution, more than half of the private farms have a size of less than 0.2 hectare. Yovchevska (2002) identified 25 million plots on Bulgaria's agricultural area in 2002. Consequently, numerous plots are scattered along the same irrigation canal, an irrigation infrastructure that is by no means adequate to serve small-scale producer needs. The duration of the controversial process of land restitution is particularly responsible for the ambiguous property rights on the irrigation infrastructure. The process for restoring land within its real boundaries took 12 years, which led to reluctance in agricultural investments – including those in the irrigation infrastructure. This resulted in the deterioration of major sections of water management facilities, currently operating in an uncoordinated or even unauthorized manner (Penov et al, 2003). This situation is frequently referred to as abandoned irrigation infrastructure.

During the period spanning 1989 to 1999, the Bulgarian governments and the changing holders of political power hardly developed any concept of how to restructure the irrigation sector and adapt it to the needs of the newly evolving land ownership and production structures. In fact, the transformation of irrigation infrastructure was more a by-product of land restitution and privatization processes in the agricultural sector.

Bulgarian privatization was a voucher privatization. Accordingly, parts of the irrigation equipment were restituted in line with voucher privatization in the agricultural sector. Within the framework of the liquidation of the socialist agricultural producer cooperatives, the cooperative farm members received vouchers for the assets of the cooperatives according to their share and their labour input. Individuals could trade the vouchers for assets at a grand auction or exchange different categories of asset vouchers and combine them to bid for larger items (Swinnen and Mathijs, 1996). Compared to the great demand for basic technical assets, such as tractors, hardly anyone was interested in irrigation equipment, except for zinc tubes, which were considered attractive. Removable technical assets that were not privatized were subject to 'spontaneous privatization' (Rabinowicz and Swinnen, 1997). In the early 1990s, concrete slabs from the irrigation canals were used for construction work in private houses and estates. Hydrants and underground tubes were dismantled and used for other purposes or sold wherever possible. Between the years 1991 and 1992 the destruction and plundering of irrigation devices reached its peak. The destruction was strongly encouraged and partly organized by the former communists, who held governmental power until 1991. With the elections of October 1991, the communist adherents wanted to show to the rural electorate that the first reformist government that did not rely on the Socialist Party for political support was unable to satisfy the basic needs of the population, i.e. secure food production and build long-term prosperity (Theesfeld, 2005). From another perspective, the reformers and anticommunists encouraged the destruction of the large-scale irrigation infrastructure in order to destroy the basis for large-scale agriculture and to hinder the reestablishment of the socialist-style producer cooperatives in the long run. Either strategy exemplifies how politicians tried to win the rural electorate support in order to regain their political leadership for the next elections, in line with favourable positions to strive for private benefits. As a result, agricultural production was at stake because numerous small-scale subsistence producers were dependent upon reliable irrigation water supply, which was of no concern to the political actors.

The outcome of irrigation infrastructure transformation was most ambiguous for the medium-scale infrastructure, which comprises midsized internal canals, pump stations and approximately 1900 microdams (World Bank Office Sofia, 1999). Until now, the ownership rights of certain parts of the infrastructure have often been ambiguous. There are various agreements in Bulgarian villages concerning ownership. The internal canal system belongs to either the newly evolving cooperatives or the municipalities. The newly evolving cooperatives are founded as successors to the socialist producer cooperatives and serve mainly to consolidate the fragmented land plots that are the result of the land restitution process. In some villages, the vouchers for the internal canal system were turned over to these successor cooperatives. There was no interest in obtaining these devices, so the cooperatives acquired them. In other villages, the ownership rights to the internal canal system fell to the municipalities. The pump stations were partly assigned to the cooperative farms or to the state, depending on the size of the command area they were intended to serve. The microdams are to a large extent in the command of the municipalities, despite the fact that they were built by the producer cooperative members during the 1960s. The municipalities frequently lease the dams to fish farmers, who hardly maintain the dams due to the lack of incentive for long-term investments in the common leasing contracts extending between one and five years only.

The ownership rights of the main distribution canals still belong to the state. According to Penov (2002), MAF is responsible for these main canals, while the ISC state firm manages them. Despite these formally well-assigned ownership rights, it is not clear who is responsible for maintaining and cleaning certain main canals.

In addition to irrigation water, the major water dams supply drinking water and, in some cases, electricity. These dams with multipurpose functions are under the shared authority of three different ministries.

Devolution focus in postsocialist legislation

In the postsocialist period, a few Bulgarian laws contain important provisions connected with the changes to the property rights regime of irrigation systems. Since 1991 the World Bank has attempted to set up water user organizations (WUOs) (World Bank Office Sofia, 1999). During the same period the Cooperative Law affected the irrigation sector. Thereafter, the Bulgarian government enacted the Water User Association Act, which had a major impact on the irrigation sector. It came into force in March 2001 and claims to reform and decentralize the former centrally planned water sector and increase the involvement of local actors.

World Bank project and the Cooperative Law

The World Bank project can be subdivided into three main phases. The pilot phase of the World Bank project lasted from 1991 until 1995. The objective was to analyse the opportunities for the foundation of WUOs according to the Turkish model. A group of experts, mainly employees from ISC, were trained by the World Bank and conducted field visits to WUOs in Turkey. Finally, four pilot WUOs were established in Bulgaria.

The second phase of the project officially pursued devolution objectives in irrigation management and ran from 1995 until 1996. The World Bank requested the establishment of WUOs as a precondition for granting a loan to Bulgaria, which was a strong incentive for the government to participate and to support the establishment of WUOs (Koubratova Hristova, 2002). The World Bank hired consultants to organize their setup. In July 1996, one consultant was employed at each ISC regional branch for at least three months. In the World Bank report these consultants were referred to as 'local facilitators ... who assisted the start of WUOs' (World Bank Office Sofia, 1999). The consultants did not have to prove their hydromeliorative expertise. Crucial for the development of the WUOs was that the consultants were paid on the basis of the number of registered WUOs, obviously a strong incentive to found as many WUOs on paper as possible. Consequently, 206 WUOs were reported to be established by the end of 1997, 128 of which were registered at courts (World Bank Office Sofia, 1999).

The third phase of the project began with the termination of the regional facilitator's work by the end of 1996. The World Bank project title, Irrigation Rehabilitation Project, is linked to this third phase. The Bank attempted to transfer management responsibilities from ISC to local WUOs. They were to take over the responsibility of operation and maintenance of the irrigation and drainage infrastructure at the local level. The basic idea behind this project was 'to manifest the WUOs' readiness and willingness to rehabilitate the irrigation facilities managed by them through their own funds' (World Bank Office Sofia, 1999).

In 1999 the project came to an end, with 172 WUOs reported to have been registered with the court. The major share (164) of these organizations was founded under the Cooperative Law. MAF reported that out of the total reported number of WUOs, approximately 30 were actively operating. In the end, only eight WUOs were listed and received a World Bank credit for rehabilitation of its irrigation facilities. In 1999 the Bank admitted that only one out of the 172 WUOs met all requirements for an operational WUO; the rest of them existed only on paper (World Bank Office Sofia, 1999). It turned out that the project was chiefly used for political purposes, varying according to the political parties in power.

Village outsiders frequently managed to receive the use rights for the canal system. By reducing maintenance work to a minimum and not ensuring a reliable water supply, they concentrated on collecting water fees, sometimes in advance. Thus, they managed to extract high personal rents, with severe consequences for the already deteriorated infrastructure. Most of the WUOs either terminated their work voluntarily as expected financial support failed to appear, or their existence was terminated by MAF after strong protest by the water users who refused to pay the overpriced water fee. In both cases, the use rights to the infrastructure fell back to ISC.

Water User Association Act and by-laws

In Bulgaria a special law for WUAs was enforced in March 2001. The main elements of the WUA Act are: first, the transferral of ownership of internal canal systems from the state to agricultural producers; and second, a change in the direction of the decision making process from top-down to bottom-up, thus delegating irrigation system management and property rights to the water users. The introduction to the WUA Act reveals the motivation of the law: to adapt the irrigation sector to the farm structures and property rights on land that evolved after 1990 as a result of Bulgaria's agricultural reform. Article 2 outlines the purpose of the WUAs:

> *Water User Associations shall be voluntary organizations of natural and legal persons, which, in accordance with the interest of their members and society and through mutual assistance and cooperation, shall perform activities related to the irrigation and drainage of agricultural lands and the maintenance of irrigation and drainage infrastructure on a specified territory.*

All WUOs that had been formally established had to reregister under the condition of the WUA Act within a period of six months from 1 April 2001. WUOs that were not reregistered by the end of this period would be terminated and taken from the register. Their irrigation infrastructure would once again fall under the management of the ISC state firm.

The operation of WUAs would be under the supervision of the state (Art. 5). MAF acts as the supervisory body with various functions. For instance, amendments in the WUAs' statutes have to be approved by the supervisory body (Art. 16). This supervisory body was specified as a Hydromeliorative Agency in subsequent by-laws. These aspects show the strong influence of the state within the WUAs, which had previsously been community organizations.

CONTESTING DEVOLUTION

The following explores the divergence between formal devolution attempts and the actual further concentration of power with ISC. Analyis of the WUA registration processes reveals the competition between the WUAs and ISC. As will be shown, the chosen formal procedure for the registration hinders rather than favours WUA foundations. Furthermore, the voluntary use rights transfer for irrigation infrastructure and aspects of the amending bills to the Water User Association Act serve as examples of pseudodevolution.

By comparison, the case of institutional change in Portugal's water sector discussed in Chapter 3 also shows a shift from regional self-governance – from a functioning institution to centralized state agencies. In contrast to the Bulgarian case, this centralization is not part of a hidden agenda; instead, actors are very outspoken about it. Chapter 3 describes a new minister's promotion in 1999 of a strong national water company that was owned by the public but controlled by the ministry. The decisions in the Portuguese case are driven by economic and environmental concerns, such as the lack of strategic water supply security and local water management capacities in the regions, as well as tourism's increasing demand for water resources. The decisions in the Bulgarian case, however, are driven by state actors' fear of losing control and influence in the irrigation sector and thereby opportunities to extract personal rents.

Decision power and membership of the temporary committee

In contrast to the registration of a WUO under the former Cooperative Law, the registration of a WUA under the WUA Act is strictly regulated. The first step in establishing a WUA is the founding of a local 'constituent committee', which is comprised of at least five people in possession of the title deeds to their land and who are served by the same single irrigation system. This group of people has to apply for the 'opening of an establishment procedure'[4] (Art. 8[2]). As a supervisory body, the Hydromeliorative Agency decides on the application and eventually ratifies the order for the opening of an establishment procedure (Art. 9). The following offers a description of the stipulation procedure for registering a WUA, once the application has reached the national authorities.

Until July 2002 no Hydromeliorative Agency was established with enough decisive power over the applications to commence the WUA establishment procedure, and instead decisions about the applications were made by a temporary committee. Insiders call this temporary committee a 'stop block', indicating its braking of the management devolution process.

An initial indication of the actual concentration of power with the state authorities is evident in the membership of the temporary committee, which cannot be regarded as neutral, as it mostly comprises specialists from ISC and MAF. There is only one participant who does not represent one of the two closely linked state authorities: a member of the union of water users. Nevertheless, he has no right to vote. The committee's composition demonstrates a crucial aspect in the competition between ISC and the planned WUAs.

There is rivalry over the midsized infrastructure between ISC and the WUAs. ISC strives to keep certain irrigation systems under its control, i.e. the profitable ones or those with well-established relationships to major individual water users, thus ensuring reliable side payments. In particular, ISC tries to keep those irrigation territories under its control that incorporate a water dam, a barrage or a main distribution canal. These so-called bottlenecks are easy to control and manageable at low cost. For the manager at ISC head office, the advantage of a WUA arises from the fact that his company has to negotiate with only one contractor for a certain territory, assuming that the water dam or the main distribution canal as a supplying infrastructure remains under ISC control. In other irrigation territories – especially those with a very small-scale, ramified and destroyed canal network – ISC wishes to outsource to the water users. Alongside a growing number of WUAs, ISC is losing its legitimation to exist. The fear of losing responsibility and hence jobs triggers competition between ISC and the WUAs. In light of the high annual subsidies paid by the state in support of the irrigation sector, the status quo puts ISC in the position of distributing and deciding over the full amount of subsidies, whereas a decentralization of management would imply a decentralized subsidy distribution, an effect not welcomed by ISC employees. Regarding the competitive situation, the empowerment of ISC department heads to decide over the establishment of WUAs through their representation in the temporary committee clearly favours the advocates of the centralized irrigation system management.

By July 2002, 150 applications had been received for 110 territories. The temporary committee held eight meetings up until July 2002 to decide on applications and offered advice to the minister to approve or dismiss the applications, which resulted in 70 orders for the opening of the establishment procedure signed by the minister. In addition to the frequent complaints of WUA initiators that ISC regional branches hindered legal establishment procedures, another indication of the strong competition is the fact that only one WUA had been registered by 2002. Moreover, this WUA did not receive water from ISC but independently from a river.

In several cases, two applications referred to an identical territory or one identical constituent committee applied for different territories. In cases where there is more than one application for commencing an establishment procedure in an identical territory, the ministry can decide how to proceed. In cases where one committee applies for different territories, the ministry assumes the role of the constituent committee with the aim of either postponing the decision on the management of the WUA by the water users or directly deciding and adjusting the boundaries of the territory.

After a constituent committee has received the order to commence the procedure, the second stage in the application procedure is reached and, in compliance with the WUA Act, further formal steps have to be taken. The initiators must organize at least two preliminary 'constituent meetings', which must be announced in local and national newspapers. The constituent meeting is legitimate if the persons described in Article 6(2) participate (Art. 11); the meeting's objective is to compile a list of all potential founders of a WUA. This refers to the rule that 51 per cent of landowners and users who own and use more than 50 per cent of agricultural land in the territory must be founding members. This requirement is restrained by Article 12, which states that each founding member may authorize another person to represent him/her in the constituent meeting with his/her signature and in witness of a notary public. In particular, this article contains opportunities to bypass the law. The participant list of the constituent meeting, as well as the statutes of the planned WUA, must be reapproved by the minister for agriculture in subsequent steps.

Voluntary use rights transfer

Another interesting issue of the WUA Act concerns the use rights of the infrastructure granted to WUAs and the ownership transfer. Article 47(1) states that:

> the associations shall be entitled to acquire use rights, free of charge, over the irrigation facilities as well as the service equipment on the territory of the association, included in the property of trade associations in which the state is a sole trader [i.e. ISC]. The terms and conditions for transferring and withdrawing use rights shall be in conformity with an ordinance issued by the Council of Ministers on a proposal from the MAF.

A WUA that uses facilities in compliance with the previous statements 'shall be entitled, within a period of up to five years from use right acquisition, to acquire property rights on them free of charge by a decision of the Council of Ministers on a proposal from the MAF' (Art. 47[4]).

At this point a digression to the Water Law should help to illustrate the deliberate fuzziness of the laws, which enable the state to exert influence over the irrigation sector at any time. For instance, the text of Article 91(1) of the Water

Law declares that, 'Owners of water economy systems shall be able to concede rights to use over the systems or technologically detached parts of them to water user association in connection with the subject of activity of the association for a term no longer than ten years.' These regulations, together with the provisions specified in the WUA Act, merely specify an opportunity for the establishment of use rights. The granting of use rights to WUAs is not a mandatory obligation but a legal option for the state firm (World Bank Office Sofia, 1999). The World Bank conceives the granting of a mere option to establish a use right an inadequate legal solution to the present crisis in the irrigation sector, which additionally hampers investment by the associations. The Bank concludes that in the Water Law the rights of ISC should be 'partially retained in full', because ISC remains owner of the infrastructure used by the WUAs. For the infrastructure that is declared public state property, a use right for the state firm should be established (World Bank Office Sofia, 1999).

Amending bills to the Water User Association Act

Two proposals to amend the WUA Act are currently circulating in Bulgaria: one was submitted by the Council of Ministers in March 2004 and one by a member of the Turkish Party in July 2004. There were a number of first and second readings of these bills in plenary sessions in the National Assembly. Nevertheless, these amendments have not been adopted by parliament. With the commencement of the preelection period and the parliamentary elections in Bulgaria in the summer of 2005, the discussion about the WUA issue was suspended.

As regards the devolution process and the redistribution of property rights in the irrigation sector, two aspects in the first amending bill are of particular interest. First, it is proposed that the rights and decision powers of the minister of agriculture be expanded (§15 Art. 66[2]). For instance, the minister should approve the statutes of the WUAs and changes to it. He can also start his own initiative to establish a WUA and can issue an order on the rules concerning infrastructure use. This opposes the decentralization objective and the claimed aim of devolving responsibilities from the state to the communities and would in fact result in a concentration of power.

Second, in reference to Article 6(2) and the 51 per cent rule, the number of people necessary to found a WUA would be reduced. At first glance, this change in procedural rules seems to lead to simplified practices and a reduction in obligation but bears the risk of misuse. Village outsiders with incentives other than organizing collective action can initiate a pseudo-WUA with more ease. It would reduce the burden of collecting a large number of signatures, a formal requirement that is already easily bypassed.

Overall, no measures in the amending bills to the WUA Act could be found that would directly facilitate the emergence of cooperation, such as disseminating information, strengthening the advisory system or increasing interpersonal trust among the rural community members – the last being a basic prerequisite for the emergence of collective action.

CONCLUSION

Bulgaria's postsocialist irrigation policies incorporate two different policy styles. In the beginning of the transition period, we observed policies dedicated to privatization and redistribution of property rights. With the enforcement of the WUA Act in 2001, devolution-oriented policy initiatives prevailed. Yet, instead of a devolution process in the irrigation sector – transfer of responsibilities and authorities from state to local communities – legislation breakdown has led to a further concentration of decision powers with the state authorities. State actors try to maintain control over irrigation and subvert devolution in the irrigation sector.

We can gain insight into the reasons for the Bulgarian pseudodevolution by relating the policies in more abstract terms to different mental models of the public–private distinction in the Introduction to this book. The redefinition of responsibilities by the state during transition and the privatization of the irrigation infrastructure correspond to the first dimension of public–private distinction as state versus market. The policies sought to reorganize the state and shift some property rights to market-based actors by way of privatization.

The second sets of policies, the ideas informing the World Bank project and the WUA Act, aim at the devolution and the promotion of cooperative structures. They relate to the second distinction between public and private. The WUAs to be founded are understood as expressions of political communities – that is, publics in the sense of the second distinction. This demonstrates that the first set of policies during the early stages of transition envisioned the state as the public, whereas the second set of policies was founded on a different notion of the public – the public as a political community including state and nonstate actors in terms of self-governance of local communities as described by Ostrom (2005).

The latest devolution-oriented reforms, which only represent pseudodevolution in practice, promote cooperative structures based on the assumption that political communities exist that could serve as foundations for WUAs. Yet in practice, state actors assert the primacy of the state as the location of the public, perceive the WUAs as a threat to their power, and react by undermining efforts to support their development. Consequently, attempts to establish WUAs will not be successful as long as, first, mental models are shaped by the first understanding of the private–public divide, and second, political actors continue to act for their own personal benefit. In order to increase support for the WUAs, it is essential that the public, including state authorities, understand political communities as building the state.

NOTES

1   As Ostrom (2005) points out, in a polycentric system 'each unit exercises considerable independence to make and enforce rules within a circumscribed domain of authority for a specified geographical area'. 'Some units are general-purpose governments while others may be highly specialized. Self-organized resource governance systems in such a system may be special districts, private associations, or parts of a local government. These are nested in several levels of general-purpose governments that also provide civil, equity, as well as criminal courts.'

2   Knox and Meinzen-Dick (2001) distinguish between devolution and decentralization, which are sometimes used interchangeably: devolution indicates the transfer of responsibility and authority over natural resources from the state to nongovernmental bodies, particularly user groups, and decentralization refers to authority and management transfers to lower levels of government (see also Introduction).

3   These pseudocooperatives were not managed and operated according to the cooperative principles set up by Schulze-Delitzsch and Raiffeisen, who created the modern cooperative system in Germany. The agricultural producer cooperatives stand for a centrally administered, hierarchically managed, nationalized cooperative system.

4   The term indicates a two-stage process. The procedure to apply for the opening of the establishment procedure is a prerequisite.

REFERENCES

Bromley, D (1998) 'Determinants of cooperation and management of local common property resources: Discussion', *American Journal of Agricultural Economics*, vol 80, no 3, pp665–668

Bromley, D and Cernea, M (1989) 'The management of common property natural resources: Some conceptual and operational fallacies', *World Bank Discussion Paper 57*, World Bank, Washington, DC

Davidova, S (1994) 'Changes in agricultural policies and restructuring of Bulgarian agriculture: An overview' in Swinnen, J (ed) *Policy and Institutional Reform in Central European Agriculture*, Aldershot, Avebury, pp36–75

Davidova, S, Buckwell, A and Kopeva, D (1997) 'Bulgaria: Economics and politics of post-reform farm structures' in Swinnen, J, Buckwell, A and Mathijs, E (eds) *Agricultural Privatization, Land Reform and Farm Restructuring in Central and Eastern Europe*, Ashgate, Aldershot, pp23–62

Dietz, T, Ostrom, E and Stern, P (2003) 'The struggle to govern the commons', *Science*, vol 302, pp1907–1912

Grafton, Q (2000) 'Governance of the commons: A role for the state?', *Land Economics*, vol 76, no 4, pp504–517

Hanisch, M (2003) *Property Reform and Social Conflict: A Multi-Level Analysis of the Change of Agricultural Property Rights in Post-Socialist Bulgaria*, Shaker, Aachen

Hanisch, M and Boevsky, I (1999) 'Political, institutional and structural developments accompanying land reform and privatization in Bulgarian agriculture', *Südosteuropa, Zeitschrift für Gegenwartsforschung*, vol 48, no 7/8, pp446–464

Hardin, G (1968) 'The tragedy of the commons', *Science*, vol 162, pp1243–1248

Knox, A and Meinzen-Dick, R (2001) 'Workshop summary' in Meinzen-Dick R, Knox, A and Di Gregorio, M (eds) *Collective Action, Property Rights and Devolution of Natural Resource Management: Exchange of Knowledge and Implications for Policy*, Zentralstelle für Ernährung und Landwirtschaft, Feldafing, Germany pp1–33

Koubratova Hristova, M (2002), 'Bulgarian Water User Associations: Situation and problems', Paper presented at the Central and Eastern European Sustainable Agriculture (CEESA) – Bulgarian Policy Learning Workshop, 18–21 July, Plovdiv, Bulgaria

Ostrom, E (2005) *Understanding Institutional Diversity*, Princeton University Press, Princeton and Oxford

Ostrom, V (1999) 'Polycentricity' (Parts 1 and 2) in McGinnis, M (ed) *Polycentricity and Local Public Economies: Readings from the Workshop in Political Theory and Policy Analysis*, University of Michigan Press, Ann Arbor, pp52–74, pp119–138

Penov, I (2002) 'The use of irrigation water during transition in Bulgaria's Plovdiv region', *CEESA Discussion Paper No. 7*, Humboldt University of Berlin, Berlin

Penov, I, Theesfeld, I and Gatzweiler, F (2003) *Irrigation and Water Regulation Systems in Transition: The Case of Bulgaria in Comparison with Latvia, East Germany and Romania*, Food and Agriculture Organization, Budapest

Rabinowicz, E and Swinnen, J (1997) 'Political economy of privatization and decollectivization of Central and East European agriculture: Definitions, issues and methodology' in Swinnen, J (ed) *Political Economy of Agrarian Reform in Central and Eastern Europe*, Ashgate, Aldershot, pp129–158

Swinnen, J (1997) 'On liquidation councils, flying troikas and Orsov co-operatives: The political economy of agricultural reform in Bulgaria' in Swinnen, J (ed) *Political Economy of Agrarian Reform in Central and Eastern Europe*, Ashgate, Aldershot, pp129–158

Swinnen, J and Mathijs, E (1996) 'Agricultural Privatization, Land Reform and Farm Restructuring in Central and Eastern Europe: A Comparative Analysis', Paper presented at the COST-Conference on 'Agricultural Privatization, Land Reform and Farm Restructuring in Central and Eastern Europe', 14–16 June, Sinaia, Romania

Theesfeld, I (2005) *A Common-Pool Resource in Transition: Determinants of Institutional Change in Bulgaria's Postsocialist Irrigation Sector*, Shaker, Aachen

Theesfeld, I and Boevsky, I (2005) 'Reviving pre-socialist cooperative traditions: The case of water syndicates in Bulgaria', *Sociologia Ruralis*, vol 45, no 3, pp171–186

Wade, R (1994) *Village Republics: Economic Conditions for Collective Action in South India*, Institute for Contemporary Studies Press, San Francisco, CA (first published in 1988 by Cambridge University Press)

World Bank Office Sofia (1999) *Irrigation Rehabilitation Project*, Main Report, World Bank Office, Sofia

Yovchevska, P (2002) 'Land relationships in Bulgaria', *Agricultural Economics*, vol 48, no 11, pp490–494

3

Water Service Provision in the Algarve, Portugal: From Local to National Publics

Andreas Thiel

INTRODUCTION

Portugal has undergone significant changes since it joined the EU in 1986. The country's European accession has led to the restructuring of the economy and to significant changes in the shape of institutions governing economic activities and in the actor constellations involved (see, for example, Magone, 1997). As will become clear, this chapter argues for a strong connection between the country's integration into the EU and the way resource governance has developed. It is illustrated by examining the implications of the emerging Algarvian tourism sector for resource governance.

The chapter reconstructs the changes in institutions and actor constellations that govern water service provision to populations in the Algarve since the accession of Portugal to the EU. In line with the topic of the volume, a specific emphasis is put on the changing role of actors in water service provision and their association with the specific understanding of the categories public and private. The question is how public, state and private sector actors have shaped water service provision. The chapter presents the contingent reasons and strategies of public and private actors on different levels of societal organization for shaping water service provision. A detailed categorization of actors' capacities helps us to understand the specific strategies and roles of private and public actors.

The case study was researched as part of a broader research project (Thiel, 2004b; 2005), conducting more than 50 interviews, covering actors at all levels of social organization and an extensive review of relevant newspapers and documents.

The chapter is divided into four sections. First, some basic definitions and the delimitation of the categories public and private are presented and related to the framework provided in the Introduction to this book. Second, a heuristic of actors' capacities is introduced to later analyse actors' strategic interaction with their environment. Third, using these conceptual tools, an account of the development of the institutions and actor constellations is provided regarding water service provision in the Algarve. Finally, the changing roles of public and private actors at different levels of societal organization are described.

Public and Private

In this chapter, institutions are perceived:

> *as sets of interrelated rules governing given aspects of social life, which*
> *are acknowledged (or sanctioned) by all or some members of society.*
> *They regulate relationships among individuals and between the social*
> *and ecological systems, ie rights and duties as well as costs and benefits*
> *of actions. Therefore, institutions link social and ecological systems.*
> *(Gatzweiler and Hagedorn, 2003)*

Institutions include formal and informal rules that fix property rights. Furthermore, Hagedorn et al (2002) include governance structures for structures that supervise and sanction property rights. By water service provision, in this chapter we understand the provision of water supply and sanitation services to permanent and temporary residents. It includes the abstraction (from surface or underground sources), treatment and provision of piped water as well as the collection and discharge (potentially after treatment) of sewage water.

Notions of public and private can have various denotations. Our delineation details the liberal-economistic distinction between state and market provided in the Introduction. For Weintraub (1997), the way economists use the terms public and private is one of the clearest examples of making distinctions with regard to the second criterion – degree of collectivity. One criterion that can delineate state/public and private action is the degree of association with the government. Weintraub emphasizes the two types of actors' diverse capacities to shape institutions and societal action. In democratic, capitalist societies, government-like actors at any level of social organizations are legitimated through elections. They make, approve and revoke regulations and employ executive/coercive powers of the state (Weintraub, 1997). The state acts as a profit oriented actor (public enterprises) or as a nonprofit oriented actor. Therefore, we introduce a subcriterion to distinguish among various types of public or private action (see Table 3.1). Both can be distinguished by the underlying rationale (nonprofit or profit orientation).

A further distinction is made with regard to the level of social organization on which public or private actors are organized and operate. Local, regional and national public actors can be distinguished on the basis of the territorially bound jurisdiction for which they are competent or the (territorial) extent of the collectivity that legitimizes their actions, which often coincide. Alternatively, nongovernmental (private), profit oriented actors at the different levels of social organization can be individuals or contractually created organizations. Their sphere of operation may comprise any territorially defined unit.

Table 3.1 *Examples of different publics and privates*

	Profit oriented	Nonprofit oriented
(Public)	Public enterprises	Administration
Governmental		
(European, national, regional, local)		
(Private)		
Nongovernmental	Private enterprises	NGOs, foundations, etc.
(Supranational, national, regional, local)		

STRATEGIC ACTORS AND THEIR CAPACITIES

This chapter reconstructs the way in which actors use their capacities to shape the institutions and actor constellations governing water use provision. Capacities are defined as 'the ability of actors (whether individually or collectively) to have an effect upon contexts which define the range of possibilities of others' (Hay, 2002). Actors are assumed to strategically act reflexively and consciously (for details see Jessop, 2001 on the strategic-relational approach). Their strategies are constrained by the physical and institutional structure in which they are embedded. Therefore, Jessop writes that action develops in a path-dependent way. Within structurally predefined bounds, however, actors similarly shape the development path (Jessop, 2002). Strategically selective structures are spatially and temporally specified and favour certain strategies over others.

This reconstruction offers more analytical depth by using a delimitation of forms of capacity with which actors exercise power over water service provision. The power to appoint an actor for a specific position is distinguished as legitimating capacity. Authoritative capacity implies authority to do or enforce something. Regulatory capacity means the capacity to draft and adopt regulations that grant authoritative power as well as legitimating, financial, physical and socially constructive powers. Most obviously, these three forms of power are genuine governmental capacities in democratic states. There are, however, so-called contractually bound organizations. Financial capacities shape water service provision by using financial means. Physical capacity implies control of the means to physically shape water use. In this chapter, the two are synonymous. Socially constructive capacities are associated with holding and producing societal knowledge and include shaping perceptions of how to combine the elements constituting water use to influence or criticize an outcome. They operate through a variety of channels such as the media, science or direct face-to-face interaction, and potentially shape all elements constituting water service provision. The various forms of power overlap each other and are interrelated.

CASE STUDY

The case study first presents the institutional, organizational and actor constellation regarding the provision of water services to the population in the Algarve at two points in time: first, when Portugal became part of the EU, and second, at present. For both moments in time, the chapter describes the role of private, nongovernmental (profit and nonprofit oriented) and public/state (governmental/profit, and nonprofit oriented) sector actors at different levels of social organization. Second, it reconstructs the explanandum, the changes in institutions and actor constellations in water service provision between these two points in time, using the conception of capacities based on strategic action as well as on a spatial and temporal context. Water provision involves infrastructures that take a relatively long time to develop as well as sets of institutions whose change involves deep restructuring. Therefore, only a few instances of decisive 'accelerated' change and development need to be examined.

The case study region comprises the southernmost region of Portugal called the Algarve, which is made up of 16 councils (see Figure 3.1). Only 'deconcentrated'[1] national administrations exist on the regional level. The Algarve has three morphological regions (see Figure 3.2). The accessible, flat Litoral along the coast has numerous sandy beaches and is the focus of tourism. The coastal hinterland of the Barrocal consists of agriculture, infrastructures and several small towns with a relatively diverse economy. Finally, there is the inaccessible mountainous Serra, which is relatively unpopulated.

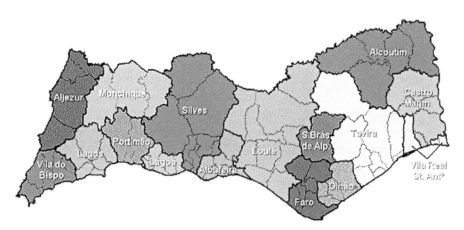

Figure 3.1   *Councils of the Algarve*

Source: CCDR, 2005

WATER SERVICE PROVISION IN THE ALGARVE: MID-1980S AND 2004

In the mid-1980s piped water service provision was relatively scarce, especially in the interior, which lacked tourism. The sector is largely unregulated, though it is formally the responsibility of local authorities to implement and charge for water services. In fact, local authorities finance water services from local tax income and operate water services disconnected from the rest of the water use sector. The regional, deconcentrated level of administration in charge of river basin protection and licensing is extremely weak and inefficient (see also Magone, 1997). Tourism development is largely uncontrolled. Hardly any data exist on the physical configuration of water availability. Technical and management capacity to implement adequate infrastructure solutions is minimal, particularly at the local level (Magone, 1997). The national public sector authorities occasionally intervene to overcome emergency situations, especially in times of drought. Water supply depends on local aquifers. Formally, the regional level is supposed to license wells; informally, however, wells are not licensed. The quality of the coastal aquifers started to deteriorate in the 1980s due to saline intrusion from overexploitation by municipalities and enterprises. This is a consequence of uncontrolled development of the tourism sector and abstraction by the agricultural sector. Coastal coverage with piped water is close to 100 per cent; in the interior it is around 60 per cent. Water pressure is variable, and quality is low. Coastal waters and beaches are increasingly polluted due to insufficient collection and treatment of mounting quantities of sewage water. Sewage water collection quota in the different areas of the Algarve are much lower than the water supply quota.

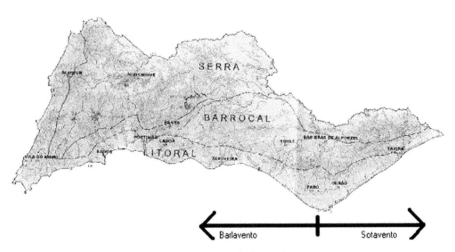

Figure 3.2 *Morphological regions*

Source: MAOT, 2000

By 2004 water service provision was segmented, regulation of the sector was enforced by the central state through its regional, deconcentrated, environmental authority. The central state is closely involved in the operation of water services and their financing. Regulatory density concerning water service provision has increased after water use licensing, planning and charging were introduced. The municipalities undertake local water distribution, water quality monitoring and sewage water collection. They fix and collect water charges. The regional, profit oriented water company in public ownership (regional organization of a national public enterprise) runs supralocal infrastructures for the provision and treatment of drinking water from dams (see Figure 3.3) and aquifers located in the interior, as well as for the treatment and discharge of sewage water. Water supply systems are regionally interconnected. The municipalities receive drinking water from the regional water company and pass sewage water on to it for treatment. They are charged for this service by cubic metre. In turn, municipalities charge citizens different prices per cubic metre for the water supply and sanitation services. In most municipalities the charges do not cover the costs of the services provided. The local authorities and the regional environmental authority follow tourism and land use development plans. The regional environmental authority enforces the licensing regime, and penalty schemes are increasingly effective, despite continuing financial and human resource constraints. Water-relevant developments lack coordination with the development of water supply to populations and the agricultural sector, specifically at the regional level. The regional water resources have been well studied, and knowledge of infrastructures and their management is high (especially at the national level) in the regional public water company, the regional environmental administration and the coastal municipalities. River basin plans have been developed in the context of development for the Water Framework Directive at the European level. Several regional interest associations effectively represent the needs of the tourism sector in the media and vis-à-vis the government. Drinking water quality, urban wastewater treatment and bathing water standards are based on European regulations and implementation efforts in the respective fields. Most infrastructures for water service provision at local as well as regional levels have been financed by European funds.

Coverage with water supply and sewage water collection is high, most of all in the coastal tourism zones. Water quality and monitoring comply with the European drinking water directive. Most coastal waters comply with the European bathing water directive. Coverage with sewage water collection and treatment significantly trail behind water supply standards. All European directives have been formally transposed and are enforced by the national state through its regional agencies. Sanitation standards (collection and treatment of sewage water) lag behind the standards of the European directives. Water consumption has greatly increased, particularly in the summer and along the coast, due to tourism expansion, use habits and golf courses. Sewage water has

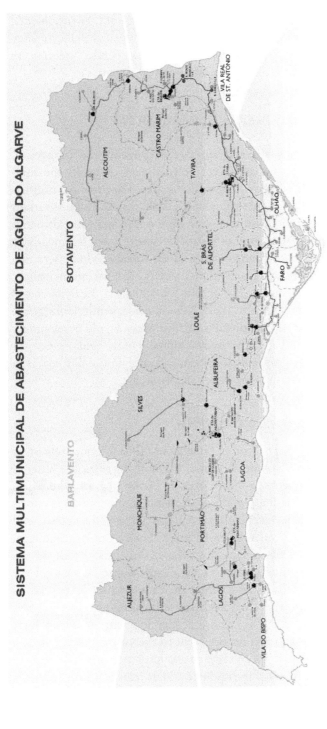

Figure 3.3 *The integrated surface water supply systems in the Algarve – Barlavento/Sotavento*

Source: Águas do Algarve, 2007

similarly increased. Coastal aquifers remain saline, and aquifers on the whole tend to be more polluted in areas of intense agriculture.

Throughout the 1990s, nongovernmental and nonprofit environmental associations increasingly interfered with water and environmental policymaking. Particularly at the beginning of the 1990s, they drew public attention to insufficient implementation of several European water directives.

STRATEGIC INERACTION ACCOUNT

The following account of the strategic interaction presents the changes in institutions, organizational set-up and actor constellations between the mid-1980s and 2004 in water service provision in the Algarve. The principal conflicts that it describes are those of setting up supralocal infrastructures and institutions to provide the initial water supply and then sanitation to the increasing demands of the coastal tourism sector. Supralocal infrastructures were supposed to strike a balance between underdeveloped municipalities in the interior, which were rich in water but poor in infrastructure and funds, and the coastal municipalities where the situation was the opposite. The account first looks at the dynamics of shaping water supply and sanitation in the 1980s. It subsequently looks at the role of regional, national and supranational actors for water supply development in the 1990s and current decade. Finally, the development of the sanitation sector in the 1990s and the current decade is described, focusing on the differences in its development in comparison with the water supply sector.

Water supply and sanitation in the 1980s

In the mid-1980s tourism lagged behind in the regions of the interior. Reliant on local aquifers, local authorities had no difficulties in supplying sufficient water of decent quality to their limited networks. Coverage of the interior with piped water, however, was much lower than on the coast. Water service provision efforts of the national public authorities were localized and sporadic and for strategic and economic reasons were focused on the coastal areas. Then as today, municipal income greatly depends on tourism and construction activity and thus on the local tax system. As a result, municipalities with a large territorial share of the interior had far less income per unit of territory than those with a large share of coastal tourism development. They had insufficient fiscal resources and know-how to improve infrastructures. The economic development of inland local authorities could not rely on tourism development to the same extent.

Administrative capacities of specifically small, local authorities were very weak. Knowledge about the status of the resource and its management was hardly available at all. No money had been spent on its study, and human resources were insufficient in this regard. Expertise was concentrated at the national level. Local administrative capacities did not match the considerable competencies that local authorities obtained after the revolution, when locally elected mayors emerged as significant independent powers in the overall structure of the Portuguese state (see also Magone, 1997). Nonetheless, they vehemently guarded their relatively strong position.

Coastal municipalities had hit the upper limit of local water resource availability at the beginning of the 1980s. Still, they used their regulatory, authoritative and fiscal capacities to promote tourism development in an almost uncontrolled fashion, during which they consistently ignored infrastructure constraints and emerging problems of increasing disfiguration of the landscape and of the appearance of coastal areas. They mainly pursued tax income from construction and local economic development. Portuguese and international private companies continued to invest in tourism development in the Algarve. Water abstraction from local aquifers spiralled out of control and soon the coastal aquifers had become saline. This situation was aggravated by occasional droughts. Water supply had to be rationed in places at the beginning of the 1980s; water quality was very poor and deteriorated further. In charge of water service provision, local authorities lacked the authoritative capacities to resort to water outside of their jurisdiction. Their fiscal resources for such complex infrastructure investments would have been insufficient. Nevertheless, the economic development of coastal municipalities depended on the water supply. Sewage water was insufficiently dealt with, leading to polluted coastal waters and a bad smell in coastal tourism areas. Tourism development became threatened by poor water supply and sanitation.

The government became conscious of these problems for the tourism sector, which by that time had started to become one of the most important economic sectors for export. Therefore, in the beginning of the 1980s it strived to reach an agreement with all (coastal and interior) local authorities to build a regional surface water supply scheme based on four dams in the interior and an extensive water distribution network covering the whole region. The basic technical dimensions and studies of surface waters underlying the project already dated back to the beginning of the 1970s, when it was supposed to provide water for intense irrigation in agriculture.

The municipalities, however, were not able to agree on a way to contribute to the funding of this scheme. In addition, given their poor administrative capacities and knowledge of water resource issues, numerous municipalities did not see the strategic dimension of and need for this project. Instead, many of the interior municipalities wanted to maintain authoritative and physical resource independence from their neighbouring municipalities and the central state. Municipalities in the interior also did not experience the water supply problems of the coastal tourism areas, as demand was much less, quality standards of provision did not have to be as high and underground water stores were greater.

Nonetheless, after these droughts and with European cofunding available after 1986, the central government used its authoritative capacity over surface waters and began to build a dam that was the first constituent of the regional scheme to provide surface water.

At the same time, some of the most affluent coastal authorities that were already dominated by tourism started to take a more strategic approach to water supply and sanitation on their own. They improved their know-how through better staffing. With substantial financial support from the European Structural funds, some of them (for example, Albufeira and Portimão) extended water supply systems in order to mobilize all water resources in their jurisdiction and include large interior aquifers. They used their authoritative capacities and increased water charges. By the end of the 1980s, they had begun to use their local capacities and improve the collection, treatment and discharge facilities for sewage water. In this way, they strived to clean beaches and coastal waters, which are essential for a successful marketing of their principal tourism product, 'sun and beach'.

Water supply in the Algarve in the 1990s

At the beginning of the 1990s there was another drought, which highlighted the long-term strategic constraints that water availability would pose for coastal tourism development. Using their socially constructive skills, national environmental NGOs simultaneously launched a media campaign revealing most municipalities' noncompliance with the European Drinking Water Directive, which had meanwhile been formally regulated (transposed) into national legislation. NGOs claimed that monitoring practices and quality standards were insufficient. Furthermore, in the wake of the negotiations on the implementation of the common internal market in the European Community, the Cohesion Fund was made available to the poorest member states, including Portugal. Approximately 50 per cent were earmarked for investments in environmental infrastructures. The EC, alerted by Portuguese NGOs, insisted that the Cohesion Fund should be spent on substantial improvements to the water supply. Furthermore, given the technical deficiencies of the water supply as well as sanitation sector and the enormous need for capital, a discussion about private sector engagement arose. Specifically, Portuguese construction companies sought and lobbied for access to the water supply and sanitation market in order to expand their businesses. Multinational companies installed representatives inside Portugal to gain access to this emerging market.

Algarvian coastal municipalities also used their socially constructive capacities to lobby and convince the government that action had to be taken to improve water supply. Bad water services and lack of compliance with EU directives could otherwise put the reputation of the Algarve and Portugal as a tourism destination at risk. This was specifically harmful to the Algarve's emerging strategic objective to establish a reputation as a destination of quality tourism. Additionally, the following countrywide issues triggered the government to reorder the sector: enforcement pressure and available funding from the EU, lack of strategic water supply security and local water management capacities in large parts of the country, the desire of the private sector to expand and, in the Algarve, tourism's increasing demand for water resources. The government decided to use its regulatory, authoritative and financial capacities to overhaul the institutional order and the organization of the sector. Its objectives at the time were: first, to implement the drinking water directive everywhere in the country; second, to secure a strategic (long-term) water supply of drinking water quality; third, to strengthen the national structure of private water service providers so they could compete with the multinationals when privatization set in; fourth, to use the European funds; and fifth, to implement economies of scale from larger supply systems. Using its regulatory capacities, it introduced so-called multimunicipal systems, which were declared to be of outstanding public interest and that comprised water supply to several municipalities in their territory. The government had the right to award concessions for these multimunicipal systems. Previously, however, the municipalities, which kept their authoritative right to provide water locally, had to agree to receive water from this segmented set-up of the system described above. Due to the specifically problematic constellation in the Algarve and its economic importance for the overall country, this set-up was initially introduced in the Algarve.

Local coastal authorities, where tourism was strong, welcomed this solution. They preferred this option to their local efforts, which in the long term were still strongly constrained by the local water resource availability. It appeared to be advantageous to them from a strategic perspective, in light of the occasional droughts and the aim to develop quality tourism products such as golf courses.

Using its regulatory power over surface waters, the government gave concessions for exploitation to a regional water company that was 51 per cent owned by the state owned company, Águas de Portugal. Together with the municipalities it founded two private companies in the Algarve, Águas do Sotavento (AdS) and Águas do Barlavento (AdB). Furthermore, central state or public sector domination of the set-up is documented by credits from the state provided to the municipalities to finance their contributions (49 per cent). They were contractually bound to procure a certain minimum amount of water from the regional water companies and to pay a preset price for it. At this time, however, not all municipalities had joined, thereby limiting the territorial coverage of the regional water supply scheme. Specifically, those municipalities in the interior that had access to large aquifers and that were not confronted with dynamic tourism development remained outside the scheme. For them, the strategic necessity to secure water supply was less significant. Until long into the 1990s, they pursued a strategy of economic diversification (rural tourism, agriculture, construction).

Founded in 1994, the task of the regional water companies in local and national public ownership was to build water treatment plants and pipes, joining the dams with the municipal water distribution networks. The state used its authoritative capacities to channel European Cohesion and Structural funds into the construction of this infrastructure. Hence, the EU paid 85 per cent of the costs of the infrastructure that the regional company implemented.

The operation of infrastructure was priced to individual consumers, leading to significant increases in water service charges raised by the municipalities. Although it was in public (governmental) shared ownership by the local and national public entities, the regional water company was intended to generate a profit, making it a public enterprise.

To secure the tourism economy it was crucial to improve water services in quality and quantity. Increasing shares of water were drawn from the surface waters in the Algarvian hinterland. Specifically, the coastal municipalities introduced stringent monitoring of water quality, given the pressure from the NGOs and media attention that endangered the reputation of the Algarve as a tourist destination. The integrated surface water supply system started to deliver water in 1999, its eastern and western sections were physically connected in 1999 and the two regional companies (AdB/AdS) were merged into Águas do Algarve by its stakeholders, reflecting the physical extent of the supply system (see Figure 3.3).

Water service provision at the national level in the 1990s and the present decade

The regulatory framework governing environmental management and water service provision management was reorganized at the national level in 1994. This reorganization put Portugal ahead of the changes in water management that discussions on the European Water Framework Directive proposed from 1996 onwards (Thiel, 2004a). At the national and regional level, water and environmental management competencies were separated from economic, regional development and planning competencies. These competencies were previously part of the regional development authority. Furthermore, new legislation was regulated in 1994 that prescribed the elaboration of river basin plans, a national water plan, licensing of pollution and abstraction, and water pricing. In subsequent years, the authoritative enforcement capacities of the regional water administration in charge of licensing gradually increased due to a reorganization of the service and growing numbers of staff. Moreover, the national administration used its regulatory and fiscal capacities to introduce an environmental inspectorate. An environmental police force was created and penalties were raised. Throughout the first half of this decade the relative share of legally licensed wells was said to be much higher than before. The national water authority believed that the background of these developments was a lack of compliance with European directives and poor quality of water resources during a heightening of quantitative and qualitative demands on them. The regional administration was additionally motivated to increase its income with penalties, one of its few sources of income.

A new minister, who took office in 1999, strived for a strong national water company in public ownership that was controlled by the ministry. He issued a strategic document that outlined the way in which Portugal would reorganize the overall water service provision sector at the national level. The whole country was to be divided into multimunicipal systems according to the set-up in the Algarve. The concession for these systems was to be given to the national water company through an authoritative act of legislation (regulation). This segmented scheme, which had partially been implemented for the water supply system, was to be extended to sanitation. The minister thus aimed to secure a further authoritative instrument over local authorities in addition to the European funds of which he was already in charge.

The new minister defended the idea of public services that enabled cross-subsidies within the system to achieve a high service standard throughout the entire territory and all social groups. He wanted to prevent private companies from 'cherry picking' or applying only for the profitable parts of the system. Together with a considerable part of the economic and political elite in environmental politics in Portugal, he also aimed to prevent foreign ownership of substantial parts of Portuguese water services. This could easily happen under Europe's free internal market regulations. He used his regulatory and authoritative capacities to these ends, specifically with regard to the instrumentalization of European funds. The private sector opposed vehemently.

Commentators say that the new plan for reorganizing the sector in 1999 was a watershed. The conservative government and the first socialist government previously aimed at establishing a strong private sector with several companies, risking eventual foreign takeover. The national water company should specifically expand abroad and should provide a platform for further Portuguese companies and their expansion into foreign markets.

The involvement of the European level in water service development in the 1990s and the present decade

Previously, infrastructure investment resorted to the general budget of the local authorities, sometimes in combination with nationally allocated European funds. In comparison to earlier times – from the 1990s until today – the central state used European funds more effectively to significantly increase its influence over the sector by means of its authoritative control over European financial capacities. The central state cofinanced large infrastructures in the water sector to improve the services and implement European directives. It used the funds to impose its will in the way water services were provided vis-à-vis the local authorities and only cofunded schemes that suited its ambitions.

Large regional infrastructures were predominantly financed by the EU. The EC had regulated the demand for water supply and sanitation standards. It used its authoritative capacity to enforce European regulations concerning drinking water quality and improve coverage of sewage water collection and treatment. Consequently, these regulations were to be implemented by the national authorities. In Portugal, however, this process was considerably delayed. The EC therefore initiated a significant change in institutions governing water service provision and indirectly shaped the efforts of the national state to achieve compliance. In other words, it exercised significant influence on the institutional landscape of the water sector in Portugal. Similarly, discussions on the Water Framework Directive at the European level interacted with the introduction and enforcement of water resource planning, licensing and water pricing in Portugal. The EC occasionally used its authoritative control over funds by imposing conditions on cofunding. It indirectly forced the Portuguese authorities to regulate and draft land use plans and to make efforts to comply with the European water directives.

In 2004 the EC used its authoritative powers to withdraw funding for the last of the four dams of the regional supply scheme, as it breached the European habitat directive. Meanwhile the expanding tourism sector in the region had come to rely on ubiquitous availability of sufficient water. Therefore, the regional associations of local authorities, founded in the mid-1990s and representing local authorities to the government, demanded that the regional water company take over the construction of the dam and that they pay for its construction with further increases in water prices.

The association of private environmental enterprises had simultaneously achieved a change in legislation in 2002, following a complaint to the EU. It argued that, in light of European regulations on tendering, the Portuguese state, which awarded the concessions for multimunicipal systems directly to the national water company, did not follow the proper tendering process. On these grounds alone, the Internal Market Directorate of the EC did not start an infringement procedure but suspended all European cofunding. As a result, the national administration granted the private sector broader access to Portugal's water service provision.

Sanitation sector in the 1990s

The Urban Wastewater Directive was adopted by the EU as early as 1991. Compliance with the challenging standards of the directive required significant investments in infrastructure in Portugal and the Algarve. Since the first half of the 1990s, participation of the private sector in mobilizing the necessary capital had been under discussion within the context of the sector's restructuring (see also above).

I have already described the set-up of multimunicipal systems. From 1999 onwards, this institutional set-up was to be transposed to the sanitation sector.

Using its authoritative capacities over the second cohesion fund period (2000 and 2006), the central administration aimed to implement the Urban Wastewater Directive after the EU started to increase its authoritative pressure on Portugal. Similar to the set-up in the water supply sector, the national level did not have the authority to provide for and charge for sewage water collection and treatment; this was the responsibility of the local authorities. In the Algarve, they strongly contested the implementation of a regional system for sewage water collection, treatment and discharge. Only a few coastal tourism municipalities with sufficient resources provided adequate wastewater treatment.

In order to gain control over the sector, the state wanted to put the national water company in charge of treatment and discharge infrastructures. Furthermore, by covering the whole region and charging municipalities the same price, it intended for ill-equipped but rich tourism municipalities to subsidize the physical improvements in badly equipped, poorer councils in the interior. As negotiations advanced, local authorities began to fiercely resist for several reasons: first, they considered the price of water treatment to be too high – many municipalities were already unable to pay for the water supply they received from the regional water company, as water tariffs remained low and they had not been collected; second, local authorities felt left alone with the most costly part of sanitation – the collection of sewage water; third, they opposed further interference of the central state into affairs of their genuine competence; and fourth, the coastal tourism municipalities wanted to sell their water treatment infrastructure to the national water company. The last issue seemed to tip the scales. Only when coastal local authorities learned that the national water authority would not pay the full value for the transfer of the existent infrastructure did they oppose vehemently. The national water company's interference into sanitation was intensely contested by the local coastal authorities, which no longer depended on national know-how and jurisdiction for improvements in sanitation.

Prior to these developments, in the second half of the 1990s, the regional water authority had negotiated and reached an agreement with all local authorities on a plan for sanitation in the region that would coordinate municipal efforts. Coastal municipalities had largely followed this plan.

At the end of the 1990s they continued to develop the infrastructure together with neighbouring councils. To implement this infrastructure, however, they required cofunding from European funds. The national authorities used their authoritative control and withheld all European funding, which forced the local authorities into segmented, multimunicipal concessions for sewage water treatment operated by the regional water company, Águas do Algarve. Financial considerations dominated the attitudes of the local authorities. It can be assumed that the negotiation position of numerous councils was additionally weakened by their enormous debts with the regional water company, since many of them did not pay for the drinking water they received. The regional water company only continued to deliver water to them after political intervention by the minister who represented the national government as majority owner of the water company.

In 2003 the local authorities finally gave in. Those who were most reluctant to agree to the regional multimunicipal sanitation system obtained side-payments from European funds for other infrastructure projects. Founded in the mid-1990s, the regional association of local authorities subsequently employed its socially constructive capacities to launch a campaign to create understanding within the local population for further drastic increases in water prices.

The progress of sewage water collection and treatment was similar to that of the water supply but was delayed due to its lower priority among most actors involved. Politicians and the population had a less developed understanding of water quality issues. The general disregard for water quality and sanitation was changed by European regulations and their increasing relevance for tourism development.

CONCLUSIONS

This concluding section analyses the case study in terms of changes in actor constellations regarding public and private/profit and nonprofit oriented actors and highlights the role of capacities in this process.

The principal issue resolved in the case study region was the disparity between areas of high demand and scarce resources and those in which the opposite was the case. In the coastal tourism zones of the Algarve, financial resources for water development were relatively large but water resources were scarce, while financial resources and water demand in the council's interior were much lower and availability higher. The solution to this mismatch reflects the temporally and spatially specific capacities of the actors involved. Water management was scaled up, and the national public sector increased its clout in water service development, thereby facilitating further expansion of the private tourism sector. The EU facilitated these developments and thus paved the way for the private sector's future involvement in water service provision.

The national public sector's growing importance in water service provision involves an increased number of regulations implemented by the deconcentrated regional public authorities (nonprofit public actor legitimated by the central state). The national, profit oriented water company developed infrastructures on behalf of the national public sector. The significant role of the national public sector can be explained through its capacities. Being a unitary state, Portugal's national public/state sector is in charge of developing, regulating and enforcing water regulations. Over time it has had to develop the capacities to actually implement these regulations; indeed, the EC demanded this of Portugal. The municipalities' competencies are limited to local water pricing and water service provision to consumers. Surface waters are under the authoritative jurisdiction of the national administration. The origin of water has shifted to surface waters. Consequently, water services are now extensively controlled at the national level. This development follows a paradigm held at the national level dating back many decades. Surface water exploitation implies the realization of economies of scale with extensive funding needs. The national authorities control the application of large European funds and in fact have an interest in finding projects to adequately spend them on, such as for example the surface water provision infrastructure in the Algarve.

While the national public sector had the capacities to exploit supralocal surface waters, the local authorities on the coast were not entitled to draw on aquifers or surface waters outside of their jurisdiction. Similarly, they had to apply for European funding to the national government/administration to undertake large infrastructure works. Conversely, interior municipalities did not have the financial or human resource capacities to accommodate even the easily solved issues surrounding drinking water and sanitation supply to populations. In this context, the central public sector was pushed by the EC and tourism demands to significantly improve water supply in the region and throughout the country. With this legitimization, it disempowered the municipalities and introduced a system in which financially weak municipalities would benefit from cross-subsidies to richer coastal areas, while coastal municipalities would benefit from the interior's surface waters. All the while the government would be making a profit from the integral commodification of water services. Hence the municipalities raised water fees immensely, a move to which they alone were entitled. The regional water company in national public ownership brought water services up to European standards. Municipalities handed over the most important segments of water service provision. In exercising their local water pricing and provision competencies, they were increasingly steered by national state authorities. Consequently, those local authorities that required a better water supply to sustain tourism supported this development.

The greater involvement of the public sector – for profit as well as nonprofit purposes – responded to the private, profit oriented tourism activity that had enlarged significantly in the area. It overstretched the local water resource base and thus made drawing in resources from the region necessary, surpassing the boundaries of the municipalities. The central level was the next highest level of government that could operate on this scale. The private tourism sector in fact pushed for the enlargement of the resource base and the improvement of water services in the region to be able to further expand the sector. The distribution of capacities forced the national state to adopt a crucial role in this. At the same time, the private sector aimed at taking over water service provision and finally received a helping hand from the EC.

The EU initiated and facilitated the portrayed development in a variety of ways. It regulated and subsequently implemented a variety of legislations to secure a European standard for water services. Furthermore, it provided a large part of the financial resources to implement the necessary infrastructure. The Portuguese national state used its allocative control over European funds and its regulatory capacities to impose a publicly owned, profit oriented water company on the localities, thereby pursuing a protectionist and redistributive rationale. In line with its Common Internal Market policies, the EC favoured neoliberal, Europe-wide free competition and private involvement in those economic sectors in which profit making was an option. Its common European policies have the authoritative capacity to impose the treaty provisions on member states, ultimately with recourse in the European court. Backed by this threat and by making the award of European funds conditional, the EC was able to prepare the ground for further private sector expansion in Portugal's water service sector.

Similar to the case of Bulgarian irrigation discussed in Chapter 2, the restructuring of the Portuguese water sector implied actual centralization of competencies and a greater role of the public sector. Supranational funds (World Bank credits in the case of Bulgaria and European structural funds in the case of Portugal) provided a decisive catalyst for this development, as the central level had great influence over their allocation. In the Algarve, European directives are close to being met in terms of water service quality standards. Therefore, at least in physical terms, this makes it a much more successful example of the restructuring of water services than that of the Bulgarian irrigation sector.

NOTE

1   In the Portuguese state structure deconcentrated administrations at the regional level are entirely dependent on their national counterparts.

REFERENCES

Águas do Algarve (2007) *Sistema Multimunicipal de Abastecimento de Água*, www.aguasdoalgarve.pt (accessed 13 September 2007)

CCDR (Commissão Coordenadora do Desenvolvimento Regional) (2005) *Mapas Temáticos*, www.dra-alg.min-amb.pt/index2.asp (accessed 12 January 2005)

Gatzweiler, F and Hagedorn, K (2003) *Institutional Change in Central and Eastern European Agriculture and Environment: Synopsis of the CEESA Project*, Food and Agriculture Organization, Budapest

Hagedorn, K, Arzt, K and Peters, U (2002). 'Institutional arrangements for environmental co-operatives: A conceptual framework' in Hagedorn, K (ed) *Environmental Cooperation and Institutional Change: Theories and Policies for European Agriculture*, Edward Elgar, Cheltenham, pp3–25

Hay, C (2002) *Political Analysis*, Palgrave, Houndmills

Jessop, B (2001) 'Institutional (re-)turns and the strategic-relational approach', *Environment and Planning A*, vol 33, pp1213–1235

Jessop, B (2002) *The Future of the Capitalist State*, Polity Press, Cambridge

Magone, J (1997) *European Portugal*, Macmillan Press, Houndmills

MAOT (Ministério do Ambiente e do Ordenamento do Território) (2000) *Plano de Bacia Hidrográfica das Ribeiras do Algarve*, MAOT, Lisbon

Thiel, A (2004a) 'Transboundary resource management in the EU: Transnational welfare maximization and shared water resources on the Iberian Peninsula', *Journal for Environmental Management and Planning*, vol 47, no 3, pp331–350

Thiel, A (2004b) 'The Role of the European Commission in the Restructuring of Water Services in Portugal: The Case of the Algarve', Paper presented at IV Congresso Nueva Cultura del Água, Tortosa, 8–12 December

Thiel, A (2005) 'Environmental Policy Integration and the Development of Water Use in the Algarve Since Portugal's Accession to the European Union', Unpublished PhD thesis, Oxford Brookes University, Oxford

Weintraub, J (1997) 'The theory and politics of the public/private distinction' in Weintraub, J and Kumar, K (eds) *Public and Private in Thought and Practice*, The University of Chicago Press, Chicago, pp1–42

PART II – PUBLIC–PRIVATE HYBRIDS

Introduction to Part II

We have looked at publics in natural resource governance in Part I. Our focus now changes to public–private hybrids, that is, actors, actions, resources or property rights that combine public and private elements (see Introduction). Part II presents three empirical analyses of public–private hybrids running through the divide between state and market, that is, the governing watersheds in the liberal-economistic model. The analyses deal with agri-environmental stewardship, biodiversity conservation and forestry, using cases from Austria, Brazil and Germany. Yet as with the contributions to Part I, the implications of the analyses in Part II extend far beyond these particular fields and cases. Chapters 4–6 engage with decentralization, public–private partnerships and labelling, which we identified as important policy issues in the Introduction.

Chapter 4 explores the range of hybrid actors and actions in Austrian landscape governance. Penker carefully surveys organizations that neither belong solely to the state nor operate purely on the self-regulating market. Furthermore, she identifies a variety of actions combining administrative and market elements by which these actors exercise agri-environmental stewardship. Agri-environmental stewardship and the preservation of cultural landscapes have become core components of the EU's Common Agricultural Policy (Brouwer and Lowe, 2000). Agriculture is no longer solely a source of food and fibre, but has now become multifunctional, producing a large variety of private and public goods for wider society (OECD, 2001). Moreover, we notice that the attention of Chapter 4 to local associations and networking connects with broader efforts to foster community based initiatives for sustainable development, such as Local Agenda 21 (Laferty, 2002).

Penker finds that landscape governance includes a large variety of organizations located between state and market in Austria. These include NGOs, the Chamber of Agriculture, tourism associations, clubs and marketing organizations. These organizations help to conserve Austria's cultural landscapes by arranging stewardship contracts with individual landholders, taking over responsibilities from the state and raising voluntary contributions of work and money from citizens, among other measures. State actors also engage in partnerships with farmers and other citizens, complementing more traditional state actions such as regulation, zoning and taxation. These insights reveal to us that Austria is witnessing the emergence of political communities concerned with the preservation of cultural landscapes and including state and nonstate actors.

This is most apparent to us in Lower Austria, where local communities are major players in landscape governance.

In addition, we note the increasing prominence of food labels created in public–private partnerships. Various kinds of organizations involved in agri-environmental stewardship have developed special food labels highlighting production in particular nature parks or localities. We recognize that these labels create different kinds of landscape publics that are not necessarily rooted in political communities. Even where labels are not supported by political communities, they may become publics by way of the publicity they attain. In this way cultural landscapes have also become focal points for publics in the sense of what is socially visible.

Chapter 5 moves from Austria to Brazil, but retains the interest in public–private hybrids. Looking at biodiversity governance, Ring diagnoses a rapid growth in public–private partnerships in the management of protected areas in several Brazilian states. She identifies intergovernmental transfers as a primary determinant of these partnerships. Transfers between central and local governments condition the ability and willingness of local governments to team up with local actors in public–private partnerships for the conservation of biodiversity. If these are tied to ecological criteria, as has happened in some Brazilian states since the mid-1990s, they may encourage local municipalities to increase their support for conservation initiatives, including public–private partnerships in protected area management. Ring's analysis thereby connects directly with work on fiscal federalism and intergovernmental transfers. This work on the distribution of state funds in relation to the tasks at hand has important implications for natural resource governance generally and decentralization in particular (e.g. Harrison, 1996; Döring, 1997). More broadly, the analysis contributes to research on so-called market based mechanisms for conservation, including public–private partnerships (e.g. Pagiola et al, 2002) and payments for environmental services (e.g. Gutman, 2003).

Ring shows that suitable fiscal relations facilitate public–private partnerships as they help to bridge the gap between global public benefits and local private costs. In Brazil, the use of ecological criteria for intergovernmental transfers has resulted in a broad range of conservation initiatives including protected areas controlled by local municipalities, Environmental Protection Areas managed by the state and landowners together, and Individual Natural Heritage Reserves established and run by landowners. In this way, the introduction of ecological transfers has created opportunities for local political communities to overcome the classical divide between state and market in biodiversity conservation. As in Chapter 1, this chapter therefore finds that state and nonstate actors come together more easily at the local level, where the integration of state actors with the broader political community is tighter than at the national level.

Chapter 6 turns to a very different kind of public–private hybrid: the media. As we all know, the media is an awkward actor. It mostly operates in self-regulating markets, yet it also serves to form and express collective preferences. As a result, it sits in an uneasy position between state and market in the liberal-economistic model. Furthermore, it *reflects* the nature of natural resource governance, yet it also assumes a formative role in the creation and sustenance of governance. In this way, Chapter 6 gets at an important issue in resource governance that has yet to be analysed in more depth. Kleinschmit and Krott make an important contribution by analysing the kinds of public actors that appear in the German and international media reporting on forestry. Nevertheless, we are also keenly aware that the role of the media and, more generally, publicity is very significant in resource governance across policy fields (Flynn et al, 2001). This becomes obvious if we recall the highly publicized campaigns undertaken by Greenpeace for the past three decades, or consider how international conservation organizations employ large mammals in their advocacy.

Kleinschmit and Krott demonstrate that the media constructs publics in the sense of what is socially visible. Media publics – or publicities – are particular, as regular citizens interviewed in opinion polls highlight a different mix of actors to those prioritized in the media. At the same time the media also reflects differences between German and international forestry publics. The German forest administration dominates media reports about forestry in Germany, portraying a forestry public firmly lodged in the state. International media reports, in contrast, display a much more balanced representation of actors concerned with forests, actors that form a broader political community beyond the confines of the state. Chapter 6 illustrates the simultaneous presence of three kinds of publics: publics as states, as political communities and as socially visible spaces. These three publics communicate with each other, yet they are distinct and cannot be conflated into one.

Taken together, the three chapters in this part of the book indicate the presence of many public–private hybrids in natural resource governance. Those highlighted in Chapters 4 to 6 are hybrid because they combine state and market elements such as NGOs providing agri-environmental stewardship in Austria, public–private partnerships in protected area management in Brazil, and the media. Nevertheless, we can easily detect examples of hybrids overcoming the divide between the political community and the more particularistic spheres of social life, such as NGOs recruiting contributions of voluntary work from Austrian citizens or commentaries written by lay experts in newspapers. Similarly, we can also think of hybrids running across the dividing line between the socially visible and the personal. For example, consider a leaflet that advertises smallholder fruit orchards as a landscape feature appealing to tourists.

At the same time, we appreciate that some of the hybridity stems more from our categorization than from actual practice (see Introduction). Some actors, actions, resources or property rights appear to be hybrid according to the presumptions of the liberal-economistic model, as they combine state and market. Yet as soon as we shift our lens to other public/private distinctions, much of the hybridity vanishes. If we shift to the notion of public as political community, it becomes easy to envision state and nonstate actors joining forces, as both are members of the political community. In Chapter 4, state agencies and farmers engage in stewardship contracts as members of political communities concerned with the preservation of Austria's cultural landscapes. Similarly, people form NGOs and other kinds of organizations that may look like hybrids from the vantage point of the liberal-economistic model but operate on the playing field provided by political communities. The very same dynamics come to light in the analysis of biodiversity governance in Brazilian states in Chapter 5.

We achieve similar clarification if we consider the third public/private distinction between the socially visible and the personal. Understanding *public* in the sense of *publicity*, we are no longer puzzled by the media's position between the state and the self-regulating market. The media contribute to and are influenced by the formation of publics understood as social visibilities. Such social visibilities are different from the other kinds of publics, as illustrated in Chapter 6. Similarly, what remains outside the limelight belongs neither to the market nor to the more particularistic spheres of social life, but is personal. Government officials, for example, belong to the state and may be important members of the political community, yet they may not receive any publicity. Another example for the creation of publics in the sense of making things visible is labels, as mentioned in Chapter 4. Labels also work by creating social visibilities, as we discuss in further detail in the introduction to Part III and in Chapter 8.

The analyses contained in Part II therefore go beyond those presented in Part I by considering all three public/private distinctions. Having extended our scope to include the distinction between what is socially visible and the personal, we can now look back at the literature cited in the introduction to Part I. We find that the analyses presented in Chapters 4–6 have much to contribute to the literature. They offer further support for the comment made at the end of the introduction to Part I: that the shift from government to governance is not just about adding further actors to the agents of state. Moreover, they indicate that the distinction between government (i.e. the state) and governance (i.e. the political community) does not exhaust the kinds of publics present in natural resource governance. There is a very important third kind of public that is distinct from the first two and cannot be reduced to either of the other two or to a combination of them: public in the sense of what is socially visible. Part II demonstrates how important it is for us to recognize all three kinds of publics in our analyses.

REFERENCES

Brouwer, F and Lowe, P (eds) (2000) *CAP Regimes and the European Countryside*, CABI Publishing, Wallingford

Döring, T (1997) *Subsidiarität und Umweltpolitik in der Europäischen Union*, Metropolis, Marburg

Flynn, J, Slovic, P and Kunreuther, H (2001) *Risk, Media, and Stigma: Understanding Public Challenges to Modern Science and Technology*, Earthscan, London

Gutman, P (ed) (2003) *From Goodwill to Payments for Environmental Services*, WWF Macroeconomics Program Office, Washington, DC

Harrison, K (1996) *Passing the Buck: Federalism and Canadian Environmental Policy*, University of British Columbia Press, Vancouver

Laferty, W M (ed) (2002) *Sustainable Communities in Europe*, Earthscan, London

OECD (Organisation for Economic Co-operation and Development) (2001) *Multifunctionality: Towards an Analytical Framework*, OECD, Paris.

Pagiola, S, Bishop, J and Landell-Mills, N (eds) (2002) *Selling Forest Environmental Services: Market-Based Mechanisms for Conservation and Development*, Earthscan, London

Governing Austrian Landscapes: Shifts along the Private–Public Divide

Marianne Penker

INTRODUCTION

Austrian landscapes are unique in their diversity and cultural information and therefore of outstanding value for the tourism industry, as well as for Austria's identity and image abroad. In discovering and publicizing the threat of landscape degradation, collectives represented by government authorities, NGOs, international organizations and local civil society movements directly challenge the rights of private land users. These struggles concern the legitimate power to control, manage and use landscapes and to benefit from their yields and scenic beauty as well as to affect the distribution of costs between the private and the public domain.

But how are public and private defined? In economic literature, public is generally attributed to the state, whereas private is associated with market-based coordination mechanisms. Most debates see public and private as irreconcilable and conceptualize human interaction as a duality of private and public activities. A closer look at actual landscape governance in Austria, however, reveals a great deal of activity in between the two poles of state and market and suggests a polarity rather than a duality of private and public.

The general hypothesis guiding this chapter is that the valorization of landscapes is reflected in changed governance structures and related shifts along the public and private divide. The meta-analysis of ten empirically founded research projects looks into the allocation of rights and duties, benefits and costs of landscape governance between the private and the public domains. Not omitting the two polar governance schemes of state and market, the analysis particularly focuses on those interesting developments on the ground that are neither clearly public nor private, such as:

- contracts between state authorities and private land users as well as other forms of private–public partnerships;
- semiprivate organizations fulfilling public tasks;
- voluntary-based collective interaction and self-governance;
- networks, strategic alliances and cooperation.

The concluding section lists possible reasons and explanations for the important role various types of hybrids play in governing Austrian landscapes.

CONCEPTS

For the reader's benefit, the following describe the basic concepts that define this chapter's approach to the main objects of analysis – landscape and private and public governance.

Landscape

Landscape has been a scientific term since the end of the 18th century, when Humboldt defined landscapes as the totality of all aspects of a region as perceived by humans (Humboldt, 1808). Ever since, the term has been the subject of broad terminological discourse and contested conceptualizations. According to the European Landscape Convention (launched in October 2000 by the Council of Europe), landscape is 'an area, as perceived by people, whose character is the result of the action and interaction of natural and/or human factors'. The definition emphasizes the cultural aspect of landscapes that are shaped by human activity. More so than the term environment, landscape first exists once people have imagined and valued it. Landscape, like beauty (with which it is often associated), develops in the eye of the beholder. The definitions constituting scenic beauty, cultural landscape amenities and conservation are contingent on social and cultural factors (cf Geisler, 2000). Landscape in all its diversity contributes to the formation of local culture and is a basic component of cultural heritage as well as collective and personal identity.

Private and public governance

The term governance stands for a more or less fragmented or integrated 'system of rule' (Rosenau, 1992). In economic and political science literature, governance is conceptualized as encompassing all relevant mechanisms for coordinating individual and collective action (Williamson, 1979; Powell, 1990; Mayntz, 2005) and is categorized either as markets, hierarchies and networks or as horizontal and top-down coordination mechanisms – or even as private and public governance, as in this chapter. Private and public can be differentiated by various pairs of antonyms (voluntary action – state coercion; individual – collectivity of individuals; personal – socially visible), which are often used inconsistently and therefore blur the discourse on public and private in resource governance (see Introduction). In this chapter, public governance is defined as state control that is characterized by the organizing principle of hierarchical coercion. Private governance, by contrast, is equated with horizontal market based mechanisms for the voluntary coordination of individuals. Whereas in common thought state intervention clearly belongs to the public sphere and individual action decisively to the private, civil society movements, NGOs and self-organized forms of cooperation combine elements of voluntary commitment (often related with private) and collective action (often associated with public). This chapter uses the term hybrids to refer to those institutions that combine public and private elements and that are neither simply state nor entirely market; that is, they are hybrid by the distinction between public and private in the liberal-economistic model (see Introduction).

META-ANALYTICAL APPROACH AND MATERIAL

The chapter is a meta-analysis drawing on several studies finished between 1999 and 2005 within the Austrian research programme, Cultural Landscapes, which involved 500 researchers, 40 disciplines, 170 research institutions and realized about 70 major research projects. Of particular relevance to this meta-analysis are ten projects that looked into the societal, institutional and economic aspects of landscape development.[1] Using the categories of private and public governance, relevant results of these ten projects (highlighted throughout this chapter by the project acronyms) are explored from a slightly different angle in order to gain a deeper understanding of the changing structures of landscape governance and related shifts along the private–public divide. The structure of the study corresponds to the three analytical components of property rights analyses as applied in legal anthropology (Benda-Beckmann, 1995):

1 private and public actors involved in landscape governance;
2 private and public landscape goods as objects of governance;
3 (new) types of relationships with respect to landscape goods (i.e. the rights, duties and possibilities pertaining to the various actors).

ACTORS INVOLVED IN LANDSCAPE GOVERNANCE

Private actors

Traditional rural land users, such as farmers and foresters, produce landscape amenities jointly with crops, dairy or forest goods. An increasing number of landholders provide remunerated landscape services. Private companies in gardening and landscaping also engage in the production of landscapes. Small- and medium-sized technical offices and consultants provide services for landscape conservation and management. Conversely, a diversified tourism and recreation industry is based on the consumption of landscape and entertainment (skiing, climbing, golf, canoeing, cannoning and so on) (IAM; Buchinger, 1998).

Regarding end consumers, we perceive rural inhabitants enjoying the landscape they live in, tourists and city dwellers looking for rural recreation and an idyll, adventurers and sportsmen. A small, but growing, group of so-called discerning consumers is willing to pay extra for food and forest products or tourism services promising sound land use and diverse and beautiful landscapes.

Public actors

Numerous specialized public organizations initiate, develop, implement, monitor and control landscape policies or directly manage landscapes in nature reserves and public gardens. These governmental organizations and state authorities are located at all levels, from the local to the European level (e.g. local municipalities, nature conservation authorities or spatial planning agencies of the nine Austrian states, the Federal Ministry of Agriculture, Forestry, Environment and Water Management or the Environment Direction General at the European level).

Hybrid actors combining private and public elements

Somehow belonging to the realism of the state and yet integrating attributes of private companies, an increasing number of semiprivate organizations fulfil tasks traditionally attributed to the responsibilities of governmental organizations or state bureaucracy. These semiprivate organizations are disentangled from federal budgets and their legal form often corresponds to those of private companies (e.g. limited liability companies such as GmbH). They work for governmental organizations and are subject to various forms of direct and indirect governmental control. Several semiprivate organizations also manage landscapes, implement landscape policies or provide services of landscape based marketing for business locations, tourism destinations, food and forest products. For instance, the Umweltbundesamt (Federal Environmental Agency) is the expert authority for environmental protection, environmental control and environmental information. In addition to its work for the federal government, it is entitled to carry out tasks for third parties that are of general interest (Environmental Control Act; § 6 [1] d). Other semiprivate organizations active in landscape governance are the Chamber of Agriculture, which plays a crucial role in the implementation of stewardship schemes, offices for regional management, regional tourism associations, the Agrarmarkt Austria marketing GmbH, organizations for location marketing and destination building, offices for the management of national parks or the Austrian Agency for Health and Food Safety.

In contrast to semiprivate organizations controlled by the government, NGOs and civil society movements are characterized by voluntary interaction. The local voluntary sector is involved in context sensitive strategies for landscape governance. Local societies or clubs provide platforms for dedicated people who invest personal time and activity, who are capable of inspiring and carrying along others with ideas to enhance their local landscapes. Other examples of voluntary-based collective action and self-governance are farmer cooperatives (Maschinenring) that provide medium- and large-scale landscape services, food processors marketing their products under local labels or voluntary based nonprofit organizations involved in ecological and cultural education. On the regional and national level, NGOs focusing on nature conservation, environmental protection and Alpinism play a crucial role in landscape governance. Among the first were alpine and nature associations and workers' bicycle clubs. (Alpenverein was founded in 1862, Arbeiter-Radfahrervereine in the 1890s and Naturfreunde in 1895; cf LQ1). Today, NGOs organized on regional, national and international levels engage in landscape governance; first and foremost are the WWF, Alpenverein, Naturfreunde and Distelverein. Once taken for granted as local space for working and living, landscapes have become issues of international organizations, just as biotic and cultural landscape features are defined as being of supraregional or even international relevance. Landscapes of high ecological and recreational value, such as the Alps, attract not only internationally active grassroots organizations (WWF, Greenpeace and so on) but also international organizations such as the United Nations Educational, Scientific and Cultural Organization (UNESCO) and the Commission Internationale pour la Protection des Alpes (CIPRA).

Typical conflict lines

Various groups represent plural and of course contradicting interests, which form the basis for various lines of conflict, many of them between individual land users and collectives such as NGOs or the general public, represented by state authorities. Conservation authorities and environmental NGOs oppose exceptions made for traditional land users – such as farmers, foresters, hunters or fishermen – that free them from legal restrictions (such as biodiversity conservation, some environmental standards, some building regulations and tax on mineral oil) (MU4). From the private landholder's point of view, NGOs and state authorities can be accused of employing ideological arguments of national good or ecological values to bring through certain landscape policies. The declining number of agricultural holdings and farmers challenges the argument that farmers are responsible for landscape stewardship (FL; Dietrich et al, 2003). Farmers argue that the responsibility for the provision of landscape goods cannot fall to them alone; the public sector should provide financial compensation for landscape stewardship. Representatives of the farmers' union argue that all agricultural subsidies are of public interest (open landscapes, food security, food safety, rural employment) rather than private interest of income support ('without farmers no cultural landscapes').

Another typical conflict can be discerned within the tourism sector, whose economic viability is dependent on beautiful landscapes resulting from morphological and biological diversity as well as characteristic forms of traditional land use. Indeed, one could argue that in no other region of the world is tourism as strongly based on the traditional forms of agricultural land use as in the Alps. At least in some parts of the Alps, recreational and tourism infrastructure may also jeopardize beautiful and unique Alpine landscapes.[2] With its significance for regional income and regional employment, the tourism sector argues in favour of permission for further development projects. Local authorities often lack the power to counter tourism's development interests. Even federal environmental impact assessments can suffer from powerful intervention in favour of (short-term) economic interests.

LANDSCAPE GOODS AS OBJECTS OF LANDSCAPE GOVERNANCE

Processes of landscape change seem to indicate an irreversible loss of ecological value as well as the limitations of socioeconomic development options in rural areas. Change is also seen as an unwelcome aesthetic phenomenon. Nevertheless, Austrian landscapes are still among those goods Austrians are most proud of; surveys emphasize the importance of landscapes as a national feature of identity (SU2; Aigner et al, 1999). Ninety per cent of interviewed inhabitants of a rural region (Aflenzer Becken) and 70 per cent of interviewed inhabitants of a smaller city (Kapfenberg), both in the Alpine region of Styria, state that they feel particularly connected to their surrounding landscapes. The contribution of local landscapes to the quality of life is rated higher than that of material standards of living (LQ1). These data provide us with evidence for the relevance of landscapes to the local population but tell us nothing about the actual object(s) of purposeful landscape intervention.

Public authorities purporting to act on behalf of society, or even on behalf of future generations, can be quite vague about the general goals of landscape governance. Therefore, it is difficult to discern priorities for the protection or creation of landscape amenities. An analysis of legal documents at the EU, national and state levels identified an abundance of varying and partly contradictory objectives for landscape development (Penker, 2005). It can be assumed, however, that landscape policies are also guided by numerous hidden intentions and inevitably driven by ideological attribution. For instance, Veichtelbauer et al (2000; KLIK) suggest that the conservation of societal structures could be an implicit intention behind the preservation of cultural landscapes. Hebertshuber (2000; KLIK) even assumes that decision makers try to keep landscapes free from strange and modern culture in order to offer an image of purity, order and traditional culture.

None of the empirical studies analysed included any typology of landscape goods such as immaterial/material, private/public or natural/cultural. Both in the analysed studies as well as in relevant legal texts, landscape is generally referred to as a bundle of valuables. Traditional farmhouses and fences, biodiversity, seminatural habitats, natural and cultural landscape features, biodiversity and running or stagnant water are all distinguished and regulated by various institutional regimes. Control and management of habitat is separated from rights to cultivate the same land or to enjoy the scenic beauty by accessing this landscape on farm or forest roads. In this way, systems of rules are individually defined for various properties of the landscape. For each of these differentiated legal components (not naturalistic categorizations; see Benda-Beckmann, 1995), the specific governance schemes can differ – private, public or hybrids are imaginable.

Regarding the World Trade Organization (WTO) debate, the distinction between public and private goods is of particular relevance, since the legitimization of agricultural subsidies is limited to nontrade concerns of agriculture that are again generally restricted to public goods provisioning (Vanslembrouck and Van Huylenbroeck, 2005). In practice, however, it is often difficult to draw a distinction between public and private goods (in this debate, public is understood as a collective), because the criteria of (non)rivalry and (non)excludability often fail to result in clear categorizations. Although landscapes encompass strictly public goods such as aesthetic and scenic beauty, most landscape components can best be referred to as impure public goods (e.g. club goods, common property resources, etc.) (Vanslembrouck and Van Huylenbroeck, 2005).

TYPES OF RELATIONSHIPS WITH RESPECT TO LANDSCAPE GOODS

The diverging interests with respect to different components of landscapes can be coordinated by different governance schemes that are private, public or – as the Austrian case demonstrates – located somewhere between the poles of (newly created) markets and state control and thus combine public and private elements (see Table 4.1).

Private governance organized by horizontal market coordination

A superficial observer might suggest that the management decisions of individual landowners alone drive landscape development. This theoretic case of full private ownership would imply that landowners are legitimated to use, control, change and destroy landscape goods, and the general public would have to bear all of the social costs. Either society would have to put up with irreversible losses of landscape goods, or it would have to compensate landowners for giving up undesirable activities. Bromley (1997) argues, however, that landowners have never been allowed to use their land against the rules of general social acceptance. This is particularly true for today's Austrian landholders, who are subject to the remarkable number of about 900 agri-environmental regulations on the regional,

Table 4.1   *Mechanisms of landscape governance and the associated distribution of costs and benefits*

Mechanisms of landscape governance		Private elements		Public elements		Distribution of	
		Voluntary action	Individual action	State coercion	Collective action	Costs	Benefits
Private	Joint production, eco-labels, entrance fees	x	x			Beneficiaries	Providers
Public	Legal restrictions, taxes, zoning			x	x	Landholders	Beneficiaries
Hybrid	Contracts between NGOs and landholders	x	x		x	Taxpayers	Providers
	Contracts between government organizations and landholders	x	x	x		Political community	Providers
	Activities of semiprivate organizations	x	x	x	x	Taxpayers	Beneficiaries
	Participation projects	x			x	Taxpayers	Beneficiaries
	Activities of civil society movements	x			x	Political community	Beneficiaries
	Cooperation and alliances	x			x	Variable	Variable

Note: Providers create, preserve and develop landscape goods. Beneficiaries benefit from cultural and ecological landscape goods. Taxpayers finance state budgets. Political community is a self-governed collective providing voluntary work and donations for their shared concern – cultural landscapes national and supranational level (Penker, 1997; see next section on public landscape governance). Austrian law favours open access in forests, on roads, on water and in the mountains. This reflects a quite common property-minded attitude towards aesthetic and recreational landscape values. In general, there are no charges for hiking, rafting, mountain biking, climbing, paragliding and other activities, whereas in other countries such use values are captured by private markets (OECD, 1996).

Those in favour of private arrangements argue for the lower transaction costs of self-regulating markets, which are based on 'the beneficiary pays principle'. Indeed, only some landscape features in specific areas allow for market creation and the capture of economic value by arrangements such as agrotourism and ecotourism, green consumerism, labels of origin, entrance fees to outstanding nature parks or for the use of (sports) infrastructure or the acquisition of ecologically valuable habitats via environmental NGOs (e.g. individuals buying symbolic square metres of river wetlands). In an exceptional example of cooperation between tourism and agriculture, a local community (Weissensee) has transferred stewardship payments to local farmers. In Austria (LQ1), as in other European countries (cf Chapter 10), the growing interest of consumers in more sustainable forms of farming and food production, as well as the characteristics of certain landscape features as joint products of agricultural commodities, opens the possibility for market creation and remunerating farmers for landscape services through increased market prices of food products. Local food in particular is closely connected with the preservation of context-specific landscapes (LQ1). Market creation, however, depends on specific marketing techniques (such as ecolabels, Nature Park label 'Naturpark Spezialitäten', or regional brands), institutional innovation (e.g. intellectual property rights of geographic indications protected by EU law), or specific marketing channels (self-harvesting projects, direct marketing, regional forms of cooperation between farmers and gastronomy and so on) (Penker and Payer, 2005; Van Huylenbroeck and Verhaegen, 2002).

Public governance organized by hierarchical state intervention

Water, air and soil as well as outstanding landscape features and endangered species are protected by legal acts and standards set and controlled by European, state and regional authorities (SU1; Penker, 1997). Particularly harmful interventions in landscapes are forbidden or are at least the subject of formal approval procedures. Codes of good agricultural practice and crosscompliance should help to integrate environmental concerns into the Common Agricultural Policy of the EU. Strict forestry legislation keeps the number and the surface of all forests constant and should prevent settlements and tourism infrastructure from penetrating into forest areas. Various Austrian federal states have introduced landscape taxes on the extraction of gravel, on ski lifts and on other forms of landscape intervention (SU1; Penker, 1997; 2003). In Lower Austria, a tax on aesthetically unwelcome telephone masts was discussed recently; the regional government and representatives of the mobile phone companies, however, were able to reach an agreement on a reduction in the number of transmitting masts by the joint use of single masts by several companies.

Various sectoral plans cover the whole country. A zoning system protects landscapes by restricting the development of settlements in rural regions and defining nature and landscape reserves with particular constraints for land use (SU1; Penker, 2003). Inventories – a broadly used instrument of nature protection acts – cover seminatural habitats such as vineyards, chalk grassland or wet meadows as well as natural amenities such as glaciers, running and stagnant water, untouched high Alpine regions or old-growth forests. Designated areas are subject to special acts that restrict human activities. All these hierarchical institutions of public governance draw on 'the land user pays principle'. The land user has to bear all of the costs (forgone profit, extra efforts and expenses, fines for incompliance and taxes).

Despite all of the regulative efforts on the EU, federal, state and local levels, there are considerable discrepancies between the overall goals driving landscape policies and their actual outcome (SU1; APK; SU2; Penker et al, 2004; Egger and Jungmeier, 2001; Hiess et al, 1999). Analyses of the Austrian spatial planning and building law (SU2; Hiess et al, 1999) as well as empirical research on federal conservation legislation, on EU co-financed stewardship schemes and on national energy taxation (SU1; Wytrzens et al, 2001; Penker and Wytrzens in press) confirm the general experience of massive implementation deficits. The gaps between the normative *de jure* level and the actual socioeconomic and ecological situation might be explained by the fact that the systems of rules regulating landscape governance are by no means well-integrated wholes. None of the nine federal states prescribes an obligatory integrative instrument for landscape planning (SU2; Hiess et al, 1999), which might help to coordinate different domains of authority such as agriculture, nature conservation, rural development, tourism development and spatial planning (MU4).

Landscapes seem to fall between the cracks of governmental and administrative competence, and therefore officials would regularly have to trespass spatial and sectoral competences for integrative landscape measures (SU2; Aigner et al, 1999). Knoflacher (1998; IAM) points out another difficulty: the limited predictability of actual impacts of human interventions in particular landscapes. Due to this uncertainty he assumes a general reluctance of officials to make decisions on landscape intervention at all. The cause of ineffective landscape policies, however, might also rest with those addressed by public regulations, i.e. the land users. Some Austrian farmers oppose growing public influence by ignoring and deliberately infringing legal regulations on land use (control and sanctions are often moderate anyway, SU1). Young farmers changing professions and rural exodus, however, might indicate a more implicit form of protest.

Hybrid forms between private and public governance

Stewardship contracts between NGOs and individual landholders
The preceding description of private and public mechanisms of landscape governance in Austria indicates a limited right of the general public to an intact landscape, that is, particularly grave interventions are forbidden by state or federal acts or at least require formal permission. The current institutional setting, however, does not oblige landholders to active landscape services (such as planting hedges, maintaining or erecting traditional stonewalls or fences). If nonlandholders or NGOs want active interventions in landscape development (i.e. landscape services) (MU4), they have to rely on financial incentives, which reflect 'the provider gets principle'. Starting in the late 1980s, NGOs, especially the Distelverein, began to draw up contracts with farmers (LQ1).

Stewardship contracts between state authorities and individual landholders
Likewise in the 1980s, the conservation authorities of various federal states successively began to design landscape stewardship schemes and entered into contracts with farmers. Payments came either from the general conservation budgets or from particular landscape funds instituted in the same period and financed by a landscape tax (e.g. on mining of gravel, waste dumps and other interventions in the landscape). When joining the EU in 1995, Austria already had considerable experience in shaping and implementing stewardship schemes and therefore was able to respond rapidly to the EU's agri-environmental regulation (for more details on the implementation of stewardship agreements in the UK see Chapter 10). By 1997, 85 per cent of the Austrian utilized agricultural area in objective 1 zones (the EU 15 average is 10 per cent) and 67 per cent (the EU 15 average being 28 per cent) in nonobjective 1 zones were already managed in accordance with at least one agri-environmental scheme (European Community, 1998). Due to the high degree of prescription and standardization, the prevailing management agreements lack certain characteristics of 'real' contracts under private law (Penker et al, 2004). These contracts represent hybrid forms between public and private.

Semiprivate organizations fulfilling public responsibilities
Several tasks traditionally considered to be clear-cut public responsibilities (such as environmental documentation, environmental information and awareness building, education, implementation of stewardship schemes, food security) have been transferred to a constantly increasing number of quasi or semiprivate organizations disintegrated from federal budgets. They are predominantly financed by tax money. Nevertheless, they are not accountable to the parliament but rather to various kinds of supervisory boards nominated by governmental organizations, the Austrian Social Partners (i.e. the official associations of farmers, industry, labour and commerce), political parties and other organizations.

Voluntary based participation projects initiated by state authorities
Participation projects could motivate locals to reveal their landscape preferences
and empower them to control their landscapes as a major determinant of their
quality of life (LQ1). Only Lower Austria, however, has provided an
institutionalized form of community based landscape governance financed by
public budgets (Penker, 2003; Penker et al, 2004). Decision makers controlling
landscape development often neither live nor work in the relevant landscapes.
The fact that locals have little influence on landscape governance and cannot
voice their preferences and fears of landscape change in the policy arena could
foster forces of collective action, civil society movements and self-governance.

Voluntary based collective action, civil society movements and self-governance
Local clubs and associations as well as national and international NGOs play
various roles in the protection and provision of landscape valuables. Receiving
little financial support from the government, they greatly depend on voluntary
work and donations ('the political community pays principle'). In 2001,
Austrians donated 45 million euros to conservation, environmental protection,
ecology and animal welfare (ÖIS, 2001). The WWF, Alpenverein, Naturfreunde,
Distelverein and other organizations bundle these ecological and aesthetic
interests, buy outstanding and threatened pieces of landscape, invest in
information and awareness building, implement or pay for management services
and lobby for landscape sensitive policies.

Cooperation and alliances between the various private and public actors
Various forms of cooperation and horizontal coordination between different sectors
aim at landscape preservation, such as the ones existing between conservation and the
food sector (food labels of nature parks and organic food in kindergartens, schools
and nursing homes; Penker and Payer, 2005), conservation and tourism (ecotourism)
and tourism and agriculture (for example, restaurants offering local food; Penker and
Payer, 2005). In some federal states, conservation authorities cooperate with
representatives of NGOs (Penker, 2003). They provide context sensitive and well-
adapted seeds and plants, point out hot spots and situations calling for action and
explore new management techniques and observe their actual landscape impacts
(Penker et al, 2004). Green labels and protected indications of origin for food and
wood products, private–public comanagement of nature reserves and other alliances
between market, state and civil society actors provide flexible means to undertake the
complex tasks of landscape governance and joint landscape management.

DISCUSSION

The relevance of landscapes to the Austrian population but also to the Austrian
key economic sector – tourism – forms the basis of a struggle for the appropriate
governance of landscape, which is also a kind of battle for the distribution of

control, benefits and costs between the public and the private sector. This meta-analysis of ten empirically founded research projects indicates that landscape governance in Austria and related shifts along the public–private divide are multifaceted and diverse. On the one hand, private landholders have been constrained by public responsibility for landscape conservation. On the other, public landscape governance has been successively enriched by voluntary based coordination mechanisms, such as participation, market creation (stewardship contracts, ecolabels) or public–private comanagement. There is no simple dichotomy between market and state, private and public and voluntary interaction and hierarchy in Austrian landscape governance.

The Austrian case study identified a broad spectrum of hybrid organizations located somewhere between the poles of state hierarchy and market that play important roles in landscape governance, such as NGOs (Diestelverein, Alpenverein, WWF), semiprivate organizations (Chamber of Agriculture, regional management offices, management organizations of national parks or nature parks), the local voluntary sector and loose networks and alliances. These hybrid organizations further blur the divide between private and public by forming coalitions with governmental actors and by linking traditionally private preference systems (e.g. markets for food or forest products) with public action (i.e. the preservation of cultural landscapes) and vice versa.

The objects of landscape governance – the landscape goods – are also diverse and are generally best referred to as impure public goods, that is, neither strictly public nor private. Different components of the same landscape are regulated by different governance schemes. For instance, the field margins, hedges, stone walls and traditional fences could be regulated by contracts between NGOs or state authorities and individual landholders, whereas the adjacent meadows are shaped by the management decisions of individual landholders. In turn, rare habitats or species located in these meadows could be subject to the protection of EU directives or state law. For example, the Alpenverein and other Alpine organizations preserve the hiking trail passing through the same landscape, and a viewing platform from which walkers and passers-by could enjoy the beautiful scenery could be built and preserved by the local club for landscape enhancement. Consumers may pay a premium for beef products originating from this landscape and marketed via labels of origin or in local restaurants. In this way, different components of Austrian landscapes are governed by diverse private, public and hybrid mechanisms, which include individual land use decisions or consumption behaviour, entrance fees, legal restrictions, taxes, zoning systems, contracts with landholders, food-related activities such as 'eat the view' or labels of origin.

CONCLUSIONS

Literature refers to the deterritorialization, centralization and publicization of natural resource governance. As a consequence of a growing number of international conventions and EU policies, we witness – despite all efforts to come to more local, community based forms of resource management – an increasing deterritorialization (Appadurai, 1990) of property rights. We also see an increasing dissociation of managerial and governance organization from the spatially grounded land through the globalization of environmental values and the construction of common goods at world scale (Benda-Beckmann, 2001). Hagedorn et al (2002) argue that dividing rights between land users and other specialized agents automatically results in a higher degree of centralization of those rights that the former holders are deprived of. Aznar and Perrier-Cornet (2004) refer to the 'publicization of rural areas'.

The Austrian case of landscape governance is not clearly driven by an increase in public control that exhorts balance with and protection of nature, with the state shielding nature from the excesses of private dominion over land (Geisler, 2000). Rather, governance structures have been evolving and converging into new hybrids and alliances between public and private actors. New institutional arrangements combining private and public elements (see Table 4.1) are used to articulate the demand for landscape amenities, to establish markets or incentives for landscape services and to coordinate landscape management across space. This might indicate a new approach towards the governance of landscape governance in particular and natural resource management in general (see Introduction and Chapter 10).

Landscape governance is passing through a fascinating period of adjustment, which finds its expression in the growth of NGOs, civil society movements and other hybrid organizations but also in an increasing importance of governance mechanisms combining private and public elements. The following preliminary theses might explain some aspects of the crucial role hybrids play in landscape governance:

- Complex regulatory tasks such as landscape development call for complex governance structures including a variety of organizations and mechanisms located somewhere between the polar solutions of markets and state control.
- New hybrid organizations react faster and more flexibly to the revalorization of landscapes than hierarchical state bureaucracy. This might explain their dominant role in this new field of resource governance.
- Hybrid organizations establish and increase their sphere of influence because of the withdrawal of the state and the outsourcing and privatization of tasks formerly fulfilled by state bureaucracy.
- Hybrids have always played a role in landscape governance; however, they have largely been ignored by research, politics and common thought due to the dialectic conceptualization of public and private.
- The relevance of hybrids rests upon a certain insufficiency of both, the outcome of private land use decisions and the actual results of state intervention in landscape development.

- Hybrid organizations themselves promote and drive collective action for the preservation of cultural landscapes.

Whatever the reasons for the perceived increase in relevance of hybrids in landscape governance, it is evident that – in contrast to other resources – we know very little about landscape governance: about societal priorities for landscape governance, the actors involved and their motivations, or about the actual effects of human intervention in landscapes. In the face of this missing knowledge, it is to be hoped that decentralized and flexible organizations and governance mechanisms meet societal needs without taking far-reaching risks of central intervention failure.

ACKNOWLEDGEMENTS

The analysis presented here draws on ten interdisciplinary research projects carried out within the Austrian Cultural Landscape Research Programme. Thanks to all the researchers, interview partners and funding organizations of these projects. In writing this paper, I am particularly grateful for helpful comments on an earlier draft provided by Thomas Sikor, David Baldock, Tim O'Riordan, Ortwin Renn and Hilary Torvey.

NOTES

1   The ten projects, their acronyms and key publications are:
   - Interaktionsmodell als Beitrag zur ganzheitlichen Kulturlandschaftsforschung (IAM; Knoflacher et al, 1998);
   - Agrarökologisches Projekt Krappfeld (APK; Egger and Jungmeier, 2001);
   - Kulturlandschaft im Kopf (KLIK; Bekesi et al, 2002);
   - Lebensqualität und Umwelthandeln: Konsens und Konflikt im Alltag einer Kulturlandschaft (LQ1; Buchinger et al, 1999);
   - Kultur – Landschaft – Entwicklung im westösterreichischen Alpenraum (MU4; Drapela et al, 1999);
   - Infrastruktur und ihre Auswirkungen auf die Kulturlandschaft (SU2; Aigner et al, 1999; Hiess et al, 1999);
   - Rechtsbestimmungen und ihre Auswirkungen auf die Kulturlandschaft (SU1; Wytrzens et al, 2001);
   - Fast Food – Slow Food (FFSF; Favry et al, 2005);
   - Flächendeckende Umstellung auf biologischen Landbau (VUBL; Bartel et al, 2002);
   - Future Landscapes (FL; Dietrich et al, 2003).
2   Alpine tourism is concentrated in 10 per cent of the western Austrian communities and even there is closely linked to agriculture and landscape based recreation (MU4).

REFERENCES

Aigner, B, Dostal, E, Favry, E, Frank, A, Geisler, A, Hiess, H, Lechner, R, Leitgeb, M, Maier, R, Pavlicev, M, Pfefferkorn, W, Punz, W, Schubert, U, Sedlacek, S, Tappeiner, G, Weber, G (1999) *Szenarien der Kulturlandschaft*, Austrian Federal Ministry for Science and Transport, Vienna

Appadurai, A (1990) 'Disjuncture and difference in the global cultural economy' in Featherstone, M (ed) *Global Culture: Nationalism, Globalization and Modernity*, Sage, London, pp295–310 [cited in Benda-Beckmann (2001)]

Aznar, O and Perrier-Cornet, P (2004) 'The production of environmental services in rural areas: Institutional sectors and proximities', *International Journal of Sustainable Development*, vol 7, no 3, pp257–272

Bartel, A, Darnhofer, I, Eder, M, Freyer, B, Hadatsch, S, Lindenthal, T, Milestad, R, Muhar, A, Payer, H, Penker, M, Rützler, H, Schneeberger, W, Velimirov, A and Walzer, A (2002) 'Flächendeckende Umstellung auf biologischen Landbau: Integrative Akzeptanz- und Wirkungsanalyse anhand ausgewählter Untersuchungsregionen', unpublished research report

Bekesi, S, Gamper, C, Haage, U, Hebertshuber, M, Kittel, G, Klaffenböck, G, Liebhart, K, Liska, G, Ross, M M, Salzuer, I, Schneider, P, Standler, K, Strohmeier, G, Veichtlbauer, J and Winiwarter, V (2002) *Zu Begriff und Wahrnehmung von Landschaft*, Austrian Federal Ministry for Science and Transport, Vienna

Benda-Beckmann, F von (1995) 'Anthropological approaches to property law and economics', *European Journal of Law and Economics*, vol 2, pp309–336

Benda-Beckmann, F von (2001) 'Between free riders and free raiders: Property rights and soil degradation in context' in Heerink, N (ed) *Economic Policy and Sustainable Land Use: Recent Advances in Quantitative Analysis for Developing Countries*, Physica-Verlag, Heidelberg, pp293–316

Bromley, D W (1997) 'Property regimes in environmental economics' in Folmer, H and Tietenberg, T (eds) *The International Yearbook of Environmental and Resource Economics: A Survey of Current Issues*, Edward Elgar, Cheltenham, UK and Lyme, NH, pp1–27

Buchinger, E (1998) 'Natur und Gesellschaft: Systemtheoretische Aspekte einer Beziehung' in Bundesministerium für Wissenschaft und Verkehr (ed) *Theorien und Modelle: Kulturlandschaftsforschung*, Austrian Federal Ministry for Science and Transport, Vienna, pp135–146

Buchinger, E, Burkart, R, Götzenbrucker, G, Halper, C, Jäger, F, Kainz, S, Knoflacher, M, Kollmann, G, Leitner, K H, Maderthaner, R, Matouch, S, Mokricky, C, Nicolini, M, Rammer, C, Schartinger, D, Stadler, M, Stalzer, L, Szynkariuk, S and Teibenbacher, P (1999) *Lebensqualität und Umwelthandeln – Konsens und Konflikt im Alltag einer Kulturlandschaft*, Austrian Federal Ministry for Science and Transport, Vienna

Dietrich, R, Dörr, H, Fiby, M, Hilbert, A, Kals, R, Pohl-Iser, E and Schiller, I (2003) 'Die Zukunft der Landschaft in Mitteleuropa. Verantwortung für die Kulturlandschaft im 21. Jahrhundert', unpublished research report in Future Landscape research programme

Drapela, J, Grabher, D, Jungmeier, M, Lechner, R, Messner, K, Matouch, S, Musovic, Z, Pfefferkorn, W, Sieber, W, Simoni, E, Tappeiner, G, Tauber, H, Walch, K, Wrbka, E and Zürrer C (1999) 'Kultur – Landschaft – Entwicklung im westösterreichischen Alpenraum', unpublished research report

Egger, G and Jungmeier, M (2001) Das Agrarökologische Projekt Krappfeld, unpublished research report

European Community (EC) (1998) State of Application of Regulation (EEC) no. 2078/92, 'Evaluation of Agri-environmental Programmes', DGVI Commission Working document VI/7655/98, DGVI, Brussels

Favry, E, Hiess, H, Payer, H, Penker, M, Schütz, O and Wytrzens, H K (2005) *Fast Food – Slow Food: Lebensmittelwirtschaft und Kulturlandschaft*, Austrian Federal Ministry for Education, Science and Culture, Vienna

Geisler, C C (2000) 'Estates of mind: Culture's many paths to land', *Society and Natural Resources*, vol 13, pp51–60

Hagedorn, K, Arzt, K and Peters, U (2002) 'Institutional arrangements for environmental co-operatives: A conceptual framework' in Hagedorn, K (ed) *Environmental Co-operation and Institutional Change: Theories and Policies for European Agriculture*, Edward Elgar, Cheltenham, UK and Northampton, MA, pp3–25

Hebertshuber, M (2000) 'Anmerkungen zur Landschaftswahrnehmung' in Békési, S, Gamper, C, Haage, U, Hebertshuber, M, Kittel, G, Klaffenböck, G, Liebhart, K, Liska, G, Ross, M M, Salzuer, I, Schneider, P, Standler, K, Strohmeier, G, Veichtlbauer, J and Winiwarter, V (eds) *Zu Begriff und Wahrnehmung von Landschaft*, Austrian Federal Ministry for Science and Transport, Vienna, pp88–99

Hiess, H, Hoffmann, H, Lechner, R, Maier, R, Schubert, U and Weber, G (1999) 'Infrastruktur und ihre Auswirkungen auf die Kulturlandschaftsentwicklung', unpublished research report

Humboldt, A von (1808) *Ansichten der Natur mit wissenschaftlichen Erläuterungen*, Cotta, Stuttgart

Knoflacher, H M (1998) 'Grundkonzept für ein kulturlandschaftbezogenes Interaktionsmodell' in Bundesministerium für Wissenschaft und Verkehr (ed) *Theorien und Modelle, Kulturlandschaftsforschung*, Austrian Federal Ministry for Science and Transport, Vienna, pp17–30

Knoflacher, H M, Bossel, H, Breckling, B, Buchinger, E, Pfister-Pollhammer, J, Raza, W G, Renn, O, Kastenholz, H G, Simonis, U E and Wiegnad, T (1998) *Theorien und Modelle, Kulturlandschaftsforschung*, Austrian Federal Ministry for Science and Transport, Vienna

Mayntz, R (2005) 'Governance Theory als fortentwickelte Steuerungstheorie?' in Schuppert, G (ed) *Governance-Forschung: Vergewisserung über Stand und Entwicklungslinien*, Nomos, Baden-Baden, pp11–20

OECD (Organisation for Economic Co-operation and Development) (1996) *Amenities for Rural Development: Policy Examples*, OECD, Paris

ÖIS (Österreiches Institut für Spendenwesen) (2001) *Spendenmarkt Österreich*, ÖIS, Vienna

Penker, M (1997) *Zusammenstellung des österreichischen Agrarlandschaftsrechts: Bestandsaufnahme landeskultureller Normen auf Europa-, Bundes- und Landesebene*, Austrian Society for Agricultural and Environmental Law (ÖGAU), Vienna

Penker, M (2003) 'Naturschutz auf landwirtschaftlichen Flächen – eine institutionenökonomische Betrachtung', *Die Bodenkultur – Austrian Journal of Agricultural Research*, vol 53, no 4, pp217–226

Penker, M (2005) 'Society's objectives for agro-landscapes as expressed in law', *Land Use Policy*, vol 22, no 3, pp197–206

Penker, M and Payer, H (2005) 'Lebensmittel im Widerspruch zwischen regionaler Herkunft und globaler Verfügbarkeit' in Brunner, K M and Schönberger, G U (eds) *Nachhaltigkeit und Ernährung: Produktion – Handel – Konsum*, Campus Wissenschaft, Frankfurt, New York, pp174–187

Penker, M, Wytrzens, H K and Kornfeld, B (2004) *Natur unter Vertrag – Naturschutz für das 21. Jahrhundert*, Facultas Universitätsverlag, Vienna

Penker, M and Wytrzens, H K (in press) 'Legal-ecological assessments: A transdisciplinary approach for evaluating landscape governance' in Hirsch Hadorn, G, Hoffmann-Riem, H, Biber-Klemm, S, Grossenbacher-Mansuy, W, Joye, D, Pohl, C, Wiesmann, U and Zemp, E (eds) *Handbook of Transdisciplinary Research*, Springer, Heidelberg, pp181–192

Powell, W W (1990) 'Neither market nor hierarchy: Network forms of organization', *Research in Organizational Behavior*, vol 12, pp295–336

Rosenau, J N (1992) 'Governance, order, and change in world politics' in Rosenau, J N and Czempiel, E O (eds) *Governance without Government: Order and Change in World Politics*, Cambridge University Press, Cambridge, pp1–29

Van Huylenbroeck, G and Verhaegen, I (2002) 'Evaluating small-scale collective initiatives producing and marketing environmentally friendly food products' in Hagedorn, K (ed) *Environmental Co-operation and Institutional Change: Theories and Policies for European Agriculture*, Edward Elgar, Cheltenham, pp362–373

Vanslembrouck, I and Van Huylenbroeck, G (2005) *Landscape Amenities: Economic Assessment of Agricultural Landscapes*, Springer, Dordrecht

Veichtlbauer, J, Liebhart, K and Kittel, G (2000) 'Politische Grammatik von Landschaften' in Békési, S, Gamper, C, Haage, U, Hebertshuber, M, Kittel, G, Klaffenböck, G, Liebhart, K, Liska, G, Ross, M M, Salzuer, I, Schneider, P, Standler, K, Strohmeier, G, Veichtlbauer, J and Winiwarter, V (eds) *Zu Begriff und Wahrnehmung von Landschaft*, Austrian Federal Ministry for Science and Transport, Vienna, pp72–85

Williamson, O E (1979) 'Transaction-cost economics: The governance of contractual relations', *Journal of Law and Economics*, vol 22, pp233–261

Wytrzens, H K, Penker, M, Reiterer, M, Tronner, R and Wittich, S (2001) *Der Rechtsökologische Befund – Ein Instrument zur Erfassung von Landschaftswirkungen des Rechts*, Facultas Universitätsverlag, Vienna

5

Biodiversity Governance: Adjusting Local Costs and Global Benefits

Irene Ring

LINKING BIODIVERSITY GOVERNANCE TO FISCAL FEDERALISM

Multilevel and multiactor governance in biodiversity conservation

The concept of governance itself is associated with a wider perspective on environmental decision making.[1] Regarding the public side with mostly hierarchical decision making, it is no longer the nationstate alone that is predominantly in charge of setting the framework for environmental decisions. Both higher and lower levels of environmental decision making come increasingly into play, for example, European directives have had a strong hierarchical impact on member states regarding the creation of the Natura 2000 network; the international Convention on Biological Diversity, although more reliant on consensual decision making, still morally binds and influences signatory states regarding its implementation. State, regional and local governments can play increasingly crucial roles for environmental decision making. On the one hand, this depends on the type of federal system in place and its associated hierarchical rules. On the other hand, new alliances emerge in the form of hybrid organizations, such as Local Agenda 21 initiatives and networks. At the same time, environmental decisions are no longer the exclusive realm of governmental agencies. The private sector – including consumers and business, as well as hybrid organizations crossing the public–private divide such as NGOs or semiprivate organizations (for example, agencies and research institutes) – play an important role in decisions on the conservation and sustainable use of biodiversity.[2]

Hence, biodiversity governance has to be seen in a context of both multilevel and multiactor governance. Another important issue is the development and implementation of policy instruments. Regulation, economic incentives, voluntary, informative and communicative instruments on the public side as well as activities initiated by civil society continuously interact and are of varying importance depending upon the concrete problem. Regulation or so-called command and control instruments have been widely used in the early phases of environmental policy, representing the coercive principle in public state management of environmental goods. Nowadays, economic incentives and voluntary instruments are in the forerun wherever feasible, allowing individuals more leeway of action and contributing to increased economic efficiency. While they are policy instruments – meaning framed and issued mainly by state action – they no longer fit the perspective of the coercive state. Jordan et al (2003) have framed the term 'new environmental policy instruments' with respect to the increasing use of these new instruments of environmental governance. The mix of instruments and thus the increasing interaction of public and private spheres, which is the larger topic of this book (see Introduction), also apply to the field of biodiversity governance.

One of the main objectives of this chapter is to link biodiversity governance to the economic theory of fiscal federalism. The latter is concerned with the assignment of public functions, expenditures and fiscal instruments to different levels of government. Therefore, we can identify an important link between multilevel governance and fiscal federalism where spatial characteristics of biodiversity conservation are of prime importance. The environmental quality of a landscape is closely linked to its land use pattern and the type of management performed by public jurisdictions and private land users. Yet, there are few incentives for local actors to encourage conservation activities when ecological benefits cross local boundaries (Perrings and Gadgil, 2003). Spatial externalities or spillovers exist that – if not adequately compensated – lead to an underprovision of the public goods and services concerned. This is the case for a number of ecological services, such as nature reserves or the conservation of endangered wildlife. Decisions on the designation of protected areas or species protection are often made by institutions above the local level, whereas the concrete consequences in terms of restrictions in land use or the damages caused by wildlife are born by local actors, often without any or sufficient compensation.

Fiscal federalism as a subfield of public finance in economics predominantly deals with the public aspect of environmental governance, implying identification with the kind of goods and services that should be provided by public institutions at different levels of government. In this context, the distinction between public and private clearly refers to the state as the public sphere and the market as the private sphere of voluntary interaction (see Introduction). Fiscal federalism already involves a truly multilevel perspective on the provision of public goods and services; analysis is not confined to the nationstate as predominant public actor. Public institutions may range from international institutions down to municipalities as the most decentralized governmental level. It is important to note the difference between the municipality – as the local authority representing the state and the local community – and the wider political community including further local associations and stakeholders. Fiscal federalism deals with the local level of government. In the first part of this chapter, two important principles in fiscal federalism are introduced – the principle of decentralization and the principle of fiscal equivalence. They are applied to environmental issues, helping to decide on adequate levels of actions and relevant policy instruments.

The second part of this chapter analyses the spatial characteristics of conservation benefits and costs in relation to governmental levels. The costs and benefits of providing public goods and services do not always match with jurisdictional boundaries, which call for adequate instruments to adjust them. It is important to check who is bearing the costs and who is benefiting from certain conservation programmes or measures. In practice, public and private actors continuously interact and commonly contribute to the final outcome in terms of successes and failures of the conservation and sustainable use of biodiversity. Therefore, one has to consider public and private actors in the course of adjusting the benefits and costs of biodiversity conservation.

The third part of the chapter is devoted to a case study, presenting an innovative instrument implemented in the 1990s in several Brazilian states: the ICMS-Ecológico (Imposto sobre Circulação de Mercadorias e Serviços-Ecológico) (Grieg-Gran, 2000; Loureiro, 2001; May et al, 2002; Ring, 2004b). It is an excellent and rare example of the consideration of ecological indicators in intergovernmental fiscal transfers from the state to the local level. The ICMS-Ecológico (ICMS-E) renders protected areas within municipal borders into communal revenues. In this way, it clearly represents an incentive for the creation of newly protected areas, mainly at local and state levels. Although a hierarchical, state-governed instrument, it is an economic instrument by nature. Furthermore, the ICMS-E emerged as an economic incentive for new forms of public–private interaction. Thus, the instrument and its effects are a good example of the shifting boundaries between notions of publics and privates in various aspects.

Environmental federalism

A central objective of fiscal federalism is to effectively and efficiently assign public functions, expenditures and revenues to the central, state and local governmental levels in federal systems. This means deciding which public functions and instruments are best centralized and which are better placed at decentralized levels of government (Oates, 1999). Concerning the allocation function of public sectors, which is of major interest for the provision of environmental goods and services, the basic principle of fiscal decentralization has been put forward (Musgrave, 1959; Oates, 1972). The provision of most public goods and services is more efficiently guaranteed when production and consumption are limited to the lowest governmental level possible. The decentralization rule is based on the following major arguments. First, the regionally differing preferences can be better considered at decentralized levels of government (Tiebout, 1956). Second, it is a requirement for more competition within the public sector. And third, many public goods and services experience cost degression due to lower coordination and transaction costs at the local level.

Nevertheless, there are exceptions from the general decentralization rule, as it only applies in the absence of economies of scale. If economies of scale exist, the provision of public goods and services concerned should be moved to the cost efficient centralized level (Postlep and Döring, 1996). In addition, due to the characteristics of nonrivalry and nonexcludability of many public goods and services, some of them are associated with spatial externalities or spillovers between jurisdictions. Concerning environmental 'bads', such as pollution, the activities of one jurisdiction can lead to negative externalities in neighbouring or even remote jurisdictions, implying that part of the costs in question are externalized. In the context of biodiversity conservation, for example, building infrastructure such as roads may cause a fragmentation of habitats for protected endangered species, eventually leading to a decline or extinction of a population. Concerning environmental goods or services, spillover benefits may be created. In this case, a jurisdiction bears the costs of providing certain environmental goods and services, but the benefits thereof also accrue to people in other jurisdictions at the same or at higher governmental levels. For example, various types of nature reserves, such as national parks or biosphere reserves, lead to costs in terms of land use restrictions for local communities but are highly valued, even on a global scale.

When spatial externalities exist, the principle of fiscal equivalence comes into play. It advocates achieving a match between those who decide on the provision of a collective good, those who receive the benefits, and those who pay for it (Olson, 1969). Social welfare is increased through the differentiation of public goods and services in accordance with spatially related costs and preferences. There are several ways of solving this problem. The implementation of fiscal equivalence may require the shifting of competence to a more centralized level of government. Other options involve negotiations between the parties concerned for more equal distribution of the costs and benefits of actions. This may include the formation of administrative institutions that map the spatial range of costs and benefits to internalize spatial externalities. In the EU, the implementation of the Water Framework Directive is currently leading to the establishment of new river basin authorities, or alternatively to cooperative arrangements among those jurisdictions that share a river basin, allowing for coordinated water management at the basin level (Petry and Dombrowsky, 2007). Yet another option relates to fiscal instruments such as transfers or compensation payments that help to internalize spatial externalities.

What are the basic consequences of the decentralization rule and the principle of fiscal equivalence for environmental issues? Following the general decentralization rule for the allocation function of public services, the provision of environmental goods and services should be assigned to lower levels of government where appropriate. But what does this exactly mean in terms of environmental policy in general and biodiversity governance in particular? Not all problems can be dealt with at the local level. What could the criteria be for deciding on the suitability of a problem's decentralization?

In an initial approximation, the spatial scale of a problem and the mobility of the respective environmental media play an important role in deciding on the appropriate governmental level (Ring, 2002). Consequently, small-scale public functions such as purely local public goods or land use related tasks are often suitable to local governmental decision making. The provision of drinking water or sewage and waste disposal are good examples of public services predominantly provided at the municipal level. By contrast, land related environmental problems accumulating at larger spatial scales, such as nitrogen emissions in agriculture, definitely need centrally set standards yet require local action. Spatial scale and mobility are also very important characteristics regarding species protection. The larger the habitat, for example, of large vertebrates, and the more mobile a species is (consider migrating species!), the greater the relevance of centrally performed services, including standards of protection. Concrete implementation of species protection policies still requires substantial local action, but this needs to be coordinated between public and private actors depending on the spatial distribution and mobility of the species concerned (Similä et al, 2006).

A closer look at the spatial distribution of the costs and benefits of biodiversity conservation enables a further assessment regarding the assignment of public goods and services to adequate governmental levels and potential needs for adjustment due to spatial externalities.

LOCAL COSTS AND GLOBAL BENEFITS OF BIODIVERSITY CONSERVATION

The spatial distribution of conservation benefits

The total economic value of biodiversity results from adding up its partial values (see Figure 5.1). In economics, the various benefits of biodiversity conservation are usually looked at from an anthropocentric perspective, hence, the value of goods and services is gained on the basis of individual preferences (e.g. Pearce and Turner, 1990). Market prices are the preferred indicator of economic value and are usually available for tangible goods and services. Positive and negative externalities, however, are rarely included in market prices. Reflecting the value of ecosystem services in market prices is also very difficult – if not impossible – in many fields of biodiversity conservation (Gowdy, 1997; Millennium Ecosystem Assessment, 2005b). There are various surrogate methods to reveal individual preferences for biodiversity goods and services when no market prices exist (Turner et al, 2003a; Turner et al, 2003b; Hein et al, 2006). They are widely used in economics, though one has to be aware of their implicit assumptions and shortcomings. Next to quantifiable economic values that at best allow an expression in monetary terms, safe minimum standards on the ecological side and

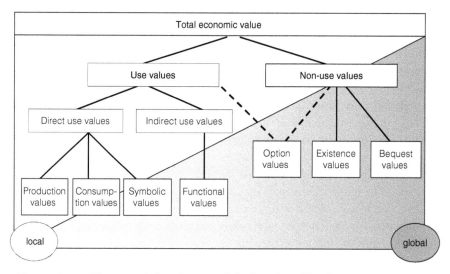

Figure 5.1   *The spatial distribution of the benefits of biodiversity conservation*

Source: Adapted from Ring, 2004a

cultural values obtained by deliberation on the social side are also part of valuing biodiversity.

The spatial distribution of conservation benefits has to be considered when decentralizing or centralizing competencies of biodiversity conservation (Döring, 1998). The spatial distribution of beneficiaries usually increases when moving from direct to indirect use values and further on to option and existence values of biodiversity conservation (see Figure 5.1). At the most general level, conservation measures can have both local and global benefits (Perrings and Gadgil, 2003). Even production values that can be captured at the local level may affect global benefits, depending on the scale and intensity of land uses and their impacts, such as local afforestation, which potentially leads to regionally changing weather conditions and helps to mitigate global climate change by carbon sequestration. There are also ecological feedback loops between local measures and higher level conservation objectives that require coordination at higher governmental levels.

It is widely uncontested in economic and legal studies of federalism that especially the non-use values associated with natural resources justify the centralization of competencies (Revesz, 2000; Oates, 2001; List et al, 2002; Ring, 2004a). Therefore, decisions on biodiversity conservation belong to the public tasks that have to be fulfilled at higher governmental levels, requiring centralized standard setting and policies. This is a fundamental difference compared to other fields of resource governance covered in this volume, particularly water and food.

The need for central standards and principles of action in biodiversity conservation is reflected in the Convention on Biological Diversity and related activities. In the EU, it is carried out by several European directives that must be implemented by member states and must set a binding framework for biodiversity policies (Similä et al, 2006). On the one hand, the loss of biodiversity belongs to the very serious problems of global change. On the other hand, decentralized activities related to local land use have – if accumulated – a tremendous influence on the state of biodiversity worldwide. As a result, centralized standard setting still requires decentralized implementation of biodiversity policies.

Perrings and Gadgil (2003) address a number of reforms necessary to reconcile both local and global public benefits of biodiversity conservation. One of them is adjusting incentives to allow local communities to be rewarded and paid for their conservation efforts (Ring, 2002).

The spatial distribution of conservation costs

From an economic perspective, biodiversity conservation is a public good. Its benefits accrue to overall society, that is, the wider political community, which ultimately relies on functioning ecosystems and their services provided to society. Therefore the state as the political representative of society has to set the framework conditions that guarantee the sufficient provision of the related public goods and services. Following the principle of fiscal equivalence, the costs of biodiversity conservation should also be borne by overall society. However, in reality the costs of biodiversity conservation are often distributed unequally among different groups of society.

First, we will consider public expenditures for nature conservation in relation to population density based on the example of Germany (see Figure 5.2). Empirical data for the various German states, or *Länder*, indicate that states with a lower population density bear the highest expenditures per capita (Ring, 2004a). This is related to the fact that nature conservation normally takes place in space. The conservation value of landscapes often increases in remote and less inhabited areas where numerous large-scale reserves can be found.

Second, the primary sector (agriculture, forestry, fisheries) is of extraordinary importance for the conservation and sustainable use of biodiversity. On the one hand, agricultural development in European landscapes has particularly contributed to the decline of biodiversity during the last century (Hampicke, 1991). According to the results of the Millennium Ecosystem Assessment (2005a), the primary sector will continue to be responsible for the destruction and degradation of valuable habitats due to substantial land use changes on a global scale in the near and medium term

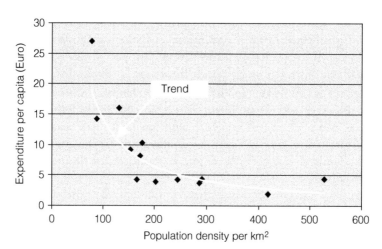

Figure 5.2   *Conservation expenditures of the German* Länder *(2001)*

Source: Bundesamt für Naturschutz, department II.1, January 2004; data: Stratmann, 2002

future, as the result of further intensification of production mainly to meet increasing global food production needs. On the other hand, the costs of biodiversity conservation must largely be borne by the primary sector (Hampicke, 2005). Current extensive and sustainable land use practices are rarely competitive in an economic sense. Whereas production schemes for intensification and enlargement of production in agriculture and aquaculture are often subsidized, payments for ecological services belong to a field in the process of development (Gutman, 2003). Without broad societal support by rewarding ecological services provided by land users, the loss of biodiversity cannot be reduced or halted (Millennium Ecosystem Assessment, 2005b; Beck et al, 2006).

Third, the unequal distribution of conservation costs also concerns the spatial distribution of nature reserves and related costs. These costs not only include measures for the conservation and sustainable use of biodiversity, but also the costs of long-term land use restrictions to be borne by communities. Depending on the protection category, local land use planning can be heavily restricted. As a result, most communities are not actively interested in the designation of protected areas. Taking Germany as an example once more, the lowest protection category of landscape reserves is still quite homogeneously distributed across the German states. However, there is an increasing concentration of protected areas for the categories of nature reserves, biosphere reserves, nature parks and national parks. Three out of 16 states (Mecklenburg-Western Pomerania, Lower Saxony and Schleswig-Holstein) hold 90 per cent of all German national park areas (Urfei, 2002).

Adjusting local costs and global benefits for public and private actors

Biodiversity conservation is a public good with its benefits mainly accruing at centralized levels – be they national, European or global. The costs of biodiversity conservation are distributed both sectorally (primary sector) and spatially (conservation expenditure per capita and protected areas) in an unequal manner. This relationship requires a centralized standard setting. In this sense, the continuing and ambitious standard setting at the European level, for example, by the Habitats Directive and the establishment of the Natura 2000 network, is justified from the economic perspective of fiscal federalism. At the same time, the increasing trend to cofinance regional, state and national agri-environmental programmes as well as environmental measures in fisheries policies with European support can be underlined.

The arguments brought forward underpin the important role of the nationstate and the increasing role of international institutions for biodiversity governance. Substantial disadvantages may exist when federal states underestimate the essential role of the nationstate, for example, by assigning decision making powers predominantly to lower governmental levels. During the recent discussion on the reform of federalism in Germany, national conservation authorities and NGOs put forward strong arguments against considerations of potentially abolishing the federal nature conservation law (Hendrischke, 2004; Ring, 2004a). Nature conservation was and still is a rather weak policy field in the overall political arena and may – despite factual evidence – be sacrificed in the course of strategic political compromises. The political results of the reform follow this line of argument. Nature conservation will be part of the German Environmental Code that is presently in design. Compared to other environmental policy fields such as water resources and emission standards, however, the German states will have far-reaching legal entitlements to derogate from the national standards (SRU, 2006). Nevertheless, the extent to which the states will make use of these derogation rights in their state conservation laws remains to be seen.

Adjusting local costs and higher level benefits of biodiversity conservation can take many different forms (Millennium Ecosystem Assessment, 2005b). The case study presented in the third part of this chapter is dedicated to protected area management, highlighting the necessity to integrate ecological indicators into intergovernmental fiscal relations. In Europe, it is common practice to compensate private land users for restrictions imposed by conservation policies. The same philosophy, however, applies to public actors on a local scale. Decentralized levels of government such as municipalities should be compensated for ecological services provided in the long run by having protected areas within their administrative boundaries. For the most part, this is still neglected in German and European fiscal relations (Ring, 2002), rendering the following case study an innovative example to learn from.

The ecological ICMS in Brazil: Fiscal transfers for local ecological services

History and basic characteristics of the ICMS-E

Brazil is a federal country consisting of 27 states, each of which has an elected government with revenue-raising power. About 90 per cent of overall state tax revenues are based on the ICMS (Imposto sobre Circulação de Mercadorias e Serviços), a tax on goods and services similar to the value-added taxes in other countries (Loureiro and de Moura, 1996; May et al, 2002). The ICMS also represents a relevant source of revenue for local governments because the Federal Constitution of Brazil decrees that 25 per cent of the revenues raised by this tax have to be allocated by the state to the local level of government. According to the Federal Constitution, 75 per cent of the total amount passed on to the municipalities is to be distributed in accordance with the share of the state ICMS that has been collected within that municipality. The state governments decide on the indicators for allocating the remaining 25 per cent.

During the early 1990s, the state of Paraná was the first to introduce ecological indicators alongside other indicators commonly used for redistribution by the states – such as population, geographical area or primary production (Grieg-Gran, 2000). The new instrument of ICMS-Ecológico or ICMS-E (May et al, 2002) was created, through which allocation of revenues is based on environmental indicators.[3] Paraná started using ecological indicators in 1992, and soon other states followed this example. The states of Minas Gerais (1996), São Paulo (1996), Rondônia (1997), Mato Grosso do Sul (2002), Tocantins and Pernambuco (2003) started operating a similar system a few years later (Grieg-Gran, 2000; May et al, 2002; Villar Martins, 2003; CPRH, 2003; Loureiro, 2004). ICMS-E legislation also exists in the states of Amapá (1996), Rio Grande do Sul (1999), Mato Grosso (2001) and Rio de Janeiro (2007). Further Brazilian states are actively engaged in introducing ecological fiscal transfer legislation, including Santa Catarina, Espírito Santo, Goiás, Bahia and Ceará. In the states of Pará and Amazonas, the ICMS-E has been under serious discussion (Bernardes, 1999; Freitas, 1999; Loureiro, 2001, 2005a; MMA, 2002; Arantes, 2006).

Each state is independent when making decisions about the indicators for distributing the 25 per cent of ICMS revenues to the local level. Therefore, different operating systems are in place regarding the consideration of ecological indicators, with one exception: all states with existing ICMS-E legislation have introduced the basic ecological indicator 'conservation unit' (CU), referring to the National System of Conservation Units in Brazil (Sistema Nacional de Unidades de Conservação). CUs include totally protected and restricted sustainable use areas that can be publicly managed (at the federal, state or municipal level), privately owned or managed by public–private partnerships.

Eligible conservation areas need to be legally defined and registered in order to be considered (Grieg-Gran, 2000).

The various categories of protected and sustainable use areas in Brazil – such as ecological research stations, biological reserves, parks, private natural heritage reserves (RPPNs) or environmental protection areas (APAs) – involve different degrees of protection and associated land use restrictions. Therefore, the states multiply the actual size of CUs with a weight reflecting its conservation value, with strictly protected areas at the top and sustainable use areas at the bottom of the scale (0 < conservation weight ≤ 1). Each state is autonomous in applying its own relative weights.

The revenues allocated to the local level are based on an ecological index that represents the weighted CUs within municipal boundaries. Again, the states use slightly different calculation systems, but the general procedure can be described as follows (compare Grieg-Gran, 2000; May et al, 2002): the municipal conservation factor is based on the total area set aside for protection in terms of CUs in relation to the total area of the municipality. The state conservation factor is given by the sum of all municipal conservation factors in the state. The ecological index is then calculated by dividing the municipal conservation factor by the state conservation factor. Finally, the municipal ecological index is multiplied by the total amount of ICMS-E revenues dedicated to CUs. For example, the ecological share of total ICMS revenues for conservation units is 2.5 per cent in Paraná, 5 per cent in Rondônia and Mato Grosso do Sul and 0.5 per cent in Minas Gerais and São Paulo (Grieg-Gran, 2000).

Most states use a purely quantitative measure in terms of the quantitative amount of CUs. Although several of the states with ICMS-E legislation call for a quality index, in most cases they are only partially implemented if at all. The state of Paraná succeeded first in considering the quality of protected areas as part of their ecological index, rendering the implementation of the instrument more complex but also more effective in terms of conservation objectives.

Financial incentive to create new protected areas

The ICMS-E has been quite effective in encouraging the creation of new protected areas (Young, 2005). In Paraná, for example, the total area in CUs grew by over 1.5 million hectares by the year 2000 (see Table 5.1), representing an overall increase of 165 per cent during the nine years since its introduction in 1992 (May et al, 2002). Municipalities in particular developed an interest in designating new public protected areas at the local level. The introduction of the quality evaluation of conservation units in Paraná also had a positive effect on the interest of municipalities to improve their management (Grieg-Gran, 2000; Loureiro, 2005b).

In Brazil, protected areas can be designated by public institutions at federal, state and municipal levels, a procedure referred to as conservation federalism

Table 5.1   *ICMS-E in Paraná: The increase in public and private protected areas*

Protected areas	Until 1991 (ha)	Total by 2000 (ha)	Increase (%)
Public			
Federal	289,582	340,428	18
State	39,859	53,663	35
Municipal	1429	4169	192
Private/mixed			
APA	306,693	1,212,324	295
RPPN	0	26,124	
Other	0	53,607	
Total	637,563	1,690,315	165

Source: May et al (2002) and own calculations. APAs can be designated at federal, state or municipal level. RPPNs can be designated at federal or state level

(Loureiro, 2005a). They can be initiated by private actors or by a collaboration of private and public actors. As can be seen in Table 5.1, the most significant increase, both in absolute and relative numbers, is related to the category of APAs. These are sustainable use areas that can easily be created and involve relatively few land use restrictions. This is also reflected in the rather low conservation weight of 0.1 associated with this conservation category in Paraná, meaning that only 10 per cent of the actual size of an APA is relevant for ICMS-E transfers. In contrast to APAs, RPPNs are of higher conservation value (conservation weight 0.8).

Since the introduction of the ICMS-E, revenues can considerably change for municipalities with a large share of CUs. In Paraná, the total amount passed through to municipalities averaged over R$50 million (US$21 million) per year between 1994 and 2000 (May et al, 2002). There are positive examples like Piraquara (90 per cent of municipal area protected watershed, 10 per cent CUs) that increased their earnings by 84 per cent in 1995 (Loureiro cited in Echavarría, 2000). Changing municipal revenues from the ICMS-E led to the creation of Brazil's first municipal consortium for biodiversity protection in 1995, which resulted in the foundation of the Ilha Grande National Park two years later (May et al, 2002).

Incentive for new forms of public–private interaction

The ICMS-E programme is clearly targeted at the local governmental level and its public actors, for ICMS-E revenues only accrue to the municipality and not to the owner of the land. The incentive effect thus primarily addresses local public authorities. There is, however, another incentive effect to encourage public–private partnerships in terms of more environmentally sound land uses. Some of the municipalities have started supporting land users in managing CUs, including provision of staff, equipment and vehicles for managing the areas (Bernardes, 1999; May et al, 2002). These activities are mostly related to a specific category of reserves, namely the RPPNs, a private reserve category specified in the national system of conservation units. RPPNs are owned and administered by a wide range of institutions, such as NGOs, industry or private landowners. These reserves are established and run by their owners, who are fully responsible for their maintenance and management (Manigel, 2004).

Both Paraná and Minas Gerais have actively been promoting the establishment of RPPNs as part of an integrated public–private partnership in buffer zones surrounding public protected areas, representing an important link between totally protected areas and intensively used landscapes for agricultural production (cf Chapter 10). RPPNs originally represented a reserve category to be designated and handled at the national level by the Federal Brazilian Institute for the Environment and Renewable Resources (Instituto Brasileiro do Meio Ambiente e dos Recursos Naturais Renováveis). The states of Paraná and Minas Gerais established state legislation in the 1990s, allowing a less bureaucratic way of designating and handling the private reserves at state level. This step, together with the financial incentive effect of the ICMS-E, contributed to a significant increase in the number and size of RPPNs. By the year 2000, some 26,124 hectares were designated in Paraná and 34,069 hectares in Minas Gerais (Bernardes, 1999). Due to the very active role of state environmental agencies in promoting private reserves, Paraná now holds the largest number and area of RPPNs (183 reserves with 36,928 hectares) protecting the remaining Atlantic Forest, one of the global hotspots of biodiversity (Mesquita, 2004).

The ecological fiscal transfers actually motivated local governments to assist landowners in measures to protect and maintain the environmental quality of their areas, and also helped them to prepare the necessary registration documentation (Bernardes, 1999). Drainage improvements as well as road maintenance and access improvement belong to the infrastructure support municipalities provide for landowners. Although RPPNs are eligible for rural land tax exemption, May et al (2002) found out that this is not much of an incentive to private owners. The hopes for a link with municipal services and the prospects of ecotourism revenues are higher.

With the rising significance of RPPNs, their owners soon founded associations of RPPN holders to better organize themselves, improve the management of the reserves, and speak with a common voice regarding their interests. State conservation authorities (public actors) and conservation NGOs (hybrid organizations) actively cooperate with these new organizations or with single potential future RPPN holders (private actors) in pursuit of creating new

RPPNs (Coneglian, 2005; Loureiro, 2005b). They join forces in talking to mayors to make them aware of the benefits from ICMS-E and encourage them to share at least part of the additional municipal revenues to help landowners manage the CUs (Mesquita, 2004; Jordan, 2005).

Nevertheless, the public–private partnerships related to RPPNs have been subject to critique. Due to the size of property and the volume of resources involved, large farmers were prioritized for the most part, leading to complaints that public money was being used to benefit a few large landowners (May et al, 2002), even though small landowners would also be interested in RPPN creation. In the meantime, new ways have been explored that also take smaller properties for RPPN creation into consideration, calling for a reduction of transaction costs associated with their management.

At a more general level, the ICMS-E has substantially improved relations between protected areas and the surrounding inhabitants (Bernardes, 1999). As with numerous other places in the world, protected areas were primarily seen as an obstacle to local development (e.g. in Germany: Bauer et al, 1996; Stoll-Kleemann, 2001). With this new instrument, local actors started perceiving them as an opportunity to generate revenue. For some municipalities, it was the additional revenue that first created a basic awareness of the existence of protected areas within municipal boundaries. In Minas Gerais, for example, only federal and state protected areas were considered during the first year of the ICMS-E's operation. Locally protected areas existed but still needed formal registration to be eligible for the programme. Municipalities reacted quickly to the new incentive programme, registering locally protected areas for inclusion in the ICMS-E programme during the second year (Grieg-Gran, 2000).

Since the new revenues, the attitudes of both public municipal actors and local citizens towards protected areas have begun to change. However, this is greatly dependent on the communication strategies of local authorities. May et al (2002) investigated the public–private relationships in municipalities belonging to the Ilha Grande National Park in Paraná, where the municipalities are actively communicating the benefits of the ICMS-E to the local population. In this way, the whole community perceives the financial importance of the ICMS-E. In São Jorge do Patrocínio, for example, the ICMS-E represented 17 per cent of the overall municipal budget in 1998 and 71 per cent of the total ICMS transfers in the year 2000. The local authorities make clear for what purposes the additional revenues are used, such as well drilling to provide drinking water, cleaning and landscaping of the urban area, garbage collection, landfills, environmental education or enforcement of land use controls in parks and APAs (May et al, 2002). Local communities are thus made aware of the link between revenues, public investments and protected areas within municipal borders.

Federal environmental institutions – including the environmental ministry – support the spread of knowledge about the effects of the ICMS-E in Brazil. Conservation NGOs, such as The Nature Conservancy of Brazil, actively work together with local networks of NGOs to promote its introduction in states where the ICMS-E does not exist yet (Veiga Neto, 2005). A variety of actors join forces – both public and private, ecologically and socially motivated. Because the ICMS-E is distributed in lumpsum payments, the revenues can be spent for conservation purposes but can also help to alleviate social and health problems or improve the educational situation in the municipalities.

CONCLUSIONS

Biodiversity governance involves different governmental levels and a variety of actors, including public authorities, private landowners and representatives from hybrid organizations. Even in the case of a purely hierarchical instrument, introduced and managed by public authorities, the ICMS-E in Brazil has shown how numerous new interactions crossing the public–private divide can follow. The rising significance of the private reserves is a good example of the blurring boundary between public and private spheres of biodiversity conservation (see Introduction). The importance of the ICMS-E's creation of these links, however, lies in the fact that there are few schemes in Brazil that directly compensate land users for ecological services on their land. In this way, the ICMS-E became the major instrument for internalizing spillover benefits of biodiversity conservation by compensating municipalities for local costs of bearing conservation measures and land use restriction.

The situation is different in the EU. A variety of agri-environmental and conservation programmes exist to compensate land users for environmental services (cf Chapter 4). Here, instruments for compensating municipalities, that is, the local public side, for their restrictions in land use planning and barriers to generating income to fulfil municipal public functions are commonly missing, although environmental advisory councils have long asked for the introduction of such instruments (SRU, 1996). Ideally, both types of instruments exist, internalizing conservation spillover benefits to the local level for both public institutions and the private sector. But in reality, there are different political cultures calling for mutual education. At least in some cases, it would certainly be more cost effective in Brazil to avoid the detour via the municipal government in compensating private landowners for their conservation activities. In Europe, by turn, there is a need to consider decentralized levels of government by introducing ecological fiscal transfers to the local level (Köllner et al, 2002; Ring, 2002; Perner and Thöne, 2005). So far, only Portugal has set up a fiscal transfer scheme that explicitly rewards municipalities for having designated Natura 2000 sites and other protected areas within their territories (de Melo and Prates, 2007).

There are also lessons at a more general theoretical level. For decades environmental economics and the theory of environmental policy predominantly focused on environmental pollution associated with negative externalities and respective policy instruments for internalization such as taxes, charges and fees. For the sufficient provision of environmental goods and services, internalizing positive externalities is just as important as internalizing negative externalities. Comparative efforts still have to be dedicated to the analysis of positive externalities and adequate policy instruments to address them.

Regarding biodiversity governance, an important task is to acknowledge and value the spillover benefits, especially of both public and private local conservation efforts. Conservation management is mostly management related to land use, where local communities play a role that is not to be underestimated. Even though some conservation related measures are paid by higher level institutions, local actors ultimately carry the costs, at least in terms of land use restrictions. Financial instruments to compensate the local costs of biodiversity conservation are a minimum requirement for the sufficient provision of biodiversity related goods and services. They can be provided by both public and private actors, although different types of instruments are needed for addressing each of them.

Agri-environmental payments constitute a common instrument for compensating private land users for their additional costs of conservation. All too often, however, agri-environmental payments in environmental economic literature and in the media continue to be summarized as subsidies (see also Introduction), frequently involving a negative connotation of market distortion. In fact, subsidies are defined in public finance literature as public transfers without equivalent market relevant services by the recipient. There is a substantial need for better differentiation in this respect, with true economic and societal recognition of the farmer's performance. If farmers provide ecological services to society in terms of biodiversity conservation, thereby producing positive externalities, they should be paid by society for these services. Otherwise, as economic reasoning tells us, there will be an underprovision of the respective goods and services, because markets are unable to cope with externalities. In economic terms, the financial instrument used for payments of environmental services should no longer be referred to as a subsidy.

Intergovernmental fiscal transfers in federal systems constitute a suitable instrument for internalizing spillover benefits between public jurisdictions at different governmental levels. So far, they have rarely been used for environmental purposes (Ring, 2002). Environmental federalism primarily deals with competencies of environmental decision making. This involves the question of devolution: which environmental goods and services should be provided by public institutions and which by private actors (e.g. Anderson and Hill, 1996)? And if this decision goes for public provision, the centralization/decentralization question arises (e.g. Harrison, 1996): Which environmental standards should be set at which governmental levels? Analysing intergovernmental fiscal relations and respective policy instruments for their potential to compensate local governments for spillover benefits associated with the provision of environmental goods and services is still a large field to explore and develop. The Brazilian case study has shown the extent of local initiative and endeavour that still lies idle in states with no adequate compensation for local conservation services.

NOTES

1   Biodiversity governance is understood as a subfield of resource governance. Environmental governance is used as the most generic term in this chapter and includes both of these fields. Concrete examples are mostly related to the conservation and sustainable use of biodiversity.
2   See Chapter 4 for a more detailed portrayal of private, public and hybrid actors related to landscape governance that is also valid for the field of biodiversity governance.
3   The ICMS-Ecológico is also known under the term 'ecological value-added tax'. However, this term is misleading from a public finance perspective. An ecological tax would be a tax assessed on the basis of ecological indicators. The ICMS-Ecológico uses ecological indicators for the allocation of its revenues. Therefore, economically speaking, the term 'ecological fiscal transfer' is more appropriate.

REFERENCES

Anderson, T L and Hill, P J (1996) *Environmental Federalism: Thinking Smaller*, Property and Environment Research Center Policy Series, No PS-8, Bozeman, MT

Arantes, A (2006) 'ICMS Ecológico, uma oportunidade histórica de Goiás', www.semarh.goias.gov.br (accessed 26 May 2006)

Bauer, S, Abresch, J-P and Steuernagel, M (1996) *Gesamtinstrumentarium zur Erreichung einer umweltverträglichen Raumnutzung*, Metzler-Poeschel, Stuttgart

Beck, S, Born, W, Dziock, S, Görg, C, Hansjürgens, B, Jax, K, Köck, W, Neßhöver, C, Rauschmayer, F, Ring, I, Schmidt-Loske, K, Unnerstall, H, Wittmer, H and Henle, K (2006) *Die Relevanz des Millennium Ecosystem Assessment für Deutschland*, UFZ Report No 02/2006, UFZ Centre for Environmental Research, Leipzig

Bernardes, A T (1999) *Some Mechanisms for Biodiversity Protection in Brazil, with Emphasis on Their Application in the State of Minas Gerais*, World Bank, Washington, DC

Coneglian, S J (2005) 'Sociedade de Pesquisa em Vida Selvagem e Educação Ambiental', Curitiba, Brazil, personal communication

CPRH (State Agency of the Environment of Pernambuco) (2003) 'Decret No 25,574', www.cprh.pe.gov.br/ctudo-secoes-sub.asp?idsecao=178 (accessed 27 May 2004)

Döring, T (1998) 'Möglichkeiten der Dezentralisierung im Bereich globaler Umweltprobleme – Das Beispiel des Natur- und Artenschutzes in Deutschland' in Renner, A and Hinterberger, F (eds) *Zukunftsfähigkeit und Neoliberalimus*, Nomos, Baden-Baden, pp425–441

Echavarría, M (2000) 'Valuation of water-related services to downstream users in rural watersheds: Determining values for the use and protection of water resources', FAO Background Paper, no 4, presented at the Electronic Workshop 'Land-Water Linkages in Rural Watersheds', 18 September–27 October 2000, Rome

Freitas, A (1999) *ICMS ecológico – Um Instrumento Econômico para Conservação da Biodiversidade*, World Wide Fund for Nature Brazil, Brazil

Gowdy, J (1997) 'The value of biodiversity: Markets, society, and ecosystems', *Land Economics*, vol 73, no 1, pp25–41

Grieg-Gran, M (2000) *Fiscal Incentives for Biodiversity Conservation: The ICMS Ecológico in Brazil*, Discussion Paper 00-01, International Institute for Environment and Development, London

Gutman, P (ed) (2003) *From Goodwill to Payments for Environmental Services*, World Wide Fund for Nature, Washington, DC

Hampicke, U (1991) *Naturschutzökonomie*, Ulmer, Stuttgart

Hampicke, U (2005) 'Naturschutzpolitik' in Hansjürgens, B and Wätzold, F (eds) *Umweltpolitik und umweltökonomische Politikberatung in Deutschland*, special issue of *Zeitschrift für angewandte Umweltforschung*, vol 15, pp162–177

Harrison, K (1996) *Passing the Buck: Federalism and Canadian Environmental Policy*, University of British Columbia Press, Vancouver

Hein, L, van Koppen, K, de Groot, R S and van Ierland, E C (2006) 'Spatial scales, stakeholders and the valuation of ecosystem services', *Ecological Economics*, vol 57, no 2, pp209–228

Hendrischke, O (2004) 'Naturschutz und Landschaftspflege in der Föderalismusreform: Stärkung der Handlungsfähigkeit durch Neugestaltung der Gesetzgebungskompetenzen', *Natur und Landschaft*, vol 6, pp276–279

Jordan, A, Wurzel, R K W and Zito, A R (eds) (2003) *New Instruments of Environmental Governance? National Experiences and Prospects*, Frank Cass, London

Jordan, D (2005) 'Incentivo a Reservas Particulares de Patrimônio Natural é Instrumento bem Sucedido para a Preservação Ambiental: Notícia do ambientebrasil', www.ambientebrasil.com (accessed 26 May 2006)

Köllner, T, Schelske, O and Seidl, I (2002) 'Integrating biodiversity into intergovernmental fiscal transfers based on cantonal benchmarking: A Swiss case study', *Basic and Applied Ecology*, vol 3, pp381–391

List, J A, Bulte, E H and Shogren, J F (2002) 'Beggar thy neighbor: Testing for free riding in state-level endangered species expenditures', *Public Choice*, vol 111, no 3, pp303–315

Loureiro, W (2001) *O ICMS Ecológico na biodiversidade*, IAP Regional de Campo, Mourão

Loureiro, W (2004) 'ICMS Ecológico – a consolidação de uma experiência brasileira de incentivo a conservação da biodiversidade', Seminário de Pós-Graduação em Engenharia Florestal, Universidade Federal do Paraná, Setor de Ciências Agrárias, Paraná, www.floresta.ufpr.br/pos-graduacao/eventos.html (accessed 12 August 2004)

Loureiro, W (2005a) 'ICMS Ecológico. Na Conservação da Biodiversidade no Brasil', Colóquio ministrado na Universidade Católica Dom Bosco, 14 March, Campo Grande

Loureiro, W (2005b) 'State Environmental Agency', Curitiba, personal communication

Loureiro, W and de Moura, R P R (1996) 'Ecological ICMS (tax over circulation of goods and services): A successful experience in Brazil', presentation at the workshop 'Incentives for Biodiversity: Sharing Experiences', 30 August–1 September, Montreal

Manigel, E (2004) *Integrating Parks and Neighbours*, Tropical Ecology Support Programme, GTZ, Eschborn

May, P H, Veiga Neto, F, Denardin, V and Loureiro, W (2002) 'Using fiscal instruments to encourage conservation: Municipal responses to the "ecological" value-added tax in Paraná and Minas Gerais, Brazil' in Pagiola, S, Bishop, J and Landell-Mills, N (eds) *Selling Forest Environmental Services: Market-Based Mechanisms for Conservation and Development*, Earthscan, London, pp173–199

de Melo, J J and Prates, J (2007) 'EcoTerra Model – economic instruments for sustainable land use management in Portugal', Paper presented at the 7th International Conference of the European Society for Ecological Economics, 5–8 June, Leipzig

Mesquita, C A B (2004) *RPPN da Mata Atlântica*, Conservação Internacional, Belo Horizonte

Millennium Ecosystem Assessment (2005a) *Ecosystems and Human Well-Being: Synthesis*, Island Press, Washington, DC

Millennium Ecosystem Assessment (2005b) *Ecosystems and Human Well-Being: Biodiversity Synthesis*, World Resources Institute, Washington, DC

MMA (Ministry of the Environment) (2002) 'National Program for the Conservation of Biodiversity–DCBIO: Second National Report of Brazil to the Convention on Biological Diversity', MMA (Ministry of the Environment), Biodiversity and Forest Secretariat – SFB, preliminary version, Brasília

Musgrave, R M (1959) *The Theory of Public Finance*, McGraw-Hill, New York

Oates, W E (1972) *Fiscal Federalism*, Harcourt Brace Jovanovich, New York

Oates, W E (1999) 'An essay on fiscal federalism', *Journal of Economic Literature*, vol 37, no 3, pp1120–1149

Oates, W E (2001) 'A reconsideration of environmental federalism', *Discussion Paper 01-54*, Resources for the Future, Washington, DC

Olson, M Jr (1969) 'The principle of "fiscal equivalence": The division of responsibilities among different levels of government', *American Economic Review*, vol 59, no 2, pp479–487

Pearce, D and Turner, R K (1990) *Economics of Natural Resources and the Environment*, Johns Hopkins University Press, Baltimore, MD

Perner, A and Thöne, M (2005) 'Naturschutz im Finanzausgleich. Erweiterung des naturschutzpolitischen Instrumentariums um finanzielle Anreize für Gebietskörperschaften' in *FiFo-Berichte*, no 3, Institute for Research on Public Finance, Cologne

Perrings, C and Gadgil, M (2003) 'Conserving biodiversity: Reconciling local and global public benefits' in Kaul, I, Conceição, P, Le Goulven, K and Mendoza, R U (eds) *Providing Global Public Goods: Managing Globalization*, Oxford University Press, Oxford, pp532–555

Petry, D and Dombrowsky, I (2007) 'River basin management in Germany: Past experiences and challenges ahead' in Erickson, J D, Messner, F and Ring, I (eds) *Ecological Economics of Sustainable Watershed Management*, Elsevier, Amsterdam, pp11–42

Postlep, R-D and Döring, T (1996) 'Entwicklungen in der ökonomischen Föderalismusdiskussion und im föderativen System der Bundesrepublik Deutschland' in Postlep, R-D (ed) *Aktuelle Fragen zum Föderalismus: Ausgewählte Probleme aus Theorie und politischer Praxis des Föderalismus*, Metropolis, Marburg, pp7–44

Revesz, R L (2000) 'Federalism and environmental regulation: An overview' in Revesz, R L, Sands, P and Stewart, R B (eds) *Environmental Law, the Economy and Sustainable Development*, Cambridge University Press, Cambridge, pp37–79

Ring, I (2002) 'Ecological public functions and fiscal equalisation at the local level in Germany', *Ecological Economics*, vol 42, no 3, pp415–427

Ring, I (2004a) 'Naturschutz in der föderalen Aufgabenteilung: Zur Notwendigkeit einer Bundeskompetenz aus ökonomischer Perspektive', *Natur und Landschaft*, vol 79, no 11, pp494–500

Ring, I (2004b) 'Integrating local ecological services into intergovernmental fiscal transfers: The case of the ICMS-E in Brazil', *UFZ Discussion Papers*, no 12/2004, UFZ Centre for Environmental Research, Leipzig

Similä, J, Thum, R, Varjopuro, R and Ring, I (2006) 'Protected species in conflict with fisheries: The interplay between European and national regulation', *Journal of European Environmental Planning and Law*, vol 5, pp432–445

SRU (Rat von Sachverständigen für Umweltfragen) (1996) *Konzepte einer dauerhaft-umweltgerechten Nutzung ländlicher Räume*, Metzler-Poeschel, Stuttgart

SRU (2006) 'Der Umweltschutz in der Föderalismusreform', communication no 10, SRU, Berlin

Stoll-Kleemann, S (2001) 'Barriers to nature conservation in Germany: A model explaining opposition to protected areas', *Journal of Environmental Psychology*, vol 21, no 4, pp369–385

Stratmann, U (2002) 'Aufgabenspezifische Erfassung der Naturschutzaufgaben von Bund und Ländern (1985-2001): Methode, Analyse, Ergebnisse', unpublished research report for the German Agency for Nature Protection

Tiebout, C M (1956) 'A pure theory of local expenditures', *Journal of Political Economy*, vol 64, pp416–424

Turner, R K, Brouwer, R, Crowards, T C and Georgiou, S (2003a) 'The economics of wetland management' in Turner, R K, van den Bergh, J C J M and Brouwer, R (eds) *Managing Wetlands: An Ecological Economics Approach*, Edward Elgar, Cheltenham, pp73–107

Turner, R K, Paavola, J, Farber, S, Cooper, P, Jessamy, V and Georgiou, S (2003b) 'Valuing nature: Lessons learned and future research directions', *Ecological Economics*, vol 46, no 3, pp493–510

Urfei, G (2002) 'Regionale Verteilung von Schutzgebieten in Deutschland – Eine empirisch gestützte Bewertung der räumlichen Implikationen des Natur- und Landschaftsschutzes per Ordnungsrecht', *Agrarwirtschaft*, vol 51, no 5, pp249–258

Veiga Neto, F (2005) 'The Nature Conservancy of Brazil', Curitiba, personal communication

Villar Martins, G I (2003) 'Análise do Efeito da Implantação do ICMS Ecológico no Pantanal Sulmatogrossense', Governmental School of Mato Grosso do Sul Secretary of Public Relations (SEGES), www.escolagov.ms.gov.br/inicial/index .php?id=29&art_id=78 (accessed 27 May 2004)

Young, C E Frickman (2005) 'Financial mechanisms for conservation in Brazil', *Conservation Biology*, vol 19, no 3, pp756–761

6

The Media in Forestry: Government, Governance and Social Visibility

Daniela Kleinschmit and Max Krott

INTRODUCTION

On the political level different notions of *public* (see discussion on three distinctions between private and public in the Introduction to this volume) dominate forest policy. In Germany, forest policy is dominated by the public in form of the government as elected representatives and the appropriate administrations. On the global level, a second notion of public dominates forest policy: a political community that leads the governing process. This new form of governance includes governmental actors as well as actors from civil society.

Both government and governance need democratic legitimacy for their political actions. In representative democracies, forest policy processes dominated by government gain legitimacy through democratic election. These elections are regarded as instrumental in bringing the governing body into agreement with the people it represents. Governance actors are not elected democratically. They need to legitimize their decisions through rational discourse led by the best argument. In both cases, a third notion of public comes into play. The public as a sphere of social visibility is needed for democratic forest policy, either in government or in governance processes. The former needs the public in order that informed citizens vote for representatives, so allowing governmental actors to reflect the preferences of society. The latter needs the public to create an open and rational discourse filtering the best argumentation.

In both cases, the public media seems to contribute to the solution of democratic legitimacy. But the media takes a special role in the discussion of the distinction of public and private (see Introduction). On the one hand, the media is regarded as public in common thinking. Connected with this perception is the characterization of the media as the voice of the interests of society and the fourth branch of governance: observing the government and taking care that political action serves the common good. On the other hand, the media is a product of either a state-owned or a private enterprise. In both cases, the enterprise competes with others in the market. Therefore, the media as a product (for example, in the form of newspaper or television) has to be oriented towards markets by fulfilling the demands of recipients and advertising customers.

The content of the media cannot mirror the whole reality, therefore the media product is a result of a selection process. The criteria used for selecting newsworthy information depend on general media rules based on the idea of gaining attention as well as on the political anchor of the owner of the media. But the selection process starts with the actors assuming that the public media has an influence on political decision making. For this reason actors compete for media attention by active event management, therefore a public media empowered by strong actors can be expected.

This combination of social visibility and private interests in the public media leads to the question of whether the media can contribute to the legitimacy of forest policy processes. This chapter focuses on two aspects of this: first, the argument that the media mirror only one perspective of the preferences of society, and second, the special character of this public media. The theoretical part of this chapter deals with the difference between the public media and popular opinion as another opportunity of representing society's preferences. Both are considered concerning their impact on policy making. Additionally, the character of the public media, regarding its feasibility as a platform of deliberative discourses for the legitimacy of governance processes, is described from the perspective of media theories. The elaborated hypotheses are tested by empirical results from media analysis and opinion polls.

THEORY

Public media and population opinion: Two different understandings of public opinion

Public, in the sense of social visibility, is an elementary societal phenomenon whose definition is not trivial. The definition of a public sphere from Habermas forms the basis of this chapter:

> *The public sphere can best be described as a network for communicating information and points of view [...] the streams of communication are, in the process, filtered and synthesized in such a way that they coalesce into bundles of topically specified public opinions. (Habermas, 1996)*

This definition includes the awareness that there is not just one public sphere with clear boundaries. Instead, different parts of the public can be differentiated by diverse criteria, for example by their content or the arena offered by different actors. Characterizing the public by the content, the political public exists next to others, for example the arts public or the scientific public (Gerhards, 1993). In the following 'the public' refers to a political public.

In the sense of the above definition, the public media is a network provided by media where topics and problems between politics and society are processed into focused opinions. These topics and problems are not independent from the existence of the public media. Actors try to put pressure on the political process by gaining media attention, actively managing events in order to be reported on by the media. The result is a media-adapted reality mirrored in the public media. Hence, this mirror of the interest of society is only one of many possibilities.

Another perspective from which to perceive the preferences of society is the results of opinion polls. These cannot be regarded as representing public opinion either. They are only the sum of individual opinions, shown as a unitary whole. The results of polls cannot be called public because the process and results are not socially visible. The poll questions are developed by polling firms and their clients. Only selected persons have a chance to answer the questions. And the results, too, are only known to the polling firm and its clients. Opinion polls are only socially visible if they are published by the media and become part of the discourse. Nevertheless, this perspective on the preferences of society can be used as a comparison with the perspective of the public media. To avoid misunderstandings, the results of these polls will be named 'popular opinion' to distinguish them from public opinion as defined above.

Different mirrors of the preferences of society

Both the public media and popular opinion influence the political process in different ways. In the following, these influences are described by findings from political and media science.

The meaning of 'public' in government

Political science approaches attach importance to public opinion in connection with elections in representative democracies (Krott, 2005). Based on the rational choice approach, and especially on economic theory of politics, the main target of political decision makers is gaining a maximum number of votes. Politicians have to adapt their actions to the expectations and needs of their potential voters. Referring to this, published opinion is used as an indicator of citizens' preferences (Gerhards, 1995). This impact increases because of the self-deception of politicians, who attach more importance to the influence of media reporting on popular opinion than it actually merits (Krott, 2005). Media theories, the influence of the media on political elites, are explained by the policy-agenda-setting approach (Linsky, 1986; Rogers et al, 1991). Hence the agenda of political decision makers is influenced by topics highly ranked in the media agenda. Results from case studies show that the attitude as well as the behaviour of political decision makers can change under certain conditions.

The impact of popular opinion on political decision makers is, in this context, regarded as the mirror of the will of the voter. It expresses a radical democratic view by referring to the bottom-up model (von Alemann, 1997). Therefore, results of opinion polls dealing with the political preferences of citizens allow responsiveness from the political elite (Hinckley, 1992). Brettschneider (1996) gives evidence of conformity between parliamentary actions and population opinion, meaning that parliamentary actions lead to a change of popular opinion as well as the other way around.

The influence of media opinion on public opinion is strongly discussed but scientifically contested. The influence on public opinion depends on a variety of factors. The public agenda setting approach assumes that the media can have an influence on the perception but not the attitude of recipients (Brettschneider, 2004). And even this influence is limited by different factors, for example the attention of recipients or the consistency of the reporting.

This rough overview of studies dealing with the impact of public media and popular opinion shows that an influence on governmental politics can be expected. Referring to the above definition of public results in the hypothesis that the public media offers only one perspective of the interests of society. The results of opinion polls are another, different way to perceive the preferences of the population.

The meaning of public in governance

In the following, 'governance' is used in a narrow sense as a normative concept of 'governance with government', as it is lately popularly used. At the heart of this concept – the so called 'new governance' – is a governing style 'in which boundaries between and within public and private have become blurred' (Stoker, 1998). This form of governance is strongly connected with the normative goal of 'shared responsibility for resource allocation and conflict resolution' (Schmitter, 2002) in which public, private and societal actors should be involved. Referring to this governance concept, the notion of public changes from public as a state authority to public as a political community involving both governmental and civil society actors, as discussed in the Introduction to this book. Habermas argues that these civil society actors are able to link political decision making with the private sphere through their 'sensitivity in detecting and identifying new problem situations' (Habermas, 1996). In some cases, this governing style takes place within the nationstate, but it is essential in political actions taking place beyond the nationstate because on a transnational level, no higher central instance exists and the rise of a world government cannot be expected in the near future. Therefore this new concept of governance is applied on a transnational level (Zürn, 1998; Keohane, 2002; Schmitter, 2002; Wolf, 2002).

In comparison with governmental forest policy, the active participation of affected private and societal actors in decision processes on forest problems is increasing. These actors are not selected by democratic process, which raises the problem of legitimacy. This can be avoided by receiving wider popular legitimacy and support for their actions through strong justification (Steffek, 2003). This argument can be strengthened by the theoretical, normative, ideal model of a deliberative democracy developed by Jürgen Habermas, which is strongly linked to his discourse theory (Habermas, 1996). At the heart of this model of discourse is the normative form of the public sphere. The argument taking place in this public sphere should be free from particular interests and led by rationality in order to reach a fair and adequate solution to political conflicts (Buchstein, 2003). Two different levels of the public sphere necessary to allow and support public deliberative processes can be distinguished. One is institutionalized through conferences, information events, documents and debates. This limited public sphere is dominated by experts. To link this level with societal problems, a second deliberative level is needed. This public sphere has to be wider, 'more public', assuring free and equal participation, and should go beyond single sectors. This discourse is conveyable only through the mass media (Arenhövel, 2003).

There is, however, a 'critical awareness of the absence of communicative space for free and equal discussion' (Torgerson, 2003), especially in the mass media. Gerhards et al (1998) link the model of deliberative democracy with the knowledge of media theories resulting from the input-hypothesis, which assumes that the opportunity to be exhibited in the media depends on the status of actors[1] and their abilities and resources to produce information in the way that the media favours. Empirical analysis of different field studies verifies this hypothesis for the national discourse (e.g. Gerhards, 1993; Gerhards et al, 1998; Weßler, 1999; Kleinschmit and Feindt, 2004) as well as for supranational discourses (Wimmel, 2004). The result is an empowered discourse dominated by government and the economy and not by civil society, contradicting deliberative principles (Trenz, 2004). This means that not everyone can state his or her arguments and interests in an appropriate framework connected with the discursive process.

This theoretical background leads to the hypothesis that forest discourse in the media is dominated by actors of high status. The hypothesis is based on Habermas' expectation that actors from the centre and periphery of a political system communicate in different ways. If the hypothesis is verified by empirical data then the legitimacy of governance decisions is lacking.

RESEARCH DESIGN

To allow testing of the hypotheses resulting from the theoretical background, existing results from different empirical studies were used. The results of these studies have been presented in other contexts (Krumland, 2004; Krumland and Krott, 2004; Kleinschmit et al, 2007a; Kleinschmit et al, 2007b). But even if the data are the result of selective analyses of different public spheres covering different time periods, the reconstructed opinions are the result of the historical development of discourses. A comparison of results allows some insights into the notions of public and private in the field of forest policy.

Data

To enable statements to be made on the differences between the public media and population opinion as two ways of mirroring the preferences of society in the field of forest policy, empirical data from media and the results of opinion polls are needed. In this chapter the latter refers to data from studies of forest and forestry in Germany presented by Bernhard Pauli (2000). The basis of Pauli's study is a representative public opinion poll, collected in 1997 and 1998 by telephone interview.

The empirical analysis of the public media here is limited to newspapers. Even if the written press today is only a minor factor in the media market, its effects should not be underestimated. Quality newspapers, as part of the prestige media, are characterized by diverse news and sound investigations. Their messages are directed to an elite readership, particularly including decision makers. This is a precondition for the media's aim for relevance across national borders (Abromeit, 2002). Therefore the impact of this kind of newspaper is enormous, even if circulation is relatively small (Noelle-Neumann and Mathes, 1987; Gerhards, 1991; Wittkämper et al, 1992; Kepplinger, 1994).

The analysis of the public media focuses on two different kinds of quality newspapers: nationwide German newspapers are used to test the hypothesis that the view of public media is only one of many perceptions of forest. The results of the analysis of these newspapers are also used to test the second hypothesis: whether the media is dominated by actors of high status. The results from analyses of internationally oriented newspapers are also considered in testing this hypothesis.

The analyses of the German quality newspapers are based on *Frankfurter Allgemeine Zeitung*, *Frankfurter Rundschau*, *Süddeutsche Zeitung* and *Die Welt*. These newspapers are, in spite of their specific distribution areas, of high relevance in Germany regarding their scope, volume of reporting, selection of topics and circulation. In the time period from 1994 to 1998, these four newspapers published 2492 articles, each with at least one paragraph dealing with forests.

Only a few quality newspapers are internationally oriented. The *Wall Street Journal*, the *Financial Times* and the *International Herald Tribune* (UNESCO, 1997) are three of them. The content of the first two newspapers is limited to economic topics. Forest topics can rarely be expected, and only with an economic bias. However, the *International Herald Tribune* publishes general news and articles, as does the weekly magazine, *TIME*, which is also distributed internationally and deals with international topics.[2] Both *TIME* magazine and the *International Herald Tribune* are suitable for a first empirical examination of whether forest articles are dominated by actors of high status.

The selection of articles is based on three topics relevant to global forest governance processes: climate change, biodiversity and forest fires. The analysis covers a time period from 1994 to 2004[3] to smooth variations and outliers as a result of topicality. In this time period, 48 articles on climate change, 29 on biodiversity and 86 on forest fires were published, all dealing with forest.

Methodology: Content analysis of media articles

All the media articles were analysed for their formal characteristics through a quantitative–qualitative content analysis. The basic category system, derived from theory, is subdivided into groups of categories. For the media analysis presented here, the variable 'speaker' is relevant.

The possible attributes of the variable 'speaker' are subdivided to allow examination of which type of actor has a voice (speaks) in the national public media. Parts of this variable are 'politics', 'administration', 'justice', 'international governmental organizations', 'scientist', 'enterprises', 'nongovernmental organizations', 'other organizations', 'media' and 'individuals'. These categories result from a combination of subcategories. The category 'politics' considers, for example, both 'government politicians' and 'nongovernment politicians'.[4] Additionally, the nationality of the variable 'speaker' is captured.

The unit of analysis for categorizing the speaker is the statement. Statements, which are identified as relevant for coding, are single verbal messages from the actors speaking in the article (Gerhards et al, 1998). Thus in one article more than one message (statement) can be coded. In the analyses of media articles in the internationally oriented media, statements referring to forest and one of the three selected topics are relevant for coding. The actor's statement can be in direct or indirect speech. It must be taken into consideration that the media itself can appear as a speaker.

The coding proceeds supported by computer. This means the data are directly entered into a developed SPSS-mask. During the analysis, frequent testing is used to check the reliability of the coding persons.

RESULTS

The results of the different empirical studies are presented in the following order to avoid repetition: first, the hypothesis that forest discourse in the media is dominated by actors of high status is tested using the results of empirical studies dealing with forest articles published in German and internationally oriented newspapers. Second, the content of the German forest articles is compared with results of an opinion poll, testing the hypothesis that the public media and opinion polls are two different ways of mirroring the interests of society.

Forest discourse in the media

Speakers have the opportunity to impose their patterns of interpretation on the description of problems reported by the media and can therefore steer the discourse in a specific direction. The debate on whether forest discourses in the media are dominated by actors of high status can be discussed by looking at the share of speakers from the categories reflecting the centre and periphery of the political system. In accordance with Habermas (1996) and resuming the characterization of Cohen and Arato (1992), the speakers are divided into the categories civil society, political centre and the economy, as well as scientists, media and a group of those who could not be associated with any of the previous groups.

National media dominated by centre actors

In Germany, forest policy is under the authority of the federal states. But there is also a national forest policy framework. Political decision making in forest policy on a national level – but also on a regional or local level in Germany – means in most cases decision making by governmental actors. Governance processes rarely take place in German forest policy. The analyses of articles dealing with forest in German quality newspapers show whether this political reality is mirrored in the public media.

Table 6.1 shows the classification of speakers belonging either to the centre or periphery of the political system. In the 'All speakers' column, all speakers giving a statement in the articles analysed are listed. More than 37 per cent of the total number of 2935 speakers belongs to the political centre. These actors are almost equally divided between administrators and politicians. The share of actors from the periphery arguing in German forest articles is far smaller (27.7 per cent).

Table 6.1   *Classification of speakers according to their belonging to the political centre or periphery in forest articles published in Germany quality newspapers 1994–1998*

Actor	All speakers N = 2935 (%)	Speakers from forest sector N = 753 (%)	Speakers from nature conservation N = 480 (%)
Centre	**1107 (37.7)**	**554 (73.6)**	**144 (30.0)**
Politics	531 (18.1)	411	61
Administration	576 (19.6)	143	83
Civil Society	**812 (27.7)**	**66 (8.8)**	**331 (69.0)**
NGOs	623 (21.2)	66	331
Individuals	64 (6.4)	–	–
Enterprises	25 (0.9)	0	0
Scientists	192 (6.5)	69 (9.2)	5 (1.0)
Media	689 (23.5)	–	–
Other	110 (3.7)	64 (8.5)	0

Source: Krumland, 2004

This result seems to verify the hypothesis that forest discourse in the public media is dominated by actors of high status.

A comparison of the share of speakers from the forest sector and those from nature conservation indicates that the reasons behind the total result are quite complex. First of all, Table 6.1 shows that a quarter of all analysed statements in the articles originate from actors in the forest sector. Most of these forest actors are part of the political centre representing the government. However, the actors from the nature conservation sector are mostly from the periphery. This mainly results from the structure of the German administrative system. In forestry offices at the regional and local levels there are many actors in forest administration dealing exclusively with forest topics. This kind of network is not so highly developed in the nature conservation sector. Additionally, the existing nature conservation administrative offices deal not only with forest but with all kinds of nature related topics.

However, in civil society the position of actors with interests in nature conservation is much stronger than that of actors from the forest sector. This result suggests the following interpretation. Nature conservation is characterized by a variety of strong nongovernmental groups with high participation of private actors. In comparison to forest administration, in most cases these groups lack direct control of specific areas legitimated by law. But beyond the structure resulting from property rights it is well known that NGOs such as Greenpeace or WWF are highly professional in their public relations.

The media devises a quarter of all statements itself. It is not surprising that journalists are an important speaker in the media. The majority of statements come from journalists in comments and reportages and from introductions, summaries and transitions from one part of the text to another. Additionally, there are a few citations from other newspapers and media. Enterprises play a minor role in forest discourse in the German national media.

The hypothesis of a forest discourse dominated by actors with high status can be verified by the results of the analysis of German quality newspapers. Actors from the centre of the political system, especially politicians and administrative actors representing forestry, dominate the discussion on forest. Hence forest discourse in the media reflects the political situation in forest policy in Germany, which is dominated by governmental decision making.

The internationally oriented media offers opportunities for the participation of civil society

But forest problems do not stop at national borders, therefore decision making in forest policy no longer stays on the national level. International forest regimes make decisions in a governance process affecting forest management all over the world. Because the actors participating in the decision making process are not legitimated by a democratic process, a more a deliberative discourse is needed.

The following results of the analyses show whether the free and equal chance to state arguments as the core idea of a deliberative discourse are complied with in internationally oriented media.

Table 6.2 makes clear that the distribution of speakers throughout these categories depends on the topic analysed. In articles about biodiversity, speakers from civil society dominate the forest discourse. A large part of these statements (35.5 per cent) are made by NGOs such as WWF, Conservation International, and Fauna and Flora International. Next to actors from civil society, many scientists from different disciplines are heard. Actors from the political centre take part in reporting on biodiversity only in minor cases (14 per cent), half of these being the statements of actors from international governmental organizations such as UNEP or UNDP.

This result shows that climate change is mainly discussed by scientists. Actors from the political centre state their arguments in the reports printed on this topic more than on biodiversity. This is because the majority of speakers are not only

Table 6.2   *Classification of speakers from the political centre or the periphery in forest articles published in the* International Herald Tribune *and* TIME *magazine 1994–2004*

Actor	Biodiversity (N = 121) n (%)	Climate change (N = 279) n (%)	Forest fires (N = 360) n (%)
Centre	17 (14.0)	64 (22.9)	95 (26.4)
Politics	1 (0.8)	10 (3.6)	9 (2.5)
Administration	7 (5.8)	28 (10.0)	77 (21.4)
Justice	0 (0)	1 (0.4)	0 (0)
International governmental organizations (UN, EU, World Bank, etc.)	9 (7.4)	25 (9.0)	9 (2.5)
Civil Society	43 (35.5)	42 (15.1)	89 (24.7)
Associations	26 (21.5)	13 (4.7)	4 (1.1)
Other organizations	4 (3.3)	16 (5.7)	37 (10.3)
Individuals	13 (10.7)	13 (4.7)	48 (13.3)
Enterprises	3 (2.5)	17 (6.1)	4 (1.1)
Scientists	28 (23.1)	97 (34.7)	42 (11.7)
Media	20 (16.5)	36 (12.9)	81 (22.5)
Other	10 (8.2)	23 (8.2)	49 (13.6)

Source: Kleinschmit et al, 2007b

from the administration and politics but also from international governmental organizations.

The topic of forest fires is likewise discussed by actors from civil society and the centre of the political system. In this case, civil society is represented less by organizations than by individuals, most of whom are personally affected by a forest fire catastrophe. The centre of the political system is, in most cases, represented by the administration of different nationstates giving information, for example about the dimensions of the fire.

The relevance of statements from the media is comparable in all three topics. A few are citations from journalists in other media products. Enterprises only play a minor role in all three topics analysed.

The hypothesis of a forest discourse dominated by actors with high status in internationally oriented media cannot be proved. Actors from civil society do have the possibility of presenting their argumentation and interests in the media analysed. Hence the forest discourse accomplishes a basic condition of an ideal process of a deliberative public sphere.

Differing perceptions of forest policy in the public media and popular opinion

Even if it is obvious that neither the media nor the results of public opinion polls can mirror reality, the hypothesis that the perception of forest policy in the public media differs from that of popular opinion is not trivial. Both the public media and the results of opinion polls are often used as an indicator of public opinion by political decision makers.

Figure 6.1 shows the frequency (percentage) of speakers in the media talking about forest topics. Additionally, the figure shows the percentage distribution of answers to the question: 'Who talks the most about forest in public in your opinion?'. The result of this question is based on a poll asking closed questions. Therefore, it is not known whether the people asked would have mentioned speakers other than those named. This has to be taken into consideration, especially in the case of the media as a speaker, because this was not an answer choice in the opinion poll.

Figure 6.1 also shows that the actual frequency of actors from the forest and nature conservation sectors speaking in the media differs from the perception of the people asked in the poll. In the opinion of the people interviewed, nature conservation institutions talk about forest most in public. The result of the media analysis shows that actors from the forest sector speak about forest in the German quality newspapers one and a half times more often than actors from the nature conservation sector. The interpretation of this result has to take into consideration the fact that the term 'public' in the opinion poll question was not explained. Therefore the results verify the hypothesis that the perception of forest differs a great deal between the media and opinion polls.

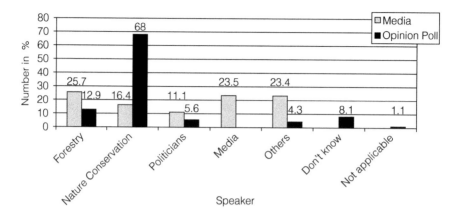

Figure 6.1   *Speakers in German quality newspapers and in the perception of citizens*

Source: Krumland and Krott, 2004

CONCLUSIONS

As a result of the shift from government to governance, the leading question in this chapter is whether the media as a public contributes to the legitimacy of forest policy processes. Based on this assumption, the chapter focused on two hypotheses. Sociological, media and political theories put forward the hypothesis that the public media presents only one perspective of the interests of society. This difference is confirmed by the comparison of results from media analyses and a public opinion poll.

What does this result mean for forest policy processes led by the government? The public media, as a biased socially visible public, influences governmental policy making in two ways. First, citizens do not have the chance to base their voting on unbiased information. Additionally, policy makers are responsive to this perspective and orient their actions and decisions towards this biased public media. This leads to a self-amplifying political process.

In governance processes, legitimacy resulting from deliberative discourses is essential. If the public media is a biased socially visible space, the forced discourse does not fulfil the precondition of open and equal access. Therefore a rational discourse led by the best argument cannot be ensured. The results of the media analysis on the national level show that the civil society periphery rarely has a chance to demonstrate its interpretative pattern. Thus a void results between policy making and the private sphere, which should be developed by civil society. In consequence, it can be said that governance processes taking place in the nationstate rarely have a chance to legitimize their actions by a deliberative discourse carried by the public media.

The hypothesis that the forest discourse in the media is dominated by actors of high status cannot be verified clearly by the results of the analyses of the internationally oriented media. The empirical results show that the kinds of actors that dominate as speakers depend on the topic of the articles. Actors from the periphery dominate the topic of biodiversity with their interpretation pattern of the problems of the forests. The proportion of centre and periphery actors is nearly equal in articles reporting forest fires. However, in the majority of articles dealing with climate change, the speakers are from the political centre. But even in this recently politically topical issue, speakers from civil society do have a chance to speak in the internationally oriented media. Therefore it can be concluded that one of the main preconditions for a deliberative discourse, open access, is fulfilled. The media seems not to sponsor the dominance of actors with high status. Considering these insights, governance processes concerning forest on a global level can be legitimized by a deliberative process reflected by the public media.

What do these results mean for the distinction between public and private, as discussed in the Introduction to this book? First of all, the empirical results emphasize the political situation in forest policy. The shift from government to governance is not as clear as is proposed. Whether the notion of *public* changes from state to a political community depends on the political level. If state actors play a strong role in the policy process, governance processes are of minor importance. This is the situation in German forest policy. On a global level, there is no competing government. Here, the notion of public can be understood as a political community.

The empirical results present another perspective on the distinction between public and private. The media, seen as a public in common understanding, shows only one perspective of society's preferences and is not necessarily compatible with other kinds of perceptions of societal preferences. This results from two factors: the media is able to make interests socially visible, but on the one hand it selects news following its own interests and particular criteria. On the other hand, it is strongly connected with the government, and therefore not independent of the political situation. If government dominates policy, the media supports this by considering governmental actors in the news selection process.

NOTES

1   The status of an actor is understood as the classification of this actor as a central or a peripheral actor (Habermas, 1996). Actors at or near the centre of the political system are of high status, while actors on the periphery of the political system, i.e. far from the political centre, are of low status.

2   There are different *TIME* editions such as *TIME Europe*, *TIME Asia*, *TIME Canada* and *TIME South Pacific*.

3   Analysis from 1994 to May 2004.

4   Whether an actor belongs to the category 'government politicians' or 'nongovernment politicians' depends on whether she/he has been elected by popular vote or not.

REFERENCES

Abromeit, H (2002) *Wozu braucht man Demokratie?*, Leske und Budrich, Opladen

Arenhövel, M. (2003) *Globales Regieren: Neubeschreibung der Demokratie in der Weltgesellschaft*, Campus-Verlag, Frankfurt/New York

Brettschneider, F (1996) 'Public opinion and parliamentary action: Responsiveness of the German Bundestag in comparative perspective', *International Journal of Public Opinion Research*, vol 8, no 3, pp292–311

Brettschneider, F (2004) 'Agenda setting. Forschungsstand und politische Konsequenzen' in Jäckel, M and Winterhoff-Spurk, M (eds) *Politik und Medien: Analysen zur Entwicklung der politischen Kommunikation*, Vistas Verlag, Berlin, pp211–229

Buchstein, H (2003) 'Jürgen Habermas' in Massing, P and Breit, G (eds) *Demokratie-Theorien: Von der Antike bis zur Gegenwart*, Bundeszentrale für politische Bildung, Bonn, pp253–260

Cohen, J L and Arato, A (1992) *Civil Society and Political Theory*, MIT Press, Cambridge

Gerhards, J (1991) 'Die Macht der Massenmedien und die Demokratie: Empirische Befunde', *Discussion Papers FS III des Wissenschaftszentrum*, Berlin, pp91–108

Gerhards, J (1993) *Neue Konfliktlinien in der Mobilisierung öffentlicher Meinung: Eine Fallstudie*, Leske und Budrich, Opladen

Gerhards, J (1995) 'Welchen Einfluss haben die Massenmedien auf die Demokratie in der Bundesrepublik Deutschland?' in Göhler, G (ed) *Macht der Öffentlichkeit – Öffentlichkeit der Macht*, Nomos Verlag, Baden-Baden, pp149–177

Gerhards, J, Neidhardt, F and Rucht, D (1998) *Zwischen Palaver und Diskurs: Strukturen und öffentliche Meinungsbildung am Beispiel der deutschen Diskussion zur Abtreibung*, Leske und Budrich, Opladen

Habermas, J (1996) *Between Facts and Norms*, Polity Press, Cambridge/Malden

Hinckley, R (1992) *People, Polls and Policymakers: American Public Opinion and National Security*, Lexington, New York

Keohane, R O (2002) 'Governance in a partially globalized world' in Keohane, R O (ed) *Power and Governance in a Partially Globalized World*, Routledge, London/New York, pp245–271

Kepplinger, H–M (1994) 'Publizistische Konflikte. Begriffe, Ansätze, Ergebnisse' in Neidhardt, F (ed) *Öffentlichkeit, öffentliche Meinung und soziale Bewegung*, Kölner Zeitschrift für Soziologie und Sozialpsychologie, Special vol 34, Opladen, pp214–233

Kleinschmit, D, Ekayani, M, Park, M and Real, A (2007a) 'Globaler medialer Walddiskurs – Beispiel für eine deliberative Öffentlichkeit?', *Politische Vierteljahresschrift*, vol 47, in press

Kleinschmit, D, Ekayani, M, Park, M and Real, A (2007b) 'Global forest governance: A fiction of democracy', *Forest Policy and Economics*, submitted

Kleinschmit, D and Feindt, P H (2004) 'Verursacher, Opfer und Helfer', *Forschungsjournal Neue soziale Bewegungen*, vol 3, pp93–98

Krott, M (2005) *Forest Policy Analysis*, Springer, Dordrecht

Krumland, D (2004) *Beitrag der Medien zum politischen Erfolg: Forstwirtschaft und Naturschutz im Politikfeld Wald*, Peter Lang, Frankfurt

Krumland, D and Krott, M (2004) 'Medienstar Forstwirtschaft. Politische Positionierung forstlicher Akteure durch Medienöffentlichkeit und Bevölkerungsmeinung', *Allgemeine Forst und Jagdzeitung*, vol 175, pp34–38

Linsky, M (1986) *Impact: How the Press Affects Federal Policymaking*, Norton, New York

Noelle-Neumann, E and Mathes, R (1987) 'The "event as event" and the "event as news": The significance of "consonance" for media effects research', *European Journal of Communication*, vol 2, pp391–414

Pauli, B (2000) 'Wald und Forstwirtschaft im Meinungsbild der Gesellschaft', *Mitteilungen aus der Bayerischen Staatsforstverwaltung*, vol 50, Munich

Rogers, E M, Dearing, J W and Chang, S (1991) 'AIDS in the 1980s: The agenda-setting process for a public issue', *Journalism Monographs*, vol 126

Schmitter, P (2002) 'Participation in governance arrangements: Is there any reason to expect it will achieve "sustainable and innovative policies in a multilevel context"?' in Grote, J R and Gbikpi, B (eds) *Participatory Governance: Political and Societal Implications*, Westdeutscher Verlag, Opladen, pp51–69

Steffek, J (2003) 'The legitimation of international governance: A discourse approach', *European Journal of International Relations*, vol 9, pp249–275

Stoker, G (1998) 'Governance as theory: Five propositions', *International Social Science Journal*, vol 50, pp17–28

Torgerson, D (2003) 'Democracy through policy discourse' in Hajer, M and Wagenaar, H (eds) *Deliberative Policy Analysis: Understanding Governance in the Network Society*, Cambridge University Press, Cambridge, pp113–138

Trenz, H-J (2004) 'Media coverage on European governance: Exploring the European public sphere in national quality newspapers', *European Journal of Communication*, vol 19, no 3, pp291–319

UNESCO (1997) *World Communication Report: The media and the challenge of the new technologies*, UNESCO, Paris

Von Alemann, U (1997) 'Parteien und Medien' in Gabriel, O W, Niedermayer, O and Stöss, R (eds) *Parteiendemokratie in Deutschland*, Bundeszentrale für politische Bildung, Bonn, pp478–494

Weßler, H (1999) *Öffentlichkeit als Prozeß*, Leske und Budrich, Opladen

Wimmel, A (2004) 'Transnationale diskurse', *Zeitschrift für Internationale Beziehungen*, vol 1, pp7–25

Wittkämper, G, Bellers, W, Grimm, J and Heiks, M (1992) 'Pressewirkungen und außenpolitische Entscheidungsprozesse: Methodologische Probleme der Analyse' in Wittkämper, G (ed) *Medien und Politik*, Wissenschaftliche Buchgesellschaft, Darmstadt, pp150–168

Wolf, K D (2002) 'Contextualizing normative standards for legitimate governance beyond the state' in Grote, J R and Gbikpi, B (eds) *Participatory Governance: Political and Societal Implications*, Leske und Budrich, Opladen, pp35–50

Zürn, M (1998) *Regieren jenseits des Nationalstaates*, Suhrkamp, Frankfurt

Part III – 'PRIVATES'

Introduction to Part III

We have looked at publics and public–private hybrids present in natural resource governance in Parts I and II. We now turn to forms of private in resource governance, that is, matters pertaining to individuals. Part III puts the analytical spotlight on market actors and market transactions, as these epitomize the private sphere in the liberal-economistic model. As we have seen in the Introduction, the model presumes that private actors engage with each other in voluntary transactions, undisturbed by coercive intervention from the state. This premise serves as a point of entry for the two analyses presented in Chapters 7 and 8. The chapters deal with bioenergy management and food safety, drawing on empirical insights from Austria, France and Germany. They attain much broader relevance, however, by examining the potentials of public–private partnerships and labelling in comparison with regulation and subsidies, the classical instruments of state action.

Chapter 7 takes a close look at private actors and their actions in relation to two bioenergy clusters in Austria and Germany. Plieninger and his co-authors identify a range of private actors involved in the growth of bioenergy production, including farmers, forest enterprises, energy companies and consumers. They examine how these private actors interact with each other, and how they respond to the actions of the EU and national and local governments. As does Chapter 5, Chapter 7 therefore engages with public–private partnerships, which have received much attention recently across policy fields (Pagiola et al, 2002). Yet the analysis by Plieninger et al gains additional relevance by dealing with a policy field – bioenergy management – that has burst forth into the open and experienced dramatic growth over the past few years (Sims, 2002; Worldwatch Institute, 2007).

The success of the Austrian bioenergy cluster, Plieninger et al show us, builds on the capacity of presumably market-oriented actors to 'go public' in the sense of becoming leaders in their community. Two local individuals took the original initiative and mobilized a local community concerned with bioenergy. These two leaders played a crucial role in setting up a cooperative to run a small plant for the production of biodiesel from rapeseed oil, the construction of a combined heat and power plant based on wood chips and the formation of a forest owners' association. In contrast, the development of the German bioenergy cluster has followed a more conventional trajectory, as market oriented actors responded to the subsidies offered by the state. Networking among the involved actors was secondary in importance to the massive financial assistance offered by the EU and German government. The governance of the German bioenergy cluster, therefore, stays close to the outline of the liberal-economistic model.

Chapter 8 examines the steps taken by various actors in the German and French markets for safe food. As we know, the safety of food is not apparent to us when we purchase it. Roosen analyses how consumers, producers and retailers in Germany and France respond to this information problem. She describes the emergence of a perplexing variety of labels promoted by single retailers, single producers and groups of producers. Such labels have mushroomed in Europe over recent years to signal the safety and quality of food (Régnier et al, 2006). At the same time they have made inroads into other policy fields, such as agri-environmental stewardship and international forestry (see Introduction and Chapter 4). Concerns over food safety, in turn, have caused European governments and the EU to initiate regulation in recent years (Ansell and Vogel, 2006; Vos and Wendler, 2006). Yet these concerns are equally significant in other parts of the world, as illustrated by international reactions to the spread of avian flu.

The labels are not only private, even though most are created and used by market-based actors. They are also public, as they operate by connecting with political communities and/or gaining social visibility. The former has existed for a while, as exemplified by the organic food movement. The latter is a fascinating new development in the food sector, where labels created by retailers and food producers have proliferated in recent years. These labels appear to us to be squarely private because they result from voluntary actions undertaken by market-based actors. Nonetheless, the individual actions attribute publicity to certain features of food production, trade and consumption. As a result, they shape the market for safe food, in turn affecting the choices available to consumers, producers and industry. What emerges, we believe, is a kind of regulation without a regulatory state – even though Roosen advises the state to define the key parameters of industry-initiated labelling.

Chapters 7 and 8 show us that there are many types of private in natural resource governance, and that these are highly heterogeneous. Even if we think in terms of the state/market distinction only, we detect a great deal of variation in the rights possessed by individual actors and the responsibilities they face. Chapter 7 highlights the subsidies that market-oriented actors receive from the state in Austria's and Germany's bioenergy clusters. Chapter 8 discusses the range of possibilities states have for the regulation of industry-initiated labels. Another example is Bulgaria's Irrigation Systems Company discussed in Chapter 2, which is listed as a stock-holding company under commercial law, yet remains very much like a state bureaucracy because the Bulgarian state subjects its operation to strict requirements. Compare this highly regulated company to the free-flying financial investors lured into the German bioenergy sector – we would not expect the two to fit into a single category. Yet both are private, according to the premises of the liberal-economistic model.

The variable nature of private becomes even clearer if we include the other two distinctions between public and private. We recognize that market-based actors may act in public ways through the very transactions conducted in markets. This is a paradox in the liberal-economistic model (see Introduction), yet it is not strange if we view market transactions in relation to the political community or what is socially visible. Market oriented actors can assume leadership roles in political communities, as the two individuals in Austria's bioenergy cluster demonstrate. In fact, many other analyses included in this book provide further examples of market based actors taking on public roles, public in the sense of political community: in Chapter 1 in forestry in Indonesia; in Chapter 4 in agri-environmental stewardship in Austria; and in Chapter 5 in biodiversity conservation in Brazil. Similarly, individual actors can create social visibility by acting on markets, as evidenced by the food labels discussed in Chapters 8 and 4.

The publicness of some private actors, actions, resources and property rights does not dissolve the distinction between private and public. In particular, we do not interpret it to imply that all private actors act public by necessity. On the contrary, we realize that attention to all three public/private distinctions helps us to understand the many kinds of private. Actors, actions, resources and property rights can be private in many more ways than are recognized by the liberal-economistic model. They can be private by relating to the more particularistic spheres of social life. The financial investors in Chapter 7 and the retailers in Chapter 8 act private in this sense. Actors, actions, resources and property rights can also be private by being personal as opposed to socially visible. The farmers discussed in Chapter 7 make personal choices about the crops they want to plant. Health ministers may enact and enforce regulations on food safety, as analysed in Chapter 8, yet when they go home they make very personal choices when shopping for groceries.

These insights equip us well to take another look at the literature on government versus governance discussed in the introductions to Parts I and II. We recognize that the literature may need to pay as much attention to privates as it has done to publics. A complementary focus on privates would help demystify the notion of private, which retains a mythical status in thought about resource governance (see Introduction). In practice, however, we observe a wide range of privates, as illustrated by Chapters 7 and 8 in conjunction with the other parts of the book. The key is to understand that the three distinctions define different kinds of private in relation to public. In fact, this helps us recognize that the very conducting of state affairs includes private dimensions. State actions can fall into the more particularistic spheres of life, such as when state agencies offer small amounts of financial aid to sports events. The conduct of state affairs can also take personal forms, which is the reason why there is so much emphasis on information sharing and transparency these days.

REFERENCES

Ansell, C and Vogel, D (eds) (2006) *What's the Beef: The Contested Governance of European Food Safety*, MIT Press, Boston

Pagiola, S, Bishop, J and Landell-Mills, N (eds) (2002) *Selling Forest Environmental Services: Market-Based Mechanisms for Conservation and Development*, Earthscan, London

Régnier, F, Lhuissier, A and Gojard, S (2006) *Sociologie de l'Alimentation*, Éditions La Decouverte, Paris

Sims, R (2002) *The Brilliance of Bioenergy in Business and in Practice*, Earthscan, London

Vos, E and Wendler, F (eds) (2006) *Food Safety Regulation in Europe: A Comparative Institutional Analysis*, Intersentia, Antwerpen/Oxford

Worldwatch Institute (2007) *Biofuels for Transport: Global Potential and Implications for Sustainable Energy and Agriculture*, Earthscan, London

7

Bioenergy Clusters in Austria and Germany: From Public Goals to Private Action

Tobias Plieninger, Andreas Thiel, Oliver Bens and Reinhard F. Hüttl

INTRODUCTION

Concerns for the exhaustibility of fossil fuels, for energy security and for climate protection have led to the increasing promotion of renewable energy sources (Mangels-Voegt, 2004). Bioenergy – the conversion of organic matter from agriculture, forestry and wastes to energy – is among the spectrum of 'renewables', the one with the largest yet unexploited potential and with the greatest impact in terms of physical area. It has a particularly high impact on agricultural and forestry lands.

The emergence of bioenergy is the result of politically defined goals and of incentives designed to achieve these goals (Ericsson et al, 2004). In most European countries there is a strong political will to make bioenergy an integrated part of the energy systems. However, the implementation of these public policies depends on predominantly private actors,[1] especially on actors in the energy, agriculture and forestry sectors (Domac et al, 2005). In many cases these actors form business clusters, defined as geographic concentrations of interconnected businesses, suppliers and associated institutions in a particular field. Governments and parliaments have initiated policies that are supposed to induce private actors to provide biomass and bioenergy – among others by tax reductions and acceptance duties for biofuels in transportation and by legally defined remunerations for green power (Sohre, 2006). The rationale of these efforts corresponds to the liberal-economistic model – some state action is required, but the development of the sector is up to market actors. Therefore, bioenergy is (next to the food sector, see Chapter 8) the field among all those covered in this book in which private, market based actions are expected to provide the main impetus for sustainable resource governance.

This chapter shows how a public agenda of bioenergy production is supported by private actors, resulting in a blend of private and public interests. It analyses the development of clusters of bioenergy actors in Germany and Austria and looks at the different motivations of private and public groups. It focuses on how these public and private actors have worked together or not, and specifically studies how far private actors match our expectations of how they should behave according to cost–benefit analysis defined in classic theory. We argue that the blend of public and private interests is complementary and as such has contributed to the rapid and large-scale dissemination of bioenergy technologies. The chapter is based on a literature review, interviews with actors from forestry and agricultural practice, science and bioenergy practice, and on several visits to the bioenergy clusters.

The following section presents an overview of the technological aspects of bioenergy and shows why this field depends so strongly on private involvement. The next section sets a theoretical framework of public and private actors in governance that is used to arrange the empirical findings of this study. The section on 'spectrum of actors' provides a first look at the motivation of the manifold actors present in the sector. These thoughts are developed in a comparative case study of the Güssing and the Barnim-Uckermark bioenergy clusters. These two cases have been selected because they represent contrasting pathways of forming bioenergy clusters – the former pursuing an endogenous and decentralized approach, the latter an exogenous and centralized approach. Finally, the empirical argument is summarized and broader implications developed in a concluding section.

THE RISE OF BIOFUELS

The fundamental objective of all forms of biomass use is the supply of fuel, heat and/or electricity. Conceivable biomass types, production systems and conversion pathways are manifold. Biofuels, the carriers of bioenergy, can either be derived from nonfossil plant or nonfossil animal biomass. Possible raw materials include wood, oil seeds, cereals, waste and liquid manure. Common conversion techniques comprise biomass combustion, gasification, fermentation and transesterification. Some bioenergy pathways are technically simple and follow a decentralized pattern, for example the use of forestry residues for heating in a domestic fireplace. Other pathways, for example bioethanol or biodiesel production, are technology intensive, require large amounts of biomass and exhibit a centralized structure (Plieninger et al, 2006). Four pathways currently dominate the sector:

1   The combustion or gasification of solid biomass for heat and power supply in small and large plants. These are the most common techniques for the conversion of woody biomass from the forestry sector and the wood processing industry.
2   The anaerobic fermentation of a range of organic substances such as food wastes, liquid manure, dung and energy crops to biogas, a mixture of methane, CO_2 and other gases. Biogas is mostly used as fuel in combined

heating and power (CHP) plants. This is the common utilization form of biomass wastes.

3 The fermentation of agricultural substances rich in carbon hydrate such as cane sugar, corn, rye or sugar beets into liquid hydrocarbons, especially bioethanol. Bioethanol can be added to gasoline or other alcohols and used as a fuel in Otto engines, fuel cells or turbines. Ethanol production is one of the most common forms of the use of plant biomass from agriculture.

4 The transesterification of plant oils, especially of rapeseed oil, or of animal fats to biodiesel, an alkyl ester and diesel equivalent, to be used as diesel engine fuel.

Three strands of argument are commonly cited in favour of an increased use of biofuels (Sims, 2003). The first is about the replacement of finite petroleum reserves. Bioenergy is renewable. As a domestic energy source and a new element in the energy mix, it diversifies energy supply, reduces the dependency on imported fossil fuels and improves energy and state security over the long term. The second strand stresses the potential of biofuels to minimize the ecological footprint of energy generation and especially to combat climate change by reducing the emission of atmospheric greenhouse gases (GHG). Energy supply from renewable resources is assumed to have far lower emissions of GHG than fossil sources. If, for example, short-rotation forest plantations are newly established on agricultural land, CO_2 will be removed from the atmosphere and stored in plants and soils. The third line of argument is about the pulses that biofuels trigger for the improvement of living conditions and for employment and business opportunities in marginal rural areas. It is argued that the energetic use of biomass from agriculture and forestry allows a diversification of land use that can stabilize the tense economic situation of many farms and forestry enterprises. Still, the rise of biofuels does not proceed without controversy. The debates concern, among other things, questions of energy and cost efficiency, the environmental impact of energy crop production and potential competition for land and natural resources.

The expectations for private involvement in bioenergy dissemination are high due to the technological nature of both biomass production and energy supply: biomass is mainly produced on agricultural and forestland, and most of this land is in private property. Energy supply in Germany is influenced by private electric power companies (although sometimes owned by public institutions) and petroleum and gas corporations.

PUBLIC AND PRIVATE ACTORS IN GOVERNANCE

In academic and everyday parlance, people frequently use the attributes of public and private to categorize actors, activities, tasks, goods or obligations. The dichotomous use of the concepts suggests a clear distinction. But in fact a variety of often overlapping categorizations can underlie the use of these terms (see Introduction). Political science and institutional economics have distanced themselves from a dichotomous view by emphasizing the study of governance or hybrids, as opposed to the study of 'the conceptual trinity of market–state–civil society' (Jessop, 1995; see also Williamson, 1998).

The biofuel production sector that we examine in this chapter principally suggests a categorization of intervening actors according to the liberal-economistic model referred to in the Introduction to this volume. In other words, state action signifies public intervention. Alternatively, voluntary interaction of participants in the market signifies private intervention. According to the liberal-economistic model, public intervention is associated with the state acting in the general interest of society, while private intervention is up to the participation of individuals in the market, which is self-regulating or regulated by the state. The delimitation described is not pronounced in the more operational motivation of the actors. Therefore, in an attempt to reach greater analytical detail within the liberal-economistic model, we distinguish between public and private actors and, within this dichotomy, between profit and nonprofit oriented intervention (cf Chapter 3).

Furthermore, whereas political processes lead to decisions about the way biofuel production is to be regulated or promoted, the public realm is in question. It illustrates the second type of differentiation between publics and privates identified in the Introduction. It refers to wider governance processes as opposed to more individualistic methods of decision making.

Political processes illustrating governance or public (state) as well as private (individual) intervention can furthermore originate from or consist of actors located at different territorially defined levels of social organization. Therefore, in order to give our analysis even more detail, we distinguish between the roles of local, regional, national or supranational publics and privates.

SPECTRUM OF ACTORS IN THE BIOENERGY SECTOR

A large number of different actor groups is involved in the bioenergy sector. Actor constellations differ along the energy supply chain, from biomass production (where farm and forestry enterprises are the dominant actors) via fuel supply and energy conversion (a domain of the power and fuel industry) to the end users of bioenergy (private households and businesses) (McCormick and Kaberger, 2005). Some actor groups such as scientists, politicians or environmental organizations are in touch with bioenergy across the entire energy supply chain.

Agricultural and forestry enterprises

Agriculture and forestry are the principal producers of biomass (Braune, 1998). Whereas in agriculture most biomass is specifically cropped, biomass from forestry is mostly a byproduct. In some bioenergy pathways, farms are nothing more than the supplier of raw materials, for example for bioethanol fuels. In other cases, further processing and energy conversion takes place on farms by means of onsite biogasification plants and generators. Accordingly, the economic impulses for agriculture are weaker or stronger. Altogether it appears that the agricultural sector is open minded towards bioenergy as a new economic branch. Forestry is the actor with the longest tradition of bioenergy use. Still, forestry acts almost purely as supplier of raw materials and does not participate further in the bioenergy value chain. Forest wood can be either combusted or gasified in a broad spectrum of plant types, whether in domestic fireplaces, CHP plants or as cosubstrate in large coal fired power plants. In the context of bioenergy, farm enterprises function as market actors in the particularistic spheres of social life and thus meet the two distinctions for private given in the Introduction of this book. Forestry enterprises in Germany are partly state owned, partly privately owned. As a supplier of biomass, however, both act in a market oriented and particularistic manner and are thus private by nature.

Energy industry

The energy industry in the EU is in a phase of transformation (Sohre, 2006). Many power plants need to be renewed in the coming years, energy prices are rising and, at the same time, public awareness for climate protection is increasing. In central Europe the energy industry is differentiated in a few large transnational corporations and smaller local enterprises, sometimes public services, sometimes private enterprises. The recent liberalization of energy markets and the introduction of competition through the breaking of the traditional regional monopolies of power companies has led to the emergence of new private energy companies. Meanwhile, even large power corporations, car manufacturers and the oil industry have committed to bioenergy, although frequent conflicts about the future role of alternative energies remain. The public or private nature of energy companies depends on whether they are state owned (focusing on services of public interest) or privately owned (with an orientation towards profits). In the course of ongoing efforts for market orientation, liberalization and privatization, however, both types are primarily market oriented and particularistic and as such private rather than public.

Environmental community

The assessment of bioenergy in the environmental community is relatively controversial. On the one hand, environmentalists have long demanded a turn from fossil and nuclear to renewable energy sources and warned about the exhaustibility of oil, coal and gas. On the other hand, many environmentalists decline new land use forms with potentially damaging effects on species and habitats (Huston and Marland, 2003). Environmental organizations are generally associations of individuals and belong as such to the private sphere of voluntary interaction. However, they enjoy a high degree of social visibility and thus create publics that are not the state.

Regional politicians

Regional policies promote the settlement of bioenergy businesses in many ways in order to boost local economies (Hillring, 2002). In the economically underdeveloped regions of the EU in particular, a multitude of public programmes offers incentives for regional development, and bioenergy projects are found in most of these programmes. In addition, local administrations often support bioenergy by heating public buildings with regionally produced biofuels. By definition politicians are part of the state and thus clearly public entities.

Private households and businesses

Private households and businesses are the potential recipients of bioenergy and finance the sector with their energy bills. There are two basic ways of financing bioenergy use. First, countries such as Austria and Germany have established renewable energy portfolio standards that require power network operators to induct renewable electricity into their networks and to pay a specified minimum remuneration. In the case of biofuels, oil companies in Germany will be legally forced to add a certain share of ethanol to gasoline, which is expected to increase gas prices, hence the costs for the promotion of renewable energies are passed on to all energy users, whether they agree or not. Second, energy consumers have the choice of paying an increased fee for green power. Certification schemes guarantee that this power has been generated from 100 per cent renewable sources. Households and businesses belong to the private and particularistic spheres of life. Nevertheless, their behaviour can be more than simply market oriented, thereby creating socially visible spaces, that is, publics, as demonstrated by the example of green power.

This overview indicates that there is a range of private actors that correspond to the definitions of the liberal-economistic model, for example certain actors in the agriculture and energy fields; however, there are other actors, for example in the environmental community, that do not fit the classical model. This calls for a closer look at two concrete case studies.

REGIONAL DEVELOPMENT THROUGH BIOENERGY

Actors in the field typically assemble in bioenergy clusters. These clusters have often become famous as bioenergy villages or bioenergy regions. Their common goal is to have all components of bioenergy systems – that is, biofuel resources, supply systems, conversion technologies and energy demands – within the area (McCormick and Kaberger, 2005).

Güssing, the bioenergy town

One of the most prominent central European cases of bioenergy's contribution to regional development is the town of Güssing in Austria (Brunner et al, 2006; Hacker, 2006). In 2001 Güssing covered an area of 49.31 square kilometres and had 3,902 inhabitants, giving a population density of 79 inhabitants per square kilometre. Declared 'Austria's first energy-autarkic town', Güssing has assumed leadership in the field of renewable energies, especially bioenergy.

Güssing is situated in Burgenland, a region in southeast Austria that had long suffered from isolation due to its proximity to communist Eastern Europe. The erection of the iron curtain at the Hungarian border shifted the region to the periphery of the Western hemisphere, which made the area of little interest for businesses. Moreover, the traditional economies of agriculture and forestry were not profitable due to an extreme parcelling of land, a consequence of traditional inheritance laws. For decades the area was considered a dying region, with typical indications of marginalization such as land abandonment, out-migration and high commuting rates. In 1988 it was considered Austria's least successful area.

Around this time, a study revealed that the population of Güssing spent 1.5 million euros per year outside of the region for fossil heating oil. The idea was formulated to keep this money in local economic cycles by using home-grown energy. The town council adopted a new energy concept in 1990, aiming at 100 per cent abandonment of fossil energy use for heating, power generation and transport fuels. The concept gradually came to life in subsequent years. First, the town evaluated its energy consumption pattern and applied energy saving practices such as optimizing streetlights. In this way, the municipal energy expenditure was reduced by 50 per cent within only a few years. The second step was the construction of a municipally owned district heating plant (with a $2MW_{th}$ and a $3.5MW_{th}$ boiler) fired with wood chips, mainly from industry wastes. More than 27 kilometres of long distance heating pipelines were built and 40 per cent of Güssing's private households, 95 per cent of public buildings and several enterprises are currently connected to the plant. In summer, heating energy is used for cooling and industrial purposes. The partial goal of heat energy self-sufficiency was thus achieved. The third step was the construction of an oil mill and a small esterification plant for rapeseed oil (and, in the meantime, it used edible oils). The initiative for this plant came from a member of Burgenland's state government who authorized the development of its conception in 1987. Organized as a cooperative, the plant was opened in 1991 and produced 2000 tonnes of biodiesel in 2005, which is more than Güssing's citizens consumed in the same year. Hence, they reached transport fuel autarchy as another partial goal. The fourth step was the construction in the year 2000 of a CHP plant (capacity: $2MW_{el}$, $4.5MW_{th}$) based on wood chips from forestry. Planners, a plant construction enterprise, a plant operator and scientists founded a network to execute this project. A state-of-the-art fluidized bed steam gasification technique came into operation for the first time. Consequently, power autarchy was achieved as the final partial goal. Subsequent to this development, a cooperation of local actors from culture, sports and tourism made the area attractive for visitors and thus created a small industry of ecoenergy tourism, with 200–300 visitors per week and special events such as Güssing's 'run in the sun' marathon. Moreover, a technology centre now harbours a number of institutions related to energy technology, among others the European Centre for Renewable Energies.

The origin of Güssing's bioenergy initiative can be clearly traced back to two individuals, a committed mayor with well developed ties to state and national politics and an engineer (the author of the seminal study on Güssing's energy consumption pattern) with great networking skills and a profound knowledge of the feasibility of alternative energy technologies. Other actors eventually joined. Initially, Güssing's town council adopted the proposed energy concept, supported the project with financial and other resources and acted as the responsible body of the initiative. Later, business actors began to collaborate. With the construction of the district heating plant, there was a surplus of heat energy in summertime. Several enterprises with high energy demands, among others two parquet manufacturers, settled in the area and now use the heat energy for their wood drying equipment. Production wastes (e.g. sawdust) are simultaneously used as fuel for the heating plant. With the smart use of existing support schemes and the establishment of a research friendly infrastructure (especially with the network of excellence 'Renewable Energy Network Austria') researchers became interested and established research in Güssing, especially on hydrogen technologies, fuel cells, methane and transport fuel generation from wood gasification and cooling techniques from district heating plants.

Another important group of actors is made up of forest owners as providers of wood fuels. The small scale pattern of forest ownership (average parcel size is 0.6ha) had often inhibited an optimal mobilization of wood resources. This structural barrier was overcome by bundling the activities of the 'Burgenländischer Waldverband', a 5200-member forest owners' association that has signed a long-term contract for the supply of the CHP plant with wood fuels and that is responsible for wood harvesting, delivery and processing. Forest owners who would otherwise be overwhelmed by managing their small forest parcel and marketing their wood by themselves have a convenient way to generate income, care for the forest and supply renewable energy sources to the community. In 2002 the volume of delivery to the CHP plant amounted to million €1, which directly benefited the forestry sector.

The trigger for the Güssing bioenergy concept came from within the region, from committed individuals who were supported by citizens, companies and the town administration. Güssing's mayor believes this is the key reason for success: 'You cannot impose anything on a region that has not grown in the region.' Nevertheless, the concept would not have been feasible without massive financial support from European, national and state schemes for regional development. Above all, the acceptance of the region as a 'target 1 region' stimulated investment and economic development.

The story of how bioenergy triggered regional development in Güssing is one of the greatest successes of the sector. The energy sector in the town created a value of 13.6 million euros per annum in 2005. The town claims that by 2005 more than one thousand new jobs in 50 new enterprises (including 250 jobs in 14 enterprises specifically in the renewable energy sector) were created as a result of the energy initiative. Municipal tax revenues have increased from about €400,000 (1990) to €1.1 million (2004). Within 15 years Güssing has evolved from the poorest area in Austria to its most innovative community with a high standard of living.

Güssing's strategy for the future is further growth of the bioenergy sector. The capacity of existing plants is to be scaled up to a permanently profitable level, and additional renewable energy technologies (e.g. solar energy and biogasification) are to be expanded, with a special focus on agricultural resources. The model is to be expanded spatially from Güssing town to the entire region of Güssing, with the aim of reaching energy autarchy for the whole region by 2010.

The Barnim-Uckermark bioenergy cluster

The Barnim-Uckermark region in Brandenburg (northeast Germany, previously part of East Germany), situated close to Berlin, has also focused on creating a bioenergy cluster. The area (4552 square kilometres) is thinly populated (317,300 inhabitants; 70 inhabitants per square kilometre as of 2004) and marked by forests, lakes and agricultural landscapes. Next to tourism, paper and chemical industries, bioenergy is currently considered one of the main pillars of the region's economy and its central field of innovation. In 2006 there were four solid biomass plants supplying electricity (total of $16.6MW_{el}$) and heat. Operated by companies of the paper and wood processing industry and by financial investors, these plants primarily use industry wood wastes. A pellet production plant (2006 production was 100,000 tonnes per year) – jointly built by a local and an outside investor – uses both industry wood wastes and forest wood. In 2005 there were nine biogasification plants operating with a total capacity of $1922KW_{el}$ and $2409KW_{th}$ (Dahle, 2005, personal communication). Three further plants were in the process of planning or construction; these have predominantly been constructed on farms and use both crop and residual biomass. Electricity is fed into the power network, while heat is mostly used for the farm buildings. Most of these farms combine bioenergy use with the use of other renewable energy sources such as photovoltaics, wind energy or plant oil for farm machinery. The number of biogas plants in Brandenburg is small compared to other German states, but the average plant size ($510KW_{el}$ in 2005) is considerably higher than the German average ($250KW_{el}$). The biofuel industry, however, has the largest demand for agricultural biomass. In Barnim-Uckermark there are one small and one large biodiesel refinery (processing rapeseed oil) and one bioethanol plant (based on rye biomass). Schwedt has a 150,000 tonne per year biodiesel plant and a 180,000 tonne per year ethanol plant. These plants emphasize the use of regional resources (produced within a radius of 100 kilometres around Schwedt), but the two large plants are located close to Schwedt's domestic port, potentially facilitating biomass importation from abroad through international shipping routes. A nearby crude oil processing plant enables the addition of these biofuels to fossil transport fuels. The bioenergy sector is embedded in a renewable energy cluster, with strong solar energy (e.g. Aleo Solar, Prenzlau) and wind energy industries (e.g. Germany's largest wind energy park near Storkow).

Agriculture has traditionally been the most important economic sector. Historically large private farm estates prevailed but were converted into large cooperative and state farms after 1945. With the transformation from a socialist to a capitalist economy in the 1990s, agriculture experienced significant changes. The number of agricultural employees in Brandenburg state sank sharply from 179,000 to 39,000 between 1989 and 1993. Cost inefficiencies, liquidity shortages and marketing problems led to a severe reduction of agricultural production, especially of animal production. Until today the region has not been very successful in coping with the economic and social transformations. The unemployment rate amounted to 16.8 (Barnim) and 29.1 per cent (Uckermark) in 2004 – the latter being one of the highest unemployment rates in Germany. From 1989 until 2002, the population of Uckermark county decreased by 14 per cent. From 2001 until 2020 a further 24.2 per cent decrease is predicted. The population decrease is an effect of out-migration, especially of younger people, women and more qualified people. As a consequence of this population exodus, many areas have fallen below a critical mass of committed actors, which often makes the establishment of regional development networks very challenging (Plieninger et al, 2005).

In the years following German unification, numerous East German enterprises found that most of the available production lines were already occupied by West German and foreign companies and that they were unable to contend with the tough competition (Jähnke and Lompscher, 1995). In this context, renewable energies appeared to be an attractive field, as it was (and still is) a newly created, emerging market. Established companies had not yet incorporated renewable energies as they did not have economic significance before the introduction of the Electricity Grid Feed Act of 1991 and later the

Renewable Energy Sources Act of 2000 and related legislation. The real boom of bioenergy use in agriculture and forestry only began in 2004, when an amendment to the Renewable Energy Sources Act made these uses economically more attractive. The eastern German agricultural sector has had a better position than most other economic sectors after reunification, as more than a third of the average European agricultural income stems from public transfer payments to which any agricultural enterprise – whether in the east or in the west – was entitled. Moreover the eastern German agricultural sector has a number of competitive advantages over its western German counterparts, above all due to its larger average farm sizes and its more professional enterprise structures. These structures seemed especially suitable for supplying large quantities of biomass to a developing bioenergy industry. Therefore, the county administrations in Barnim and Uckermark defined the increased supply of renewable energies, and especially of bioenergy, as a primary goal. The decisive arguments were the creation of employment and the promotion of regional economic development.

The carriers of the development of a bioenergy sector in Barnim-Uckermark are diverse and comprise idealistic citizens, entrepreneurs and local politicians. Nevertheless, external actors are also of outstanding importance for the region. Since the year 2000, public support from the outside has enabled effective regional clusters, networks and public–private partnerships such as the ENOB (Energie Nord-Ost-Brandenburg) and barum111 initiatives. Funded by the European Social Fund, ENOB brings together 12 farms, 14 companies and six public institutions and aims to optimize bioenergy supply and marketing in the area and intelligently combine bioenergy use with other renewable and fossil energy sources. 60 new plants are to be constructed within three to five years and will be integrated into a regional energy development concept. A basic goal is to keep the largest part of the supply chain within the area. Important activities include consulting, training farmers, research and development projects and public relations work (e.g. declaration of biomass farms that present efficient forms of biomass cultivation, biogas production and solar and wind energy use to an interested public) (ENOB, 2006). barum111 is an initiative of the Barnim and Uckermark county administrations. Its main objective is to act as an umbrella organization, interlinking all actors within the region's renewable energy supply and demand. Its name expresses the overall objective that 111 per cent of the regional energy demand should be supplied from regional renewable sources by 2010 (so that 11 per cent can be exported) (barum111, 2006). Scientists and research institutions, such as the Centre for Energy Technology (CEBra) at the Brandenburg University of Technology, act as intermediaries between regional and outside actors and provide the region with access to international science and technology networks. Since the clusters' initial creation by the regional actors themselves, large outside actors have come aboard. Large biofuel plants have been erected by outside companies, such as the Southern German Sauter enterprise group. Biogasification plants were originally the domain of farmers but are gradually being established by external investors, in part by large international corporations like the Doric Asset Finance Group. There are initial indications of heavy competition for biomass, especially between the large and the small biomass consumers.

Barnim-Uckermark has become known as one of Brandenburg's bioenergy regions. It is noticeable that the region decided on large centralized plants (e.g. biodiesel plants) rather than small-scale decentralized plants (e.g. biogasification plants). It is not clear whether this trend towards large-scale biofuel production will continue in the face of the 2006 reduction of tax privileges for transportation biofuels. But a plant for the production of 200,000 tonnes per year of synthetic BtL (Biomass-to-Liquid) fuels is scheduled to open in 2009 in a region close to Barnim-Uckermark, giving a further boost to large-scale biofuel production. Close to the district, in the town of Penkun, a biogas park comprising 40 modular fermenters with a capacity of $20MW_{el}$ is under construction. Around 400,000 tonnes of biomass will be needed annually as substrates input, which makes the operation the largest biogas park in the world. A trend to centralized plants can also be noted by observing solid biomass power plants. A large-scale $20MW_{el}$ plant was begun in 2006 and will lead to an additional wood fuel demand of approximately 100,000 tonnes per year. Altogether the renewable energies sector has proven of great economic importance, with evidently 660 employees – and more than 1,500 jobs – stabilized through biomass supply in agriculture and forestry in Uckermark county in 2005 (barum111, 2006). There are, however, signs of increasing competition for land and biomass in the area. It will be interesting to witness whether the centralized or the decentralized models of bioenergy use will be more successful in securing the limited regional biomass resources.

PUBLIC AND PRIVATE IN THE BIOENERGY SECTOR

The overall spectrum of actors in the bioenergy sector is vast. In the current phase of its establishment, new linkages are promoted in an inclusive manner, including the agriculture or forestry sectors into the establishment of supply chains. Supplying energy resources instead of food does not alter the private profit oriented motivation and roles of local farmers, although the biomass they produce finally contributes to the supply of a public good – the reduction of atmospheric CO_2 levels. However, the actor constellations involved in the establishment and operation of these new supply chains significantly differ from the traditional ways in which either the forestry or the agricultural sector were embedded. The new linkage to the energy sector implies new products, new actors and a new self-conception in agriculture and forestry. Furthermore, the promotion of the bioenergy sector has become one component of cross-sectoral regional economic development policies, specifically in deprived rural areas that lack alternatives for economic development (Hillring, 2002). Therefore, it draws in a broad range of actors and establishes new cross-links between actors, overcoming traditional sectoral delimitations. The establishment of new interlinkages is specifically dynamic, as the European energy sector as well as the agriculture policy sectors is in a phase of significant transformation.

The most obvious differences between the Güssing and Barnim-Uckermark cases are presented in Table 7.1. Both areas are committed to establishing a bioenergy industry in order to make use of the economic opportunities during the postcommunist transformation since 1989, but Güssing was a few years ahead of Barnim-Uckermark.

In both cases it seems that individual, private and public actors have played a leading role in promoting bioenergy development. In Güssing, however, most private actors were situated at the local level. In a situation of general economic despair, two individuals were able to unleash broader support due to their know-how and enthusiasm. They first convinced the local council. Later, facilitated by local public incentives, the local business sector came on board. Bioenergy development seems to have been built on a strong community in which different actors complemented each other's actions, thereby reinforcing social ties. In this way, bioenergy development took hold of the local community in Güssing until numerous members of the community were involved, pursuing profits and identifying themselves with the overall nonprofit oriented strategy of the locality. Consequently, infrastructure solutions drawn up by the community were tailored to the limited material needs of this community.

In the case of Barnim-Uckermark, local support of public and private, profit and nonprofit oriented actors was also of great importance. However, the

Table 7.1   *Characteristics of the Güssing and Barnim-Uckermark cases*

	Güssing	*Barnim-Uckermark*
Start of bioenergy development	Earlier	Later
Main initiative	Bottom-up	Top-down
Infrastructure	Small, decentralized plants	Large, centralized plants
Main biomass source	Forestry	Agriculture
Quality of social ties and complementary action	Higher	Lower
Involvement of processing enterprises	High	Average
Spatial level	Municipality	Two counties

initiative does not seem to involve the same quality of social ties and complementary actions within the area. Social ties across the much larger area of Barnim-Uckermark may be less well developed, which might be explained by its greater geographical extent combined with the fact that there has never been much feeling of connectivity within the district. Some individual and collective actors in the area strongly promote the initiative, but the quality of overall engagement observed in Güssing has evidently not been attained. Both national and international profit oriented companies expressed their interest in investing in Barnim-Uckermark. Public nonprofit oriented governmental actors at the state level also played a significant role, as Brandenburg state launched an overall bioenergy strategy for regional economic development purposes (Land Brandenburg, 2002).

The differences between the two cases with regard to directions of diffusion are explained by their timing in the overall cycle of bioenergy diffusion as an innovative energy source. Güssing developed the initiative on its own at a time when biomass was not high on the agenda in Europe and Germany. It was a strategy adapted to local needs and problems, aimed at putting Güssing on the map and trying to establish an innovative economic sector in the area. The Austrian state did not provide the regulatory framework and subsidies to push for the development of the sector. However, developments in Barnim-Uckermark are closely related to the increasing role of the bioenergy sector on the European and national levels, which are promoted by regulations and subsidies. In other words, Güssing is one of the pioneers of bioenergy strategies for development and could thus gain first-mover advantages, while Barnim-Uckermark followed developments that had already taken hold at higher levels. It therefore follows external changes and drivers, rather than initiating them. It shows that an avantgarde of nongovernmental actors who enter the public realm of social life at a local level can be more successful in the diffusion of innovations than the state, although the latter usually disposes of far more financial and regulatory resources.

We assume that the two regions' differences in bioenergy development have remained, playing out as different paths of subsequent development. Güssing has steadily focused on smaller, decentralized plants and on woody biomass from forestry. In Barnim-Uckermark agricultural crop biomass and its processing in large centralized plants dominate. Due to the smaller structures and the greater diversity of the bioenergy sector, the number of actors profiting from bioenergy is larger in Güssing than in Barnim-Uckermark, where large-scale structures in agriculture and energy conversion focus bioenergy on a smaller number of actors. In Güssing the integration of bioenergy into a broad cluster of biomass processing, energy conversion, energy delivery and energy demanding companies has been the key for its great success, whereas the development of infrastructures in Barnim-Uckermark is not tailored exclusively to resources and energy supply and demand in the area. This may be due to the role of external public and private actors in the case of Barnim-Uckermark. By the time bioenergy was developed in this area, large profit oriented companies had discovered the sector as a potential field of economic expansion and regional and national policy makers promised themselves economic development and employment. In this context, investment decisions were less cautious, leading to larger plants although this involved conflicts over the factors necessary in producing biomass. On the other hand, when bioenergy was developed in Güssing, uncertainties were higher.

In both regions, engagement of public and private actors in the area, or with great interest in the area, were a necessity but not a sufficient condition for bioenergy development. Supranational and national public nonprofit oriented actors played a key role in handing out subsidies for overcoming the risks of investment in bioenergy. Changes in funding regulations may well have played an additional role in the greater size of infrastructures developed later in the Barnim-Uckermark area.

As in any process of diffusion of new technologies, nonprofit oriented, nongovernmental research and science at the regional and national levels played a key role in communicating what is possible and accompanying the implementation of the innovation on the ground. On the one hand, the initiative in the case of Güssing emerged from the bottom up, from the experience of individuals that subsequently tried to develop ties to research. On the other hand, scientists and governmental actors in Barnim-Uckermark were strongly involved in launching the development and communicated its potential into the case study zone, illustrating the more top-down, externally steered developments in East Germany. As is often the case, nongovernmental nonprofit associations adopted various attitudes to this innovation. The ideologies these groups hold hereby play a significant role. The central difference between the two cases seems to be the diverse forms of prevailing governance. Güssing shows community centred forms of governance, while Barnim-Uckermark has been stamped by state centred approaches (similar to the Indonesian case in Chapter 1). With regard to Barnim-Uckermark, however, we have to qualify our conclusions, as several initiatives emerged simultaneously that rely on the local and regional endogenous potential.

CONCLUSIONS

What can be learnt from the analysis of actors in the bioenergy sector about the relations between public and private that might have a larger applicability to other fields? The bioenergy sector suggests good examples of changing configurations of public and private actors establishing the governance structure throughout the diffusion of bioenergy.

At first sight, the development of bioenergy can be perfectly explained with the liberal-economistic model: certain knowledge and values held by society and specific interest groups were reflected in the policy aim to increase bioenergy generation, and state agencies were charged to develop a regulatory framework for these developments. Financial incentives and aid for private enterprises were provided to overcome risks and uncertainty in favour of the desired economic change. The private, profit oriented, nongovernmental agricultural, forestry and energy enterprises and individual consumers reconfigured their strategies in this context. This was eventually to benefit overall society. The empirical findings from Barnim-Uckermark confirm that this approach led to an extensive diffusion of bioenergy, but they also show that it entailed a series of unintended consequences, for example predominantly profit oriented financial investors with little environmental commitment have entered the stage. While they are the key drivers of bioenergy expansion, they have occasionally foiled the original policy targets, as with the construction of large centralized plants with inferior energy efficiency and severe environmental impacts.

The sector has not only been shaped by market oriented private actors and the state – the pioneering activities in the field have been provided by committed private individuals who emerged from a political community surrounding the bioenergy issue. This community finds its expression in the bottom-up nature of bioenergy development, as exemplified by the numerous individuals, cooperatives and networks described in the Güssing case. These actors enjoy social visibility and, although private according to classical theory, have entered the public realm of social life, reshaping governance. Numerous actors have contrived to mix the public realm and the particularistic spheres in the bioenergy issue. They speak out for bioenergy as a community and pursue their individual profit interests at the same time. This combination of principally local nongovernmental public and private action has proven successful at the beginning of the technology development and set an example and prepared the ground for subsequent state action. At the same time, the societal commitment and the integration of these actors into local communities has prevented countless aberrations and triggered regional development to a far greater extent than a purely liberal-economistic approach.

The lesson from this analysis might be that both profit and nonprofit oriented private actors (have to) complement each other in the development and diffusion of innovative technologies. Nonprofit oriented actors are more prepared to take risks and commit to societal aims and thus often stand at the beginning of new developments. Charismatic individuals who create a strong cross-sectoral narrative of regional or local economic development can take an outstanding role in shaping their initiatives. For bottom-up initiatives at the early stages of technological diffusion, it seems to be beneficial if the sectoral development can be linked to a broader strategy for economic development in a relatively small territory. In other words, the way the promotion of a new technology is embedded seems to matter for the benefit that a region can reap from it. Where profit oriented actors operate on a larger scale, they seem to be focused more on profit maximization and less on the benefits for the overall development of a region. Large-scale profit oriented actors are less prepared to take risks. They are nonetheless indispensable for the wide appeal of a new technology. To encourage these private actors to invest in production requires that public regulation stabilize their expectations and that financial incentives are provided by the public sector. So far the state has supported the predominantly nonprofit oriented actors with (relatively modest) funds for the establishment of clusters and networks and the profit oriented actors with (very comprehensive) subsidies. The challenge for future state action in the field will be to ensure that the effects of its support programmes better meet the intended policy aims and to develop new tools to further stimulate nonprofit oriented action.

NOTE

1   The term 'private' refers to market actors and 'public' to the state throughout this chapter unless otherwise stated (following the second public/private distinction discussed in the Introduction).

REFERENCES

barum111 (2006) *barum111 – Kompetenzregion für die Nutzung erneuerbarer Energien Barnim-Uckermark*, www.barum111.de/ (accessed 20 September 2006)

Braune, I (1998) 'The contribution of agriculture and forestry to climate protection: Agriculture and forestry policy in Germany', *Berichte über Landwirtschaft*, vol 76, pp580–597

Brunner, C, Hotwagner, M and Kopitar, A (2006) 'Güssing/Südburgenland – erste energieautarke Stadt Österreichs', *Informationen zur Raumentwicklung*, vol 1/2, pp93–101

Domac, J, Richards, K and Risovic, S (2005) 'Socio-economic drivers in implementing bioenergy projects', *Biomass and Bioenergy*, vol 28, pp97–106

ENOB (2006) *Clusterinitiative Energie Nord–Ost–Brandenburg*, www.energie-nord-ost-brandenburg.de (accessed 20 September 2006)

Ericsson, K, Huttunen, S, Nilsson, L J and Svenningsson, P (2004) 'Bioenergy policy and market development in Finland and Sweden', *Energy Policy*, vol 32, pp1707–1721

Hacker, J (2006) 'Kommunales Energiekonzept mit Wärme und Kraft(stoff) aus Biomasse', *AFZ–Der Wald*, vol 61, pp552–553

Hillring, B (2002) 'Rural development and bioenergy: Experiences from 20 years of development in Sweden', *Biomass and Bioenergy*, vol 23, pp443–451

Huston, M A and Marland, G (2003) 'Carbon management and biodiversity', *Journal of Environmental Management*, vol 67, pp77–86

Jähnke, P and Lompscher, K (1995) 'Tendenzen des siedlungsstrukturellen Wandels in den dünnbesiedelten Räumen Brandenburgs', *Berichte zur deutschen Landeskunde*, vol 69, pp327–363

Jessop, B (1995) 'The regulation approach, governance and post-fordism: Alternative perspectives on economic and political change?', *Economy and Society*, vol 34, pp307–333

Land Brandenburg (2002) *Energiestrategie 2010: Der energiepolitische Handlungsrahmen des Landes Brandenburg bis zum Jahr 2010*, Ministry for Economic Affairs, Potsdam

Mangels-Voegt, B (2004) 'Erneuerbare Energien – Erfolgsgaranten einer nachhaltigen Politik?', *Politik und Zeitgeschichte*, vol 37, pp12–17

McCormick, K and Kaberger, T (2005) 'Exploring a pioneering bioenergy system: The case of Enköping in Sweden', *Journal of Cleaner Production*, vol 13, pp1003–1014

Plieninger, T, Bens, O and Hüttl, R F (2005) *Zukunftsorientierte Nutzung ländlicher Räume – Naturräumlicher und sozioökonomischer Wandel, Innovationspotenziale und politische Steuerung am Beispiel des Landes Brandenburg*, Working Paper no 2, Berlin-Brandenburg Academy of Sciences, Berlin

Plieninger, T, Bens, O and Hüttl, R F (2006) 'Perspectives of bioenergy for agriculture and rural areas', *Outlook on Agriculture*, vol 35, pp123–127

Sims, R E H (2003) 'Bioenergy to mitigate for climate change and meet the needs of society, the economy and the environment', *Mitigation and Adaptation Strategies for Global Change*, vol 8, pp349–370

Sohre, A (2006) 'Strategien für eine umweltverträgliche Energieversorgung – Deutschland und Großbritannien im Vergleich' in Reiche, D and Bechberger, M (eds) *Erfolgsbedingungen für einen ökologischen Transformationsprozess der Energiewirtschaft*, Erich-Schmidt-Verlag, Berlin, pp239–256

Williamson, O E (1998) 'The institutions of governance', *American Economic Review*, vol 88, pp75–79

8

Marketing Safe Food by Labelling: The Pros and Cons of State Regulation

Jutta Roosen

INTRODUCTION

Access to a sufficient amount of safe food is one of the basic human needs. While the very personal act of eating mainly takes place in private households (Meier, 2004), many aspects of the production and processing of food and the control of these processes have been brought from the private to the public forefront. There has always been an urge for governmental control of certain aspects of the food system. With the advent of the industrial revolution, food adulteration has become an issue of systematic regulation by the state (Tannahill, 1973). Since then, the realm of the state and of private actors in the market (i.e. firms and consumers) has constantly been changing. The BSE crisis in Europe, the associated revision of European food law and globalization are driving forces that have lead to a heated debate on the division of coercive (state) and voluntary (market) aspects of food safety regulation. In addition, as argued by Reich (1994), the enlargement of the European market has modified legislation, shifting the focus from a credulous consumer to one who is critical and of average sophistication.

The regulation of food safety influences consumer welfare in at least four dimensions (Hamilton et al, 2003). Health and safety regulation obviously affects the safety of products and, due to market repercussions, their price. Environmental and ethical aspects of production and product trade, however, are also influenced by regulation, and the overall variety of products on the market is restricted. While economists consider the aspects of product safety and price to be private good characteristics, environmental and ethical aspects as well as questions of product variety are deemed public goods. Restricting the use of growth hormones, for example, limits the choice of meat available on the market. Certainly, in a transparent and free market consumers can choose to buy hormone-treated or hormone-free meat and in this way make a private choice. Yet, they may see their role as consumer as differing from theirs as a citizen, because the application of the Kantian imperative appears to be of limited value when the choice of a single consumer has little influence on the overall market outcome. As a citizen, a person may regard the restriction of hormone use in animal production an appropriate legal activity whereas as a consumer, he would not bother to make a distinction between these different types of meat.

Contention in the debate about food safety regulation is related to the establishment of new public spheres. As indicated in the Introduction to this volume, public and private dimensions of food safety regulation can be defined by governance through coercion (state) or voluntary action (market). Concerning food safety, pure coercion no longer seems effective in many respects, as food risks are difficult to detect. The compliance with safe handling procedures and the cooperation between production and control are major issues. Furthermore, players and markets in the food sector are becoming increasingly global, leading to international quality and safety standards in the private sphere that must be compatible with multiple national (public) regulations. More trade means that products have to become more standardized and homogeneous to enable trade and make it transparent.

Therefore, we observe that private market participants form their own public. Agricultural marketing groups or NGOs, for example, form production standards according to which their product can be marketed (organic, fair trade, regional origin etc.). In addition, consumers act as citizens, simultaneously influencing market and political outcomes. Examples from consumer boycotts of genetically modified food since the 1990s or of Shell in the wake of public discussions on submerging the oil platform Brent Spar in the North Sea in 1995 have shown that intervention by NGOs can create powerful publics that answer civil questions not only through political processes but also by applying market pressure (for an economic argument explaining how firms respond to political activists see Hudson and Lusk, 2004).

Finally, certain aspects of food consumption at home are becoming more public. Food consumption away from home is increasing (Meier, 2004) and can generally be used as a public expression of the self (vegetarian diet, organic consumption etc.). Retailers and food producers are also making a public effort to market safe food, as it increases chances for market share and shareholder value.

This introduction reveals that the shifts in the public and private domains in food marketing are complex due to the different interrelating levels. The objective of this chapter, therefore, is to discuss the interaction between state regulated and private strategies for marketing safe food. As outlined above, the definition of public and private is multifaceted; however, this chapter predominantly uses the definition according to the distinctions (a) and (b) identified in the Introduction as it coincides with that of public economics. The chapter sets out by discussing why product safety is an issue that cannot be left to the market – a sphere of private actors – and why governmental regulation is necessary. It offers ways in which the information failure in unregulated markets may be overcome by different publics. It analyses the decision to use governmental regulation and standardization of product quality or information policies such as labelling.

If labelling is considered a suitable solution, the role of private (firms) and governmental or nongovernmental public parties involved in the process needs to be discussed. A case study that examines the rise in premium quality retail labels exemplifies the shifts in private and public governance in food safety information. The chapter presents results from consumer studies that observe consumer interest in and use of labels as well as their trust in information sources. Before concluding, the complementarities between public and private labelling schemes are discussed in the context of the German market for organic milk.

INFORMATION FAILURE IN THE MARKET FOR FOOD SAFETY

Rising consumer affluence has led to a diversified demand for food quality. The term food quality circumscribes a large number of attributes that can or may not be restricted to the issue of consumer safety. These food quality attributes include: food safety attributes such as food-borne pathogens, heavy metals or pesticide residues; nutritional attributes such as fat, fibre and protein; value attributes including purity and appearance; package attributes such as packaging material and atmosphere; and process attributes regarding questions, for example, of animal welfare, environmental protection or use of genetic modification (Hooker and Caswell, 1999).

In this context of vertical diversification of product quality, regulators may have several reasons to be hesitant in severely limiting quality choice by strong standardization. First, if quality is costly then consumers having a low willingness to pay will be excluded from the market and lose consumer surplus. Preferences may also be heterogeneous for reasons of taste or safety. If health characteristics and vulnerability differ by population segment, it may not be efficient to apply the same standard to all. For instance, children or old people may be more vulnerable to certain risks than others. If it turns out to be desirable to allow for product differentiation – with regard to safety characteristics as well – a suitable communication policy is needed so that consumers can decide among various product qualities.

In many situations a consumer has to rely on product information supplied by sellers who are affected by consumer choice. Nevertheless, although the interested parties (firms) have an incentive to conceal or distort information, their efforts do not always succeed. Generally it has been argued that free and open discussion or competition in the marketplace of ideas will result in the truth becoming known, leading to appropriate decisions in the marketplace (Milgrom and Roberts, 1986a).

This tenant of the efficient disclosure of relevant information in markets relies on the assumption of a sophisticated consumer who knows how to interpret and judge the information provided in the face of self-interested suppliers or the verifiability of information (Milgrom and Roberts, 1986a). These conditions, however necessary for efficient information disclosure, are quite restrictive and are unlikely to be fulfilled for questions of food safety.

According to Nelson's (1970) classification, products subject to asymmetric information can be classified according to search characteristics if consumers can inspect and verify quality before purchase, experience characteristics if quality is revealed only after purchase and consumption, and credence characteristics if quality is not revealed even after purchase. Food safety attributes often fall under this category of credence characteristics and are thus not verifiable by the consumer. In this instance Akerlof (1970) has shown that markets may not work efficiently and that adverse selection may lead to a breakdown of market transactions. The pure reliance on private action in the market for safe food is thus doomed to lead to inefficiencies, and food suppliers may therefore face difficulties in finding efficient and credible means to signal their product quality.

This has resulted in multifaceted approaches to regulation by the state or by groups of consumers or producers in order to mitigate potential inefficiencies ensuing from asymmetrically distributed information.

A pure market solution to the problem lies in consumers looking for different food quality signals. These signals can be intrinsic (tangible) or extrinsic (intangible) to a product's quality. Signals that consumers perceive as extrinsic are of particular interest in the context of credence goods. Therefore, some quality attributes may serve as food safety signals, even if there is no strong cause and effect relationship between the signalling attribute and the resulting product safety attributes. Such attributes signalling quality include brand names (Akerlof, 1970; Ross, 1988) or brand advertising (Milgrom and Roberts, 1986b), product appearance (Nelson, 1970), price (Milgrom and Roberts, 1986b) and product or retail reputation (Cooper and Ross, 1985).

Another solution that leaves the purely private sphere of market interactions between a selling firm and the consumer and that creates a new public is the use of third party accreditation of a food safety communication strategy. The involvement of an independent actor capable of controlling quality opens a path for truthful disclosure of information.

Common labels are used by several producers or firms complying with the label rules and/or having a common characteristic that is not particular to a single product. There is a plethora of common labels in Europe (McCluskey and Loureiro, 2003) relating to safety, freshness, geographic origin, organic status, fair trade or respect for the environment. Some of them are regulated at the EU level as with labels relating to geographic origin (EEC 2081/92 and EEC 2082/92) or organic production (EEC 2092/91). Since these quality attributes are shared by numerous products, firms cannot build a unique reputation in these quality dimensions, which leads to complex strategies of common labelling as a tool for promotion (Boizot-Szantai et al, 2005).

A recurrent problem with the use of these different common labels is the information overload of consumers that may result. Verbeke (2005) underlines the importance of information being well targeted to the recipient consumer. Labelling campaigns need to understand, segment and identify the target population if the consumer is to understand and use the information provided in his or her purchasing choice.

Regulation by the state strengthens the market for label information in several ways. First, even if information provided by interested parties such as suppliers is not verifiable, efficiency can be achieved through penalties for perjury, false advertising or warranty violations, if these penalties are sufficiently certain and heavy to discourage false reporting (Milgrom and Roberts, 1986a). If the government uses tort laws to encourage truthfulness in advertising and claims, then private citizens need be able to take civil action. Therefore the legal system must be accessible, efficient and effective (Hennessy et al, 2003). In the case of food safety, liability laws are rarely used due to difficulties in relating an incident, such as a salmonella infection, to a source, unless there is a large-scale outbreak (Segerson, 1999). In addition, it is argued that legal controls and penalties in the German food system are too weak to provide sufficient incentive for adhering to legal standards (Lippert, 2002). It is this observation that has led retailers to take a leading role in the market for quality by using private label products (Loader and Hobbs, 1999; Bazoche et al, 2005).

An additional task for state regulators consists of providing a framework for the application of common labels that allow firms to signal quality. Using common labels in place of individual labels permits firms to reduce the complexity of information that consumers face in the marketplace. The absence of standards in food labelling may make it difficult for consumers to understand the messages the sender seeks to convey. Labelling standards improve the consumer's information environment and improve the credibility of information provided by sellers (Hennessy et al, 2003).

Finally, the public sector can provide and regulate third party control that is needed to send credible messages for credence attributes. To work satisfactorily, consumers must understand and trust the role of the third party. The government might affirm and assure the independence and competence of testing firms, for example, by providing public control authorities or accreditation mechanisms of private firms (Hennessy et al, 2003).

RETAILER ACTION IN LABELLING FOOD SAFETY

In recent years, there has been a strong proliferation of retail brands or private-label products in the market for food. They present an additional effort of retailers to differentiate themselves from competitors in terms of higher product quality. Retail brands serve different purposes, such as building customer loyalty and signalling quality and credence attributes (Treis and Gripp, 2001). In the German food sector they have achieved a 30 per cent share of sales value (ACNielsen, 2005). While retail brands were originally introduced in the early 1970s as so-called no name products on a price competitive level, retailers have recently used them in an attempt to position themselves in the premium quality segment (Jonas and Roosen, 2005).

Bazoche et al (2005) discuss how the French retail sector has engaged in its own certification standards in order to both reassure and strengthen customer loyalty and to develop differentiation strategies in a highly competitive retail market. These retail brand efforts have led to new developments in the agro-food sector. First, these initiatives have resulted in increased segmentation of product offerings in retail stores. In addition to generic products and national brands, retailers now offer premium retail brands that have particularly proliferated in fields where national brands are sparse and generic products are ubiquitous (cf. Bazoche et al, 2005; Jonas and Roosen, 2005).

The introduction of premium retail brands necessitates private production standards that are more stringent than those of state regulations. These requirements need to be subject to regular controls performed by third party certification organizations.

In order to successfully communicate the improved quality characteristics of their premium brand, retailers have developed two strategies. One is to build a reputation for their own brands. Once they can convince their customers that they have a reputation to lose, consumers may be confident in the quality provided, allowing efficient market transactions to prevail. As discussed by Swinbank (1993) and by Henson and Traill (1993), however, firms may seek vigorous protection of brand reputation if a whole product line is at risk in a food safety scandal. A producer in the situation of monopolistic supply will target the marginal consumer, whereas the average consumer determines the market outcome under perfect competition (Nicholson, 1998). Therefore private food safety efforts may deviate from the socially efficient level.

As an alternative to establishing their own reputation, firms may combine their private label with common labels. This action strengthens the recognition of a differentiated product and helps the producer to reduce the investment in label reputation. Although a retail label can be understood as a new private action, it forms a new public between food producers and retailer, who are now vertically coordinating their quality efforts, and between retailer and consumers as a means of communication. The basis for this coordination consists of commonly agreed upon production rules, for instance, when a private label is established for organic food. In this respect, such labels allow for a market solution of cooperation (between privates), hence reducing the need for individual contractual coordination (in a new public).

CONSUMER USE OF FOOD LABELS

The success of retailers and producers in communicating quality and safety through labels will depend on consumers' perception of labelled product attributes and their trust in the message. Consumers may choose specific labels for their own private quality and safety concern, to be congruent with their civil viewpoints, or to communicate certain lifestyle choices via public consumption. The following section reviews some empirical evidence on how German consumers view and use quality and safety information through labels.

A survey of 240 consumers was conducted in Kiel in 2004 to evaluate consumer concern and perception of various food safety issues relating to meat (Goldberg, 2005). Regarding the potential of producers or supermarkets to be the sole providers of food safety information, it was found that producer labels and producer information was used only by a third of the queried consumers as a source of information about food safety (see Figure 8.1). Only 14 respondents used producer information as their main source, and only eight deemed it their most trusted source. Similarly only 13 per cent of all surveyed consumers state that supermarkets are important as an information source for food safety (Goldberg, 2005). These results are not surprising and demonstrate that private parties have to rely on supplementary strategies when signalling food safety characteristics to consumers. Credible communication seems to require the involvement of a sort of public. As evidenced by Figure 8.1, the media is one important public actor that serves as consumers' primary source of food safety information.

It should be noted, however, that information rarely used in the final purchasing decision may nevertheless be of importance to consumers. Labels of food quality characteristics serve as signals to consumers and increase their discriminatory power in the marketplace. Consumers value the opportunity for freedom of choice and diversity (Drescher et al, 2006; on limits to the freedom of choice, see Schwartz, 2004). Citizens may also strongly favour mandatory food labels without choosing such products as consumers.

In the spring of 2005, Christoph (2005) queried a sample of 5000 randomly selected consumers on their attitudes towards several types of common labels describing process attributes. Respondents were prompted to indicate: (1) the importance attributed to labels on a five-point likert scale from 1 = very important to 5 = not at all important; (2) if they use these labels for their purchase decision (1 = always... 5 = never); and (3) if they buy the products carrying that label (1 = always... 5 = never). The results are summarized in Table 8.1. Consumers seem to attribute importance to all types of labels even if they do not always look for them when buying products. They may also decide not to buy the products carrying the label, even having paid attention to them. One obvious explanation for the observed disparity is that although consumers may consider a label important, they may not be willing to pay for it.

The label that received the highest average score for importance (lowest number) is a label about animal welfare. Indeed in Germany almost 50 per cent of all eggs sold directly to consumers come from alternative (non-cage) production systems (ZMP, 2004). Labels relating to animal welfare are often used in the purchase decision.

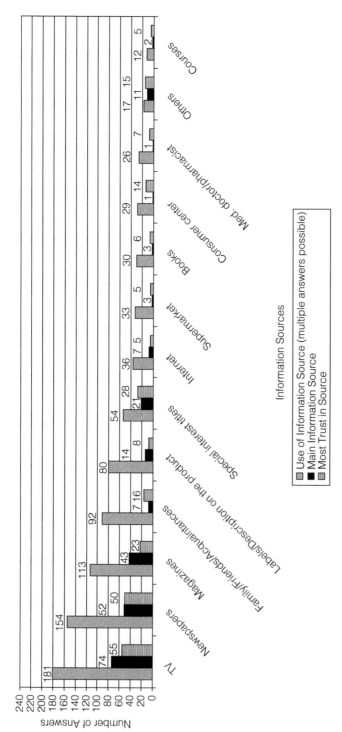

Figure 8.1 *Use of information sources and trustworthiness of information sources*

Source: Goldberg, 2005

Table 8.1   *Importance and use of common labels for German consumers (average scores)*

	Organic	GMO-free	Contains GMO	Animal welfare	Environmentally friendly	Fair trade
Important (1 = very... 5 = not at all)	2.21 (1.09)	1.94 (1.15)	2.12 (1.21)	1.68 (0.85)	2.00 (0.92)	2.07 (1.03)
Use labels in purchase decision (1 = always... 5 = never)	2.57 (1.67)	2.44 (1.35)	2.70 (1.37)	2.08 (1.07)	2.47 (1.15)	2.63 (1.28)
Buy products with the label (1 = always... 5 = never)	2.85 (1.28)	2.56 (1.30)	3.60 (1.47)	2.20 (0.98)	2.56 (1.01)	2.69 (1.12)

Note: Figures in parentheses are standard error
Source: Christoph, 2005

Labels for organic food are considered least important but are still frequently used. In Germany the share of consumers buying organic food is estimated at about 44 per cent (Kunz and Reuter, 2005). Regarding genetically modified organisms (GMOs) in food products, most consumers look for a label on products that are GMO free. Given that there are very few products containing GMOs, which must be labelled as such to be sold in German retail outlets, the result is hardly surprising.[1]

These results testify that labels not only play a role in effective consumer choice but also in empowering consumers to differentiate among products and thus to make an informed decision. Therefore, a label's value may be underestimated if one only considers changes in choice. This is because ignorance regarding product attributes may make choices excessively costly to consumers (Foster and Just, 1989). This is in line with results in Roosen et al (2003), who find that a majority of consumers in France, Germany and the UK are in favour of labelling genetically modified feed in animal production, even if this leads to an increase in product price.

Roosen et al (2003) also analysed how consumers take product labelling into consideration in making their purchasing decision. The consumer survey in the three European countries asked for the role of brand (producer or retailer) and common label of origin in beef purchasing decisions. For consumers in all three countries, beef brands were of less importance than origin labels. The regression of the importance score attributed to brand and to the origin label on sociodemographic characteristics and food safety concerns suggests that concern about production technologies has a larger impact on the perceived level of importance of origin labels than branding does. Indeed, concern about mad cow disease in European countries may explain the importance that consumers attribute to regional discrimination of producers by origin labels. Another aspect that explains the varying perception of brand and origin labels could be that meat is commonly sold as a generic product in France and Germany. Therefore, brands are perceived as more important in the UK.

The results in this section suggest that consumers value label information as a way to differentiate between products. Concern about production technologies is one of the driving forces behind their interest in labels. Knowledge about these technologies may be related to consumers' civil concerns but may also be used as a signal for private food quality and safety attributes.

THE PROLIFERATION OF LABELS: COMMON LABELS AND BRANDS

The above mentioned results suggest that interactions are to be expected between brands and common labels. Producers and retailers will particularly benefit from a reputation that has been built on the publics of state supported common label organizations when consumers do not accept brands as communication tools for generic products. This section reviews some of the recent developments in European food markets.

Boizot-Szantai et al (2005) present a study of common labels in the French egg market. They show that common labels (organic, free-range and open air systems) increased between the years 1996 and 2002. While both retail brands and producer brands have increased in market share, the increase is much more pronounced for retail brands bearing a common label. Using price differences between products with and without labels as a possible indicator of consumers' measurement of quality perception and label reputation, they find that eggs are more expensive when sold as a producer brand rather than a retail brand. In addition, the price premium associated with common labels is larger for producer brands than for retailer brands. A theoretical analysis of the interactions between common labelling and market structure has shown that a situation of multiple equilibriums may emerge when the cost of the label is relatively high. In this case, the label can be used solely by either the high quality or the low quality seller.

The accumulation of common labels and private labels is observed equally in German general retailing. For organic products in particular, retail brands have attained a large market share, and producer brands only comprise a share of 32 per cent of organic products sold in general retailing (BNN, 2003).

Using data from the GfK[2] ConsumerScan for the years 2000 to 2003, Jonas (2005) analyses the market for organic milk in German retailing.[3] Figure 8.2 presents milk-consuming households' annual expenditure for

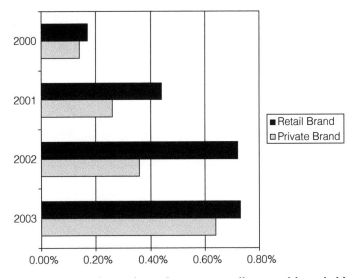

Figure 8.2   *Expenditure shares for organic milk in total household milk expenditures*

Source: Jonas, 2005

organic milk. The market share of organic milk in the national milk market is estimated at 3.3 per cent (Jonas, 2005). The GfK data attribute an expenditure share to organic milk that grew from 0.31 per cent in 2000 to 1.37 per cent in 2003 (see Figure 8.2).[4] This increase has been faster for retail brands than for producer brands for most of the time period, although to a large extent the latter caught up in 2003.

Table 8.2 shows the prices calculated as unit values from the household expenditure data of the GfK panel. It is obvious that milk with an organic label can achieve a considerable price premium of up to 0.30 euros. This corresponds to more than 50 per cent of the price of conventional milk. This high premium was achieved for producer branded milk in 2000. However, the table also shows that organic retail brands were much more successful in stabilizing the price difference between milk with and without common labels.

The own price elasticities estimated for the different milk product groups are given in Table 8.3. Those for conventional milk are about unity, whereas the one for retail branded organic milk is –2.5, demonstrating a significant ability of retailers to exert market power and obtain a premium. The price elasticity of producer branded organic milk is positive and not significant. Overall the results suggest that retail brands can make use of quality reputation by using state supported common labels to convey credibility to their premium quality strategy.

Table 8.2   *Price for milk in German retail market (cents per litre)*

	RB-NL	PB-NL	RB-OL	PB-OL	Label value RB	Label value PB
2000	47.16	53.32	75.94	83.34	28.78	30.02
2001	55.69	60.64	81.05	88.83	25.36	28.19
2002	54.97	59.87	80.34	82.16	25.37	22.29
2003	52.41	58.27	81.35	81.93	28.94	23.66

Note: RB-NL: retail brand, no label; PB-NL: private brand, no label;
RB-OL: retail brand, organic label; PB-OL: private brand, organic label
Source: Jonas, 2005

Table 8.3   *Expenditure and own-price elasticities for milk in German general retailing*

	Expenditure elasticities	Own-price elasticities
Retail brand, no label	0,986** (0,005)	–0,903** (0,048)
Private brand, no label	1,009** (0,004)	–1,124** (0,051)
Retail brand, organic label	0,974** (0,075)	–2,502** (1,131)
Private brand, organic label	1,033** (0,075)	0,937 (1,064)

Note: ** and * signify statistically significant at 5 per cent and 10 per cent levels. Standard errors in parentheses
Source: Jonas, 2005

CONCLUSIONS

This chapter has discussed the potential of food labels to avoid inefficiencies in the food market due to information asymmetries relating to food safety. Safety characteristics are mostly credence attributes of food products, rendering the information on product labels nonverifiable to consumers. Hence producers face a challenge in credibly communicating food safety attributes.

Public authorities have an important role to play in assuring the functioning of the market for information on food safety. First, the government should build a legal system assuring truthfulness in advertising and claims as well as empower the consumer to use tort laws effectively and efficiently. Second, the government could organize one market for common labels with product attributes that are indiscriminate among producers. Assuring the coherence of labels being used, the government can undertake an important step in limiting the information overload facing today's consumers. Finally, the government can provide a legal framework for credible institutions of third party certification by installing public controls or accrediting private ones. Indeed, an effective system of third party certification is crucial in any private effort of firms when communicating credence attributes to consumers.

This chapter's arguments show that public and private institutions are both substitutes and complements in efforts to assure a safe food supply. While public institutions can lay the groundwork by imposing rules of information provision, market competition and private incentives lead to a differentiation in food safety and quality characteristics that meets the consumer's ever growing demand for product variety.

Globalization and its related enlargement of food markets lead to a need for homogenized and easily tradable product qualities. The previously fixed bundling of product attributes has become more and more resolved and products more anonymous. Whereas, in former times, close links between actors of the food chain were observed (the consumer buying at the local butcher who personally knew the farmer who raised the animals), nowadays impersonalized market transactions require alternative communication channels. This can only be achieved through the standardization of information. Hence, the increase in product diversity due to the enlargement of markets comes at the cost of reduced nonharmonized product variety.

ACKNOWLEDGEMENTS

I thank Inken Birte Christoph, Isabell Goldberg, Astrid Jonas and Stephan Marette for useful discussions on the issues presented in this chapter.

NOTES

1   The author knows of no example of a food product labelled as containing GMOs according to Regulation (EC) 1830/2003.
2   Gesellschaft für Konsumforschung, Nuremberg.
3   The data refer only to the general retail sector, which represents about 30 per cent of the sales value of organic products in Germany over a given period of time.
4   The difference may be explained by the large share of organic milk in specialized organic food stores and *Reformhäuser* outside of general retailing that is not captured in the ConsumerScan panel.

REFERENCES

ACNielsen (2005) 'The Power of Private Label 2005', www.acnielsen.de/ news/ documents/ThePowerofPrivateLabel2005.pdf (accessed 22 December 2005)

Akerlof, G A (1970) 'The market for lemons: Quality, uncertainty and the market mechanism', *Quarterly Journal of Economics*, vol 84, no 3, pp488–500

Bazoche, P, Giraud-Héraud, E and Soler, L-G (2005) 'Premium private labels, supply contracts, market segmentation, and spot prices', *Journal of Agricultural & Food Industrial Organization*, vol 3, no 7, pp1–28

BNN (Bundesverbände Naturkost und Naturwaren) (2003) 'Trendbericht – Die Naturkostbranche zwischen Nitrofen und BSE. Zahlen und Fakten 2002', http://62.112.68.138/input/pdf/Trendbericht.pdf (accessed 5 December 2004)

Boizot-Szantai, C, Lococq, S and Marette, S (2005) *Common Labels and Market Mechanisms*, Working Paper 05-WP 405, Department of Economics, Iowa State University, Iowa

Christoph, I B (2005) 'Consumers' Perception of Genetically Modified Products', unpublished Working Paper, Department for Food Economics and Consumption Studies, University of Kiel, Kiel

Cooper, R. and Ross, T W (1985) 'Product warranties and double moral hazard', *Rand Journal of Economics*, vol 16, no 1, pp103–113

Drescher, L S, Thiele, S and Weiss, C (2006) 'The Taste for Variety: A Hedonic Analysis', Contributed Paper at the International Association of Agricultural Economists Conference, August, Goldcoast, Australia

Foster, W and Just, R E (1989) 'Measuring welfare effects of product contamination with consumer uncertainty', *Journal of Environmental Economics and Management*, vol 17, no 3, pp266–283

Goldberg, I (2005) *Ergebnisbericht zur Verbraucherbefragung: Lebensmittelqualität und Fleisch*, Department for Food Economics and Consumption Studies, University of Kiel, Kiel

Hamilton, S, Sunding, D and Zilberman, D (2003) 'Public goods and the value of product quality regulations: The case of food safety', *Journal of Public Economics*, vol 87, no 3/4, pp799–817

Hennessy, D A, Roosen, J and Jensen, H H (2003) 'Systemic failure in the provision of safe food', *Food Policy*, vol 28, no 1, pp77–96

Henson, S and Traill, B (1993) 'The demand for food safety', *Food Policy*, vol 18, no 2, pp152–162

Hooker, N H and Caswell, J A (1999) 'A framework for evaluating non-tariff barriers to trade related to sanitary and phytosanitary regulation', *Journal of Agricultural Economics*, vol 50, no 2, pp234–246

Hudson, D and Lusk, J L (2004) 'Activists and corporate behaviour in food processing and retailing: A game theoretic approach', *Journal of Agricultural and Resource Economics*, vol 29, no 1, pp79–93

Jonas, A (2005) *Vermarktung ökologischer Produkte über den Lebensmitteleinzelhandel: Eine empirische Analyse der Hersteller-Händler Beziehung und der Nachfrage nach Milch*, Cuvillier Verlag, Göttingen

Jonas, A and Roosen, J (2005) 'Private labels for premium products: The example of organic food', *International Journal of Retail & Distribution Management*, vol 33, no 8, pp636–653

Kunz, J and Reuter, K (2005) *Category Management für Bioprodukte. Teil 1: Anforderungen und strategische Ansätze*, ÖkoStrategieBeratung, Berlin

Lippert, C (2002) 'Zur Ökonomik der Kontrollmaßnahmen bei Lebensmitteln und Futtermittel', *Agrarwirtschaft*, vol 51, no 3, pp142–155

Loader, R and Hobbs, J E (1999) 'Strategic responses to food safety legislation', *Food Policy*, vol 24, no 6, pp685–706

McCluskey, J and Loureiro, M (2003) 'Consumer preferences and willingness-to-pay for food labeling: A discussion of empirical studies', *Journal of Food Distribution Research*, vol 34, no 3, pp95–102

Meier, U (2004) 'Zeitbudget, Mahlzeitenmuster und Ernährungsstile' in *Ernährungsbericht 2004*, Deutsche Gesellschaft für Ernährung, Bonn, pp72–94

Milgrom, P and Roberts, J (1986a) 'Relying on the information of interested parties', *Rand Journal of Economics*, vol 12, no 1, pp18–32

Milgrom, P and Roberts, J (1986b) 'Price and advertising signals of product quality', *Journal of Political Economy*, vol 94, no 4, pp796–821

Nelson, P (1970) 'Information and consumer behavior', *Journal of Political Economy*, vol 78, no 2, pp311–329

Nicholson, W (1998) *Microeconomic Theory: Basic Principles and Extensions*, Dryden Press, Orlando, FL

Reich, N (1994) 'Zur Theorie des europäischen Verbraucherrechtes', *Hauswirtschaft und Wissenschaft*, no 6, pp259–272

Roosen J, Lusk, J L and Fox, J A (2003) 'Consumer demand for and attitudes toward alternative beef labelling strategies in France, Germany, and the UK', *Agribusiness*, vol 19, no 1, pp77–90

Ross, T W (1988) 'Brand information and price', *The Journal of Industrial Economics*, vol 36, no 3, pp301–313

Schwartz, B (2004) 'The tyranny of choice', *Scientific American*, vol 290, no 4, pp70–75

Segerson, K (1999) 'Mandatory vs. voluntary approaches to food safety', *Agribusiness*, vol 15, no 1, pp53–70

Swinbank, A (1993) 'The economics of food safety', *Food Policy*, vol 18, issue 2, pp83–94

Tannahill, R (1973) *Food in History*, Eyre Methuen, London

Treis, B and Gripp, H (2001) 'Die Funktionen der Handelsmarke und ihr Schutz durch das Markenrecht' in Bruhn, M (ed) *Handelsmarken – Entwicklungstendenzen und Perspektiven der Handelsmarkenpolitik*, Schäffer-Poeschel, Stuttgart, pp165–185

Verbeke, W (2005) 'Agriculture and the food industry in the information age', *European Review of Agricultural Economics*, vol 32, no 3, pp347–368

ZMP (2004) *Noch jedes zweite Ei aus Käfighaltung: Eierkäufe der privaten Haushalte nach Haltungsformen, Jan. bis Sept. 2004*, ZMP/CMA-Marktforschung: Rohdatenanalyse auf Basis des GfK-Haushaltspanels n=13.000 inkl, Ausländerhausalte, www.zmp.de

PART IV – VISIONS FOR A SUSTAINABLE FUTURE

Introduction to Part IV

We have set out to examine the relations between public and private in natural resource governance. Part I examined various kinds of publics and their foundations in states and political communities. Part II looked at hybrid actors and actions combining public and private elements. Part III focused on market oriented actors, which we may consider to be private according to the state–market dichotomy, yet may also act public as members of political communities or by attaining social visibility. In this way we have gained a much richer understanding of public–private relations in natural resource governance.

Part IV now turns from analysis to prescription. What, we ask, does this enriched understanding of public–private relations imply for efforts to create a sustainable future? Two chapters develop visions for a sustainable future. Although their immediate concern is with food safety and biodiversity conservation, their relevance goes much beyond these particular policy fields. The chapters demonstrate that participation and public–private partnerships can help form political communities and social visibilities in support of sustainable resource governance.

Chapter 9 develops key features for inclusive risk governance dealing with food safety. Renn identifies different risk situations encountered in the production, processing, distribution, consumption and disposal of food. As the situations differ in our knowledge about the linkages between choices and outcomes, he argues, they require different procedures for making decisions. Renn's analysis comes at a time when food risks have become a primary international concern (Hoffmann and Taylor, 2005). Moreover, his argument bears important implications for risks in other policy fields, such as water quality hazards in the agri-environmental field, species loss in biodiversity conservation, fire management in forestry and droughts in rural water management. Risk has become an influential frame for the challenges faced by societies in dealing with nature (Jäger et al, 2001; Renn, 2006), associated with calls for citizens' participation in environmental decisions (Beierle and Cayford, 2002).

Renn proposes that inclusive risk governance needs to accommodate all three kinds of publics. The relevant kind of public depends on the specific risk situation. The state cooperates with the food industry on decisions made under certainty, that is, when the outcomes of different choices are known. In contrast, decisions made under risk need to include not only the state and industry but also all other members of the political community, such as NGOs and experts outside the state. Decisions made under ignorance or ambiguity, finally, need to incorporate quasi groups and non-organized voices in a reflective discourse. This can happen by way of citizen panels, consensus conferences or citizen advisory committees as means of making the required choices and normative evaluations socially visible.

Chapter 10 develops the contours of sustainable landscape governance that provide ecosystems services and extended biodiversity. O'Riordan looks at key parameters of such governance, in particular property rights, citing supporting evidence from the UK. Nevertheless, his proposal attains much wider relevance in the light of the 2006 Communication by the EC about landscape governance, which links the protection of ecosystem services to human well-being. This notion of an intimate interplay between human and ecological systems has gained worldwide acceptance through the Millennium Ecosystem Assessment. In addition, O'Riordan's emphasis on property rights connects with renewed attention to land rights in industrialized, developing and postcommunist countries (Geisler and Danecker, 2000; Richards, 2002; see also Chapter 4 and the Outlook). This is particularly interesting in the context of the UK, where the notion of private property retains a more mythical status than in other countries despite the assertion of public rights in the 1947 Town and Country Planning Act and 2000 Countryside and Rights of Way Act.

O'Riordan suggests that landscape governance in the UK incorporates increasingly diverse publics rooted in the state, political community and social visibility – and needs to become even more diverse in the future. The state is important for creating organizational and regulatory frameworks and contributing finances. The broader political community assumes a crucial role as it helps bring together state agencies, companies and NGOs for the provisioning of ecosystem services, as evidenced by initial experience with the new agency Natural England. In the future, O'Riordan argues, the political community will also serve as a foundation for new kinds of property rights that attend to individual *and* collective interests. And finally, the creation of social visibilities will encourage additional initiatives by market based actors to provide ecosystem services. A concrete example is the labels created to mark locally produced food, as also highlighted by Chapter 8.

The two chapters help us to develop visions for a sustainable future; visions informed by the empirical insights gained in the first three parts of the book. We recognize that the relations between public and private are a critical element of sustainable natural resource governance. We also understand that sustainable governance will not arise from public–private relations arranged in the form of a singular dichotomy, but incorporate multiple public, private and public–private hybrids. Moreover, sustainable governance will simultaneously encompass publics, privates and hybrids according to all three distinctions: between state and market, between political community and the more particularistic spheres of social life, and between the socially visible and personal.

What does this imply for efforts to promote sustainable natural resource governance? First, we need to enhance and create resource publics founded in the state, political community and social visibility. Second, we need to develop new forms of private, including those centred on the market, the more particularistic spheres of social life and the personal. And third, we need to creatively explore new forms of hybrids combining public and private elements according to all three distinctions. In other words, moving from government to governance will not be enough. We will need to attend to all three kinds of public–private relations identified in this book, including their public *and* their private elements.

REFERENCES

Beierle, T C and Cayford, J (2002) *Democracy in Practice: Public Participation in Environmental Decisions*, Resources for the Future, Washington, DC

Geisler, C and Danecker, G (eds) (2000) *Property and Values: Alternatives to Public and Private Ownership*, Island Press, Washington, DC

Hoffmann, S and Taylor, M R (eds) (2005) *Toward Safer Food: Perspectives on Risk and Priority Setting*, Resources for the Future, Washington, DC

Jäger, C C, Renn, O, Rosa, E A and Webler, T (eds) (2001) *Risk, Uncertainty and Rational Action*, Earthscan, London

Renn, O (2006) *Risk Governance: Coping with Uncertainty in a Complex World*, Earthscan, London

Richards, J F (ed) (2002) *Land, Property, and the Environment*, ICS Press, Oakland, CA

9

Food Safety Through Risk Analysis: The Role of Private and Public Governance

Ortwin Renn

INTRODUCTION

In an interdependent world, the risks faced by any individual, company, region or country depend not only on its own choices but also on those of others (IRGC, 2005). Nor do these entities face one risk at a time: they need to find strategies to deal with a series of interrelated risks that are often ill defined or outside of their control. In the context of terrorism, the risks faced by any given airline, for example, are affected by lax security at other carriers or airports. There are myriad settings that demonstrate similar interdependencies, including countless problems in computer and network security, corporate governance, investment in research, and vaccination. A good example of these interconnections is food. Food safety depends on the cooperation of actors belonging to a whole value chain. It starts with the producers, continues over to the food processing industry, the grocery stores, the consumers and the waste disposal services. At each step food risks are being addressed and managed. The main problem with food is the character of its hazards. Food is incorporated into human bodies and makes humans more vulnerable. In addition, the main risks here are biological in nature. Biological hazards are characterized by their dynamic growth pattern. The risks multiply over time. A small contamination at the beginning of the food chain can lead to disastrous results at the end of the chain. Because interdependence does not require proximity, the antecedents to disasters can be quite distinct and distant from the initial triggering event, as in the case of determining the necessary temperature for hygienization for animal feed in the case of BSE. Similarly, a disease in one region can readily spread to other areas with which it has contact, as was the case with the rapid spread of Severe Acute Respiratory Syndrome (SARS) from China to its trading partners.

In addition, due to the numerous interaction effects between and among food items and the potential for synergetic impacts with other lifestyle factors, most food risks show a high degree of scientific complexity as well as uncertainty. Identical diets often lead to different health consequences in different individuals and different cultural contexts. Furthermore, what is feared as a health threat is not only a matter of scientific inquiry but also a topic of cultural construction. In the context of risk we refer here to the term ambiguity.

The more uncertainties, ambiguities and interdependencies there are within a particular setting (be this a set of organizational units, companies, a geographical area, a number of countries and so on) and the more this setting's entities – or participants – decide not to invest in risk reduction while being able to contaminate other entities, the less incentive each potentially affected participant will have to invest in protection. At the same time, however, each participant would have been better off had all the other participants invested in risk reducing measures. In other words, weak links may lead to suboptimal behaviour by everyone.[1] This is the main argument against a purely market driven approach.

THE NEED FOR PUBLIC–PRIVATE PARTNERSHIPS

For situations in which participants are reluctant to adopt protective measures to reduce the chances of catastrophic losses due to the possibility of contamination from weak links in the system, a solution might be found in public–private partnerships. This is particularly true if the risks to be dealt with are associated with competing interpretations (ambiguities) as to what type of cooperation is required between different epistemic communities as well as risk management agencies in order to deal with various knowledge and competing value claims. Public–private partnerships also provide an interesting alternative in cases in which perceptions differ strongly and external effects are to be expected.

One way to structure such a partnership is to have government standards and regulations coupled with third party inspections and insurance to enforce these measures. Such a management based regulatory strategy will not only encourage the addressees of the regulation, often the corporate sector, to reduce their risks (from e.g. accidents and disasters), but also equally shift the locus of decision making from the government regulatory authority to private companies and civil society actors, who are thus required to do their own planning as to how they will meet a set of standards or regulations (Coglianese and Lazer, 2003). This, in turn, can enable companies to choose those means and measures that are most suitable for the purpose within their specific environment and may eventually lead to a superior allocation of resources compared to more top-down forms of regulation. The combination of third party inspections in conjunction with private insurance is consequently a powerful combination of public oversight and market mechanisms that can convince many companies of the advantages of implementing the necessary measures to make their plants safer and encourage the remaining ones to comply with the regulation to avoid being caught and prosecuted.

Highly interdependent risks that can lead to stochastic contamination of third parties pose a specific challenge for food safety management (i.e. the management of multiple biological and chemical risks). Due to the often particularly decentralized nature of decision making in the food chain, a well balanced mix of consensual (e.g. agreements and standards along the value chain, including regulators and consumers), coercive (e.g. government regulation) and incentive based (e.g. certificates or labels) strategies is necessary to deal with such risk problems. Again these strategies can be best developed in close – international and transnational – cooperation between the public and the private sectors.

THE EMERGENCE OF INCLUSIVE GOVERNANCE

Public–private partnerships are reliant on cooperative models between political, economic and civil society actors (so-called stakeholders). In the context of this chapter, stakeholders are defined as socially organized groups that are or will be affected by the outcome of the event or the activity from which the risk originates and/or by the risk management options taken to counter the risk. Involving stakeholders is not enough, however. Other groups – including the media, cultural elites and opinion leaders, the nonorganized *affected* public and the nonorganized *observing* public – all have a role to play in risk governance.

In accordance with the terminology suggested in the Introduction to this volume, the dualism between private (market) and public (government) will be enriched by two additional hybrid actors: civil society groups such as NGOs and different types of quasi groups within the public. Those quasi groups could be affected groups such as the consumers or the neighbours of a food processing plant or observing groups such as local opinion leaders or the many contributors to 'public opinion' whose views are made public by surveys and opinion polls. Organized groups with a specific interest in food issues are partially demanding to be involved in risk governance, yet they have something to contribute to improved risk management. NGOs can insert their specific knowledge about risks that matter to them and can contribute to the evaluation of risks based on their sets of preferences and values. The nonorganized quasi public groups have the power to respond to positively or negatively perceived signals from risk management agencies and to initiate actions such as consumer boycotts.

Each decision making process has two major aspects: what and whom to include, on the one hand, and what and how to select (closure), on the other (Hajer and Wagenaar, 2003; Stirling, 2004). *Inclusion* and *selection* are therefore the two essential parts of any decision or policy making activity. Classic decision analysis offers formal methods for generating options and evaluating these options against a set of predefined criteria. With the advent of new participatory methods, the two issues of inclusion and selection have become more complex and sophisticated than purported in these conventional methods.

Food regulation should aim at the goal of inclusive governance, in particular with respect to global and systemic risks. First and foremost, this means that the major actors in risk decision making – i.e. political, business, scientific and civil society players (organized and nonorganized) – should jointly engage in the process of framing the problem, generating options, evaluating options and coming to a joint conclusion. This has also been the main recommendation of the EU White Paper on European Governance (EC, 2001). This document endorses transparency and accountability through formal consultation with multiple actors as a means for the EU to address the various frames of governance issues and to identify culture sensitive responses to common challenges and problems. Similar to the actors determining the governance of a political union, it is obvious that the actors participating in risk related decision making are guided by particular interests that derive not only from the fact that some of them are risk producers – whereas others are exposed to it – but equally from their individual institutional rationale and perspective. Such vested interests require specific consideration and measures to make them transparent and, if possible, reconciled. Inclusive governance, as it relates to the inclusion part of decision making, requires that (Trustnet, 1999; Webler, 1999; Wynne, 2002):

- there has been a major attempt to involve representatives of all four actor groups (if appropriate);
- there has been a major attempt to empower all actors to participate actively and constructively in the discourse;
- there has been a major attempt to codesign the framing of the (risk) problem or the issue in a dialogue with these different groups;
- there has been a major attempt to generate a common understanding of the magnitude of the risk (based on the expertise of all participants) and the potential risk management options as well as to include a plurality of options that represent the different interests and values of all parties involved;
- there has been a major effort to conduct a forum for decision making that provides equal and fair opportunities for all parties to voice their opinion and to express their preferences;
- there has been a clear connection between the participatory bodies of decision making and the political implementation level.

If these conditions are met, evidence shows that, along with developing faith in their own competence, actors use the opportunity and start to trust each other and have confidence in the process of risk management (Kasperson et al, 1999; Beierle and Cayford, 2002; Viklund, 2002). This is particularly true for the local level at which the participants are familiar with each other and have more immediate access to the issue (Petts, 1997). Reaching consensus and building trust on highly complex and transversal subjects such as global change, however, is much more difficult. Therefore, being inclusive and open to social groups does not guarantee constructive cooperation by those who are invited to participate. Some actors may reject the framing of the issue and choose to withdraw. Others may benefit from the collapse of an inclusive governance process. It is essential to monitor these processes and make sure that particular interests do not dominate the deliberations and that rules can be established and jointly approved to prevent destructive strategizing.

Inclusive governance also needs to address the second part of the decision making process, that is, reaching closure on a set of options that are selected for further consideration, while others are rejected. *Closure* does not mean having the final word on a development, a risk reduction plan or a regulation. Rather, it represents the product of a deliberation, that is, the agreement that the participants reached. The problem is that the more actors, viewpoints, interests and values are included and thus represented in an arena, the more difficult it is to reach either a consensus or some other kind of joint agreement. Hence, a second set of criteria is needed to evaluate the process by which closure of debates (be they final or temporary) is brought forth as well as the quality of the decision or recommendation that is generated through the closure procedure.

The first aspect, the quality of the closure process itself, can be subdivided into the following dimensions (Webler, 1995; Wisdon and Willis, 2004):

- Have all arguments been properly treated? Have all truth claims been fairly and accurately tested against commonly agreed standards of validation?
- Has all the relevant evidence been collected and processed in accordance with current state-of-the-art knowledge?
- Was systematic, experiential and practical knowledge and expertise adequately included and processed?
- Were all interests and values considered and was there a major effort to come up with fair and balanced solutions?
- Were all normative judgements made explicit and thoroughly explained? Were normative statements derived from accepted ethical principles or legally prescribed norms?
- Were all efforts undertaken to preserve plurality of lifestyles and individual freedom and to restrict the realm of collectively binding decisions to those areas in which binding rules and norms are essential and necessary to produce the desired outcome?

Turning to the issues of outcome, additional criteria need to be addressed that have long been discussed in political science and governance literature (Dryzek, 1994; Rhodes, 1997): effectiveness, efficiency, accountability, legitimacy, fairness, transparency, acceptance by the public and ethical acceptability.

What are the advantages of inclusive governance approaches?

- More inclusive procedures enrich the generation of options and perspectives and are therefore more responsive to the complexity, uncertainty and ambiguity of the risk phenomena being assessed.

- More rational closure processes provide fairer and socially and culturally more adaptive and balanced judgements.
- The combination of voluntary and regulatory actions in the form of public–private partnerships can be improved through early and constructive involvement procedures.
- Inclusive governance provides a middle path between the private (neoliberal) market concept and the (neosocialist) government concept of strict regulation.
- The outcomes derived from these procedures are of higher quality in terms of effectiveness, efficiency, legitimacy, fairness, transparency, public acceptance and ethical acceptability than the outcomes of conventional decision making procedures.

The potential benefits resulting from stakeholder and public involvement, however, depend on the quality of the participation process. It is not sufficient to gather all interested parties around a table and merely hope for the catharsis effect to emerge spontaneously. In particular, it is essential to treat the time and efforts of the participating actors as spare resources that should be handled with care and respect (Chess et al, 1998). The participation process should be designed so that the various actors are encouraged to contribute to the process in those areas in which they feel they are competent and can offer something to improve the quality of the final product.

A RISK MANAGEMENT AND PARTICIPATION PROPOSAL FOR FOOD SAFETY

With respect to food risk and risk in general, it helps to distinguish among risk situations on the basis of the three characteristics of complexity, uncertainty and ambiguity (Renn, 2004; IRGC, 2005). One can construct different variations in the composition of complexity, uncertainty and ambiguity. If all three characteristics are low in intensity, risks are obvious and simple. A well-known natural poison, for example, has highly complex but rather certain and unambiguous risks, which are a particular challenge to scientists as they need to reveal the causal chain between a known agent and its health consequences. For instance, a known carcinogenic substance might qualify for this category. If a thorough risk assessment cannot resolve the complexities involved in the causal chain, our knowledge about the potential threat becomes blurred and uncertain. In such a case there would be evidence for the possibility of harm, but neither the extent nor the probability of such harm is clearly known to science. The risk of Creutzfeldt-Jacob disease caused by the consumption of BSE-infected beef could be cited as an example of such an uncertain situation. Lastly, the risk may be judged differently depending on social preferences, cultural values and historical traditions. For example, the risk caused by the consumption of cholesterol in food is judged to be highly problematic by American physicians, while most European physicians regard this risk as less relevant. Nevertheless, both sides base their arguments on the exact same studies and investigations. This difference in interpreting results can be labelled ambiguity.

More specifically, using the distinction of complexity, uncertainty and ambiguity, one can compose four prototypes of risk situations that are in need of different assessment and management strategies.

Simple risk problems

This class of risk problems requires hardly any deviation from traditional decision making. Data are provided by statistical analysis, goals are determined by law or statutory requirements, and the role of risk management is to ensure that all risk reduction measures are implemented and enforced. Traditional risk–risk comparisons (or risk–risk tradeoffs), risk benefit analysis and cost effectiveness studies are the instruments of choice for finding the most appropriate risk reduction measures. Additionally, risk managers can rely on best practice and, in cases of low impact, on trial and error. It should be noted, however, that simple risks should not be equated with small or negligible risks. The major issues here are that the potential negative consequences are obvious, the values applied noncontroversial and the remaining uncertainties low. Examples are known food and health risks with worldwide experience in the validity of observed thresholds. A sophisticated approach to involving all potentially affected parties is not necessary in making judgements about simple risk problems. Most actors would not even seek to participate, since the expected results are more or less obvious. In terms of cooperative strategies, an *instrumental discourse* among agency staff, directly affected groups (such as product or activity providers and immediately exposed individuals) and enforcement personnel is advisable. One should be aware, however, that risks that appear simple often turn out to be more complex, uncertain or ambiguous than originally assessed. It is therefore essential to revisit these risks regularly and monitor the outcomes carefully.

Complex risk problems

Complexity refers to the difficulty of identifying and quantifying causal links between a multitude of potential causal agents and specific observed effects. The nature of this difficulty may be traced back to interactive effects among these agents (synergism and antagonisms), long delay periods between cause and effect, interindividual variation, intervening variables and others. Complex risk problems are often associated with major scientific dissent about complex dose effect relationships or the alleged effectiveness of measures to decrease vulnerabilities (for complexity refers to both the risk agent and its causal connections as well as the risk absorbing system and its vulnerabilities). The objective for resolving complexity is to receive a complete and balanced set of risk and concern assessment results that fall within the legitimate range of plural truth claims. The proper handling of complexity in risk appraisal and risk management requires transparency regarding the subjective judgements and the inclusion of knowledge elements that have shaped the parameters on both sides of the cost–benefit equation.

Resolving complexity necessitates a discursive procedure during the appraisal phase with a direct link to the tolerability and acceptability judgement and risk management. Input for handling complexity could be provided by *epistemological discourse* aimed at finding the best estimates for characterizing the risks under consideration. This discourse should be inspired by different science camps and the participation of experts and knowledge carriers. They may come from academia, government, industry or civil society but their justification for participation is their claim to bring new or additional knowledge to the negotiating table. The goal is to resolve cognitive conflicts. Exercises such as Delphi, Group Delphi and consensus workshops would be most advisable to serve the goals of an epistemological discourse (Webler et al, 1991; Gregory et al, 2001).

Risk problems due to high unresolved uncertainty

Uncertainty is different from complexity but often results from an incomplete or inadequate reduction of complexity in modelling cause effect chains. Whether the world is inherently uncertain is a philosophical question that I will not pursue here. It is essential to acknowledge in the context of risk assessment that human knowledge is always incomplete and selective and thus contingent on uncertain assumptions, assertions and predictions (Functowicz and Ravetz, 1992; Laudan, 1996; Bruijn and ten Heuvelhof, 1999). Although there is no consensus in the literature about the best means of disaggregating uncertainties, the following categories appear to be an appropriate means of distinguishing the key components of uncertainty (cf van Asselt, 2000):

- target variability (based on the differing vulnerability of targets);
- systematic and random error in modelling (based on extrapolations from animals to humans or from large doses to small doses, statistical inferential applications and so on);
- indeterminacy or genuine stochastic effects (variation of effects due to random events, in special cases congruent with statistical handling of random errors);

- system boundaries (uncertainties stemming from restricted models and the need for focusing on a limited amount of variables and parameters);
- ignorance or nonknowledge (uncertainties derived from lack or absence of knowledge).

The first two components of uncertainty qualify as epistemic uncertainty and therefore can be reduced by improving the existing knowledge and by advancing the present modelling tools. The last three components are genuine uncertainty components (random events) and thus can be characterized to some extent using statistical distribution techniques but cannot be reduced to finite probabilities. If there is a high degree of random uncertainty, risk management needs to incorporate hazard criteria – which are comparatively easy to determine and include aspects such as reversibility, persistence and ubiquity – and select management options that empower society to deal with even the worst case scenarios (such as containing food contaminants, close monitoring of risk bearing activities, and securing reversibility of decisions in case risks turn out to be higher than expected). The management of risks characterized by multiple and high uncertainties should be guided by the *precautionary approach*. Since high, unresolved uncertainty implies that the (true) dimensions of the risks are not (yet) known, one should pursue a cautious strategy that allows learning by restricted errors. The main management philosophy for this risk class is to allow small steps in implementation (containment approach) that enable risk managers to stop or even reverse the process as new knowledge is produced or the negative side effects become visible. The primary thrust of precaution is to avoid irreversibility (Klinke and Renn, 2002).[2]

High uncertainties pose special challenges for stakeholder involvement. How can one judge the severity of a situation when the potential damage and its probability are unknown or highly uncertain? In this dilemma, risk managers are well advised to include the main stakeholders in the evaluation process and ask them to find a consensus on the extra margin of safety in which they would be willing to invest in exchange for avoiding potentially catastrophic consequences. This type of deliberation, called *reflective discourse*, relies on collective reflection on balancing the possibilities for overprotection and a lack thereof. If too much protection is sought, innovations may be prevented or stalled; if we offer too little protection, society may experience unpleasant surprises. The classic question of 'how safe is safe enough?' is replaced by the question of 'how much uncertainty and ignorance are the main actors willing to accept in exchange for a given benefit?'. Policy makers, representatives of major stakeholder groups and scientists are advised to take part in this type of discourse. In the terminology of the Introduction, the cooperation between markets and governments needs to be enhanced by a third party, in this case the potential victims of risks. For a collective representation of potential victims including future generations, organized stakeholder groups are probably best suited. They represent special interests and value formations within the civil society sector. The reflective discourse can take different forms: round tables, open-space forums, negotiated rule-making exercises, mediation or mixed advisory committees including scientists and stakeholders (Amy, 1983; Perrit, 1986; Rowe and Frewer, 2000).

Risk problems due to high ambiguity

(Interpretative and normative) ambiguity is the last term in this context. Whereas uncertainty refers to a lack of clarity over the scientific or technical basis for decision making, (interpretative and normative) ambiguity is a result of divergent or contested perspectives on the justification, severity or wider 'meanings' associated with a given threat (Stirling, 2003). The term *ambiguity* may be misleading because its connotations are different in everyday speech.[3] In relation to risk governance it is understood as 'giving rise to several meaningful and legitimate interpretations of accepted risk assessments results'. It can be divided into *interpretative ambiguity* (different interpretations of an identical assessment result, for example as an adverse or advantageous effect) and *normative ambiguity* (different concepts of what can be regarded as tolerable referring, for example, to ethics, quality of life parameters, distribution of risks and benefits and so on). A condition of ambiguity emerges where the problem lies in agreeing on the appropriate values, priorities, assumptions or boundaries to be applied to the definition of possible outcomes. If major ambiguities are associated with a risk problem, it is not enough to demonstrate that risk regulators are open to public concerns and address the issues that many people wish them to take care of. In these cases, the process of risk evaluation needs to be open to public input and new forms of deliberation. This starts with revisiting the question of proper framing. Is the issue really a risk problem or is it in fact an issue of lifestyle and future vision? The aim is to find consensus on the dimensions of ambiguity that need to be addressed in comparing risks and benefits and balancing the pros and cons.

High ambiguities require the most inclusive strategy for participation since not only directly affected groups but also those indirectly affected have something to contribute to this debate. Resolving ambiguities in risk debates requires a *participative discourse*, a platform where competing arguments, beliefs and values are openly discussed. This includes the more general (personalized) public referred to in the Introduction as the third dimension of the public dimension, including the media and quasi groups such as the consumers. The opportunity for resolving these conflicting expectations lies in the process of identifying common values, defining options that allow people to live their own vision of a 'good life' without compromising the vision of others, to find equitable and just distribution rules when it comes to common resources and to activate institutional means for reaching common welfare so that the many can reap the collective benefits instead of the few (coping with the classic commoners' dilemma).[4] Available sets of deliberative processes include citizen panels, citizen juries, consensus conferences, ombudspersons, citizen advisory commissions and similar participatory instruments (Dienel, 1989; Fiorino, 1990; Armour, 1995; Durant and Joss, 1995; Applegate, 1998).

Managing the discourse allocation

Categorizing risks according to the quality and nature of available information on risk may, of course, be contested among the stakeholders. Who decides whether a risk issue can be categorized as simple, complex, uncertain or ambiguous? It is possible that no consensus may be reached as to where to locate a specific risk. The best means to deal with this conflict is to provide for stakeholder involvement when allocating the different risks into these four categories. Allocating risks to the four categories needs to be done before the commencement of assessment procedures. Over the course of further analysis of risks and concerns the categorization may change, since new data and information are being collected that may necessitate reordering the risk. It seems prudent to have a screening board perform this challenging task. This board should consist of members from the sciences (natural and social), regulators and stakeholders. The type of discourse required for this task is called *design discourse.* It is aimed at selecting the appropriate risk assessment policy, defining priorities in handling risks, organizing the appropriate involvement procedures and specifying the conditions under which the further steps of the risk handling process will be conducted.

Figure 9.1 provides an overview of the various requirements for participation and stakeholder involvement for the four classes of risk problems and the design discourse. As is the case with all classifications, this scheme shows an extremely simplified picture of the involvement process and has been criticized for being too rigid in its linking of risk characteristics (complexity, uncertainty and ambiguity) and specific forms of discourse and dialogue (van Asselt, 2005). In addition to the generic distinctions shown in Figure 9.1, it may be wise to distinguish, for instance, between participatory processes based on risk agent or risk absorbing issues. To conclude these caveats, the purpose of this scheme is to provide general orientation and explain a generic distinction between ideal cases rather than to offer a strict recipe for participation.

CONCLUSIONS

This chapter first discussed a comprehensive approach to public–private partnerships in food risk handling. The main idea was to use the distinction of the three different types of publics made in the Introduction to this book and assign to each of them a specific role based on the characteristics of risk. The chapter then addressed the three conditions of risk management: complexity,

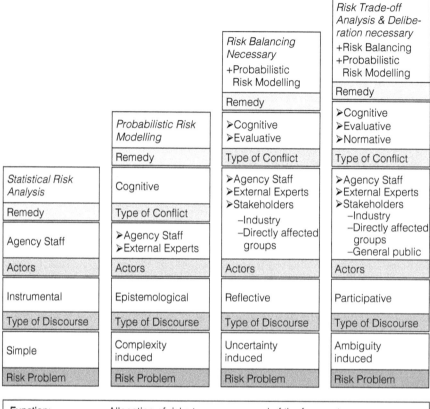

Figure 9.1   *The risk management escalator and stakeholder involvement (from simple via complex and uncertain to ambiguous phenomena)*

Source: Adapted from IRGC (2005), p53

uncertainty and ambiguity. What lessons can be drawn when linking these challenges to the application of public–private partnerships? It may be helpful in this respect to resort to a differentiation that Resnik (2003) has proposed:

- Decisions under certainty – the outcomes of different choices are known. Under these conditions we only need cooperation between governments and corporations.
- Decisions under risk – probabilities can be assigned to the outcomes of different choices. Under these conditions we need to include the major stakeholders in the decision making process, thus including the second type of public.

- Decisions under ignorance – it is not possible to assign probabilities to the outcomes of different choices. Under this condition we also need to include quasi groups and nonorganized public voices. These voices can be heard through methods such as citizen panels, consensus conferences or citizen advisory committees.

This distinction does, however, entail a major problem: looking only to the uncertainties does not provide risk managers with a clue to setting priorities for risk reduction. How can one judge the severity of a situation when the potential damage and its probability are unknown or highly uncertain? In this dilemma, risk managers are well advised to resort to deliberative methods in the entire risk governance process. In this chapter we have coined this type of deliberation *reflective discourse* since it rests on a collective reflection about balancing the possibilities for overprotection and a lack thereof, based on uncertain data and ignorance.

The first question for which deliberation is necessary relates to the task of screening. Who decides whether a risk is complex, uncertain or ambiguous? Further questions arise in later processes of the risk governance framework. How should one exercise precaution if indeed there is a consensus that a risk is characterized by high uncertainty and ambiguity? What management options are best suited to avoid irreversibilities, and what discursive methods are advisable in situations of high ambiguity?

There are no substantive solutions to these questions. The classification suggested here may help to assign risk to different classes of concern, but these do not offer any foolproof recipes or automatic rules. These questions demand deliberative methods of procedures that act as catalysts in the debate about what society regards as acceptable and intolerable. Deliberation implies inclusion and selection. It is important to include representatives of politics, industry, civil society and the public at large. The new angle is on integration, not specialization. This is also true for selecting the proper frame for subject areas. Often the debate is not about risks, but about the desirability of the envisioned benefits. Often the debate is about the choice of technology, not the acceptability of risks. This needs to be clarified in the framing phase using discursive methods of deliberation. With respect to selection it is crucial to find transparent and consensual means of generating, evaluating and choosing options for risk prevention, reduction or mitigation. Methods for conducting meaningful and effective deliberation are available and have been tested all around the world (Stern and Fineberg, 1996; Beierle and Cayford, 2002; Mitchell et al, 2006). It is up to the risk management agencies to put them into practice.

NOTES

1   A more formal game theoretic treatment of this problem has been published in Kunreuther and Heal (2003).

2   The link between precaution and irreversibility was also mentioned in the latest report on risk management by the UK Treasury Department (UK Treasury Department, 2004).

3   With respect to risk and decision making, the term ambiguity has been used with various meanings. Some analysts refer to ambiguity as the conflicting goals of participants in the process (Skinner, 1999), others use the term ambiguity to refer to the inability to estimate probabilities of an event (Gosh and Ray, 1997; Ho et al, 2002; Stirling, 2003). In the context of the present framework, ambiguity denotes the variability in interpretation and normative implications with respect to accepted evidence.

4   For a more detailed analysis of participatory methods for reaching consensus refer to Barber (1984), Webler (1999) or Jaeger et al (2001).

References

Amy, D J (1983) 'Environmental mediation: An alternative approach to policy stalemates', *Policy Sciences*, vol 15, pp345–365

Applegate, J (1998) 'Beyond the usual suspects: The use of citizens advisory boards in environmental decisionmaking', *Indiana Law Journal*, vol 73, p903

Armour, A (1995) 'The citizen's jury model of public participation' in Renn, O, Webler, T and Wiedemann, P (eds) *Fairness and Competence in Citizen Participation: Evaluating New Models for Environmental Discourse*, Kluwer, Dordrecht and Boston, pp175–188

Barber, B (1984) *Strong Democracy: Participatory Politics for a New Age*, University of California Press, Berkeley, CA

Beierle, T C and Cayford, J (2002) *Democracy in Practice: Public Participation in Environmental Decisions*, Resources for the Future, Washington, DC

Bruijn J A and ten Heuvelhof, E F (1999) 'Scientific expertise in complex decision-making processes', *Science and Public Policy*, vol 26, no 3, pp151–161

Chess, C, Dietz, T and Shannon, M (1998) 'Who should deliberate when?', *Human Ecology Review*, vol 5, no 1, pp60–68

Coglianese, C and Lazer, D (2003) 'Management-based regulation: Prescribing private management to achieve public goals', *Law and Society*, vol 37, pp691–730

Dienel, P C (1989) 'Contributing to social decision methodology: Citizen reports on technological projects' in Vlek, C and Cvetkovich, G (eds) *Social Decision Methodology for Technological Projects*, Kluwer, Dordrecht and Boston, pp133–151

Dryzek, J S (1994) *Discursive Democracy: Politics, Policy, and Political Science*, Cambridge University Press, Cambridge

Durant, J and Joss, S (1995) *Public Participation in Science*, Science Museum, London

EC (European Commission) (2001) *European Governance: A White Paper*, EC, Brussels

Fiorino, D J (1990) 'Citizen participation and environmental risk: A survey of institutional mechanisms', *Science, Technology, & Human Values*, vol 15, no 2, pp226–243

Functowicz, S O and Ravetz, J R (1992) 'Three types of risk assessment and the emergence of post-normal science' in Krimsky, S and Golding, D (eds) *Social Theories of Risk*, Praeger, Westport and London, pp251–273

Gosh, D and Ray, M R (1997) 'Risk, ambiguity and decision choice: Some additional evidence', *Decision Sciences*, vol 28, no 1, pp81–104

Gregory, R, McDaniels, T and Fields, D (2001) 'Decision aiding, not dispute resolution: A new perspective for environmental negotiation', *Journal of Policy Analysis and Management*, vol 20, no 3, pp415–432

Hajer, M and Wagenaar, H (2003) *Deliberative Policy Analysis: Understanding Governance in the Network Society*, Cambridge University Press, Boston

Ho, J L L, Keller, R and Keltyka, P (2002) 'Effects of probabilistic and outcome ambiguity on managerial choices', *Journal of Risk and Uncertainty*, vol 24, no 1, pp47–74

IRGC (International Risk Governance Council) (2005) *Risk Governance: Towards an Integrative Approach*, White Paper No 1, IRGC, Geneva

Jaeger, C, Renn, O, Rosa, E and Webler, T (2001) *Risk, Uncertainty and Rational Action*, Earthscan, London

Kasperson, R E, Golding, D and Kasperson, J X (1999) 'Risk, trust and democratic theory' in Cvetkovich, G and Löfstedt, R (eds) *Social Trust and the Management of Risk*, Earthscan, London, pp22–41

Klinke, A and Renn, O (2002) 'A new approach to risk evaluation and management: Risk-based, precaution-based and discourse-based management', *Risk Analysis*, vol 22, no 6, pp1071–1094

Kunreuther, H and Heal, G (2003) 'Interdependent security', *Journal of Risk and Uncertainty*, vol 26, no 2/3, pp231–249

Laudan, L (1996) 'The pseudo-science of science? The demise of the demarcation problem' in Laudan, L (ed) *Beyond Positivism and Relativism: Theory, Method and Evidence*, Westview Press, Boulder, pp166–192

Mitchell, R B, Clark, W C, Cash, D W and Dickson, N M (2006) *Global Environmental Assessments: Information and Influence*, MIT Press, Cambridge, MA

Perritt, H H (1986) 'Negotiated rulemaking in practice', *Journal of Policy Analysis and Management*, vol 5, pp482–495

Petts, J (1997) 'The public-expert interface in local waste management decisions: Expertise, credibility, and process', *Public Understanding of Science*, vol 6, no 4, pp359–381

Resnik, D (2003) 'Is the precautionary principle unscientific?', *Studies in History and Philosophy of Biological and Biomedical Sciences*, vol 34, pp329–344

Renn, O (2004) 'The challenge of integrating deliberation and expertise: Participation and discourse in risk management' in MacDaniels, T L and Small, M J (eds) *Risk Analysis and Society: An Interdisciplinary Characterization of the Field*, Cambridge University Press, Cambridge, pp289–366

Rhodes, R A W (1997) *Understanding Governance: Policy Networks, Governance, Reflexivity and Accountability*, Open University Press, Buckingham

Rowe, G and Frewer, L (2000) 'Public participation methods: An evaluative review of the literature', *Science, Technology and Human Values*, vol 25, pp3–29

Skinner, D (1999) *Introduction to Decision Analysis*, Second edition, Probabilistic Publishers, London

Stern, P C and Fineberg, V (1996) *Understanding Risk: Informing Decisions in a Democratic Society*, National Research Council, Committee on Risk Characterization, National Academy Press, Washington, DC

Stirling, A (2003) 'Risk, uncertainty and precaution: Some instrumental implications from the social sciences' in Berkhout, F, Leach, M and Scoones, I (eds) *Negotiating Change*, Edward Elgar, London, pp33–76

Stirling, A (2004) 'Opening up or closing down: Analysis, participation and power in the social appraisal of technology' in Leach, M, Scoones, I and Wynne, B (eds) *Science and Citizens: Globalization and the Challenge of Engagement*, Zed, London, pp218–231

Trustnet (1999) *A New Perspective on Risk Governance*, EU, Paris, www.trustnet governance .com (accessed 8 November 2005)

UK Treasury Department (2004) *Managing Risks to the Public: Appraisal Guidance*, Draft for Consultation, HM Treasury Press, London, www.hm-treasury.gov.uk (accessed 8 November 2005)

van Asselt, M B A (2000) *Perspectives on Uncertainty and Risk*, Kluwer, Dordrecht and Boston

van Asselt, M B A (2005) 'The complex significance of uncertainty in a risk area', *International Journal of Risk Assessment and Management*, vol 5, no 2/3/4, pp125–158

Viklund, M (2002) *Risk Policy: Trust, Risk Perception and Attitudes*, Stockholm School of Economics, Stockholm

Webler, T (1995) 'Right discourse in citizen participation. An evaluative yardstick' in Renn, O, Webler, T and Wiedemann, P (eds) *Fairness and Competence in Citizen Participation: Evaluating New Models for Environmental Discourse*, Kluwer, Dordrecht and Boston, pp35–86

Webler, T (1999) 'The craft and theory of public participation: A dialectical process', *Risk Research*, vol 2, no 1, pp55–71

Webler, T, Levine, D, Rakel, H and Renn, O (1991) 'The Group Delphi: A novel attempt at reducing uncertainty', *Technological Forecasting and Social Change*, vol 39, pp253–263

Wisdon, J and Willis, R (2004) *See-Through Science. Why Public Engagement Needs to Move Upstream*, DEMOS, London

Wynne, B (2002) 'Risk and environment as legitimatory discourses of technology: reflexivity inside out?', *Current Sociology*, vol 50, no 30, pp459–477

10

Connecting Ecosystem Services to Biodiversity: Designing Sustainable Landscapes by Linking the Public and Private Sectors in Common Cause

Tim O'Riordan

KEY SUMMARY

Ecosystem services are the myriad of natural functions that maintain the self-organizing services of planet Earth. Without them, the globe would revert to the lifeless mix of carbon dioxide, methane and unbearable heat that would otherwise pervade an orb lying between Venus and Mars in the solar planets (see Lovelock, 2006).

Nowadays, ecosystem services are beginning to be valued for what they do to maintain life and absorb, buffer or otherwise offset costly replacements of their functions by artificial means. More to the point, these services are also seen as miraculous, spiritual manifestations of original planetary processes that reflect a mysterious force that, in part, gives humans life and consciousness.

The EU has followed the example of the Millennium Ecosystem Assessment and given ecosystem services provision formal significance in the maintenance and extension of biodiversity. In a communication (EC, 2006) the EC has linked the protection of these services to human well-being, recognizing that these functions provide a barometer for human survival.

This recognition in turn has led to a reassessment of how biodiversity may be enhanced in a climate changed world, where thresholds of tolerance for species survival could be surpassed. Study after study by the United Nations Environment Programme and the World Conservation Monitoring Centre have shown that all manner of species life is being lost, stressed or seriously threatened.[1]

For both ecosystem services to be enhanced and biodiversity to be extended, it will be necessary to cross the line between public and private property rights. This message is the essence of this entire volume. New forms of cooperation and funding will be required, involving complexes of organizations and governing forms. This chapter argues for the inevitable emergence of a joint property right for landowners, especially farmers, that transcends the conventions of the private ownership responsibility in favour of a sustainable landscape covenant. This will lock landowners into a common endeavour, acting as wards for the maintenance of biodiversity and associated ecosystem services.

The chapter reflects the public–private hybrid approach taken in the Introduction to this volume. Increasingly, the assumed dichotomy between a state centred public regulatory or custodial role and a market driven private responsibility has become so blurred as to lose its distinctiveness. For truly sustainable landscapes there can be no pure 'private' role as most natural resource land managers are receivers of one form or another of state subsidy. All of these subsidies are tied to a public centred responsibility. This may be ecological in the form of maintaining a water resource, absorbing floods or protecting soils from erosion. It may be aesthetic in the manner of reality and respecting science theory and public enjoyment via recreational or educational access. Or it may be social in that healthy landscapes encourage healthy minds, and all are a source of healthy living (see Pretty, 2004). So the 'hybrid' perspective offers an opportunity to reassess the mutual obligation that binds the subsidized owner to the public interest in creating and maintaining a sustainable landscape. In this last sense, Penker's notion of a 'socially visible' covenant to landscape care is also relevant (see Chapter 4).

SUSTAINABLE LANDSCAPE STEWARDSHIP

In 1987, the EU created the designation of environmentally sensitive areas (ESAs). These were landscape units for practising agriculture and associated land use that were to be safeguarded by special incentive payments linking farm to neighbouring farm, administered by a project officer with power to negotiate and cajole, and aimed at maintaining the intrinsic features of ecosystem functioning and heritage features of special landscapes. The environmentally sensitive area was an EU wide designation though many member states supplemented the basic provisions of landscape based payments with additional schemes of their own. Chapters 4 and 5 are relevant in addressing this aspect of supportive funding for a longer term stewardship covenant for the landscape.

Penker provides a valuable matrix of public–private property rights in her useful chapter on this topic (Chapter 4). She notes that there are many motivations for protecting sustainable landscapes – cultural, historical, economic (for tourism and food identity) and spiritual. Increasingly landscapes are being used as 'labels' for marketing specific services. Notable here are specialized foods, imaginable leisure usage and cultural-historical identity. There may even be an educational element for a sustainable landscape – namely how such a notion can be put into effective practice. Penker also points out a hybrid mix of payment arrangements, ranging from EU wide to local. These tend to direct management in certain directions and may impose management regimes (e.g. noncompliance or landscape care covenants) to ensure appropriate and empathetic management practice.

The outcome following the introduction of the ESAs into the member states was patchy in terms of effective compliance. The UK government embraced the notion as it was deemed politically expedient to start paying farmers positively to manage the land for biodiversity and public enjoyment, given the hostility to the Common Agricultural Policy at the time. The Germans, by contrast, regarded the establishment of a federally imposed regulation over private property rights as a matter for the Länder, and hence stalled the designation of all protected landscape designations (Stoll-Kleemann, 2001).

Nevertheless, the concept of a whole landscape basis for farm by farm management had taken official hold. The strengths of the arrangement lay in its EU wide designation, its mix of ecology, heritage and public access – enjoyment, and its willingness to encourage landowners and tenants to cooperate across private property boundaries. The advent of the project officer was a particularly important development. This individual had powers and an element of freedom to negotiate a range of management agreements so that landowners could cooperate and effectively maintain ecosystem services. This is a particularly important aspect of the public–private reformulation inherent in this volume of essays. The application of any notion of a 'whole' landscape needs both some sort of visual aid to enable landowners to see just where their part of the jigsaw fits in, and a catalyst figure who can work the motivations and the underlying enthusiasms in almost every landowner in pride over the property.

The EU Habitats Directive extended this basic notion to the special area for conservation (SAC) under its Habitats Directive of 1992. Like the ESA, the SAC is also an EU based scheme, set in member state biodiversity managing arrangements that embraced the notion of integral ecosystem maintenance. The SAC was part of an EU wide set of linked designations for species and habitats aimed at ensuring the long-term survival of critical European wildlife. As for the environmentally sensitive areas, the special area of conservation has robust protection, management agreements that cross private property boundaries, along with site managers with powers to encourage cross boundary compliance.

In its communication (EC, 2006), the Commission admits that the emergence of the SAC designation has not stopped the loss of biodiversity throughout the Union. Indeed the net losses are still rising. Despite the aspiration for a halt to this loss by 2010, it is very unlikely that this will occur without the kind of new organizational initiative of public–private blending promoted by this volume.

This new initiative comes at a time when official protected area status in the EU is still lamentably failing (see O'Riordan et al, 2002). Few key sites have complete protection; land managers can alter designated protective practices with little likelihood of serious penalty, and at least a third of possible habitats are not yet properly identified as formerly protected sites. The general policy of connecting fundamental biodiversity as intrinsic to any traditional interpretation of an economic, investment led, developmental perspective is too demanding for innovation/competition minded national governments to swallow. Thus, there may be a labelling of protected areas, giving the appearance of safeguard. But there is no delivery mechanism for converting this to sustainable and fully functioning landscapes based on ecosystem function, establishing first initiatives for food sales and ecotourism related activities.

The notion of *landscape integrity* is now with us. It is weak. It is finely balanced in the face of huge competing pressures. It is still hugely dependent on farmer cooperation; their ecological understanding and commitment; excellent project managers with vision; knowledge of ecological functioning and huge powers of persuasion; and a lively negotiable budget. It will also require sensitive cooperation between planning authorities, environmental custodial bodies and nongovernmental wildlife and recreational charities. The exciting sense is that this kind of organizational fusion is beginning to be established.

Chapter 4 is also helpful here. Penker points to a number of hybrid arrangements, notably around ecotourism, local food enterprise and the marketing of particular historical landscape features. This is also beginning to occur in the UK, though the experience is at an early stage.

These are still not common arrangements. Still the best bet is the ESA/SAC. But, as mentioned already, they exist in very small pockets of Europe. And they are beginning to wane. The budgets for ESA are dropping, project officers are being moved on and made redundant, landowners are becoming restless and do not want to commit themselves to ten year agreements or more. Ten years as an 'opt in-opt out' covenant is too minimal for establishing and maintaining sustainably ecologically functioning landscapes. Yet few landowners are willing to commit their land to longer periods of management obligation unless the terms of such landscape agreements address the uncertainties of reliable income that any owner will reasonably expect.

This is a critical point. There is no clearly defined property right in a socially maintained landscape. The onus of management remains with the occupier or owner. There are few compulsory arrangements to precise management measures. Certainly it is not yet legally possible for a landowner to be required to be consistent with neighbours in managing for an ecosystem function overall. Even the Water Framework Directive, coming into force in the EU in 2007, does not mandate compatible farm to farm, land to land coordination of water resources. So the tools are feeble, and the funds for encouraging voluntary compliance are insufficient and short term. Yet there is also the work of Rose (1994) suggesting that US land property rights can extend to a social-ecological obligation in ecosystem functioning and species protection. Similarly, Penker hints that a public right over private land ownership is being drafted, though by informal encouragement, rather than by formal legal means (Chapter 4).

So we are currently in a dilemma. The early promise of whole landscape care is falling away. There has been no progress over the precise coordination of a private land property right and a public interest in permanently sustaining landscapes and ecosystem services. Funds are drying up and may not be replenished. Above all, there is no appropriate landscape right in functioning ecosystem services.

POSSIBLE WAYS FORWARD

We face an insecure ecological age. Climate change is real and unavoidable. All the signs are that biodiversity as we know it in critical protected areas will not be maintained in a climate changing world. Even if buffer zones for the key sites are also included, and assuming some form of miraculous landowner compliance, it is extremely unlikely that future biodiversity and ecosystem services can be maintained and enhanced. Yet this is an EU policy imperative for 2010 and beyond.

What will be needed to meet the EU commitment to halting and reversing biodiversity loss and to enhancing ecosystem services by 2010?

1. *There will need to be a fresh approach to a joint property right that links public interest in sustainable landscape care to the private interest and managing land.* At present this is still a distant prospect. Land law theory and practice have not evolved to bring such an arrangement about.

This raises the need for land lawyers and public interest NGOs to work together with the planners and the custodial agencies to establish a new form of private–public covenant for the landscape. Such a covenant will require the kind of blend of incentives and regulatory controls that bind the landowner to stewarding the ecosystem services of the land via informed agreements and improved understanding of the ecology and landscape amenities involved.

To do so will require visions and scenarios of how sustainable landscapes might look, under various conditions of management. For example, upland boggy areas may be safeguarded for floodwater absorption. Soft sandy soils may be seeded or planted with low growth grasses or heather to establish zones of soil stability during periods of intense rainfall. It is even possible that such arrangements could be paid for in part by water companies, whose cleanup costs would be lowered by reducing damaging soil erosion. Indeed, new areas of heath for soil stabilization could become the next phase of mature heath in two generations' time, when climate change may preclude existing heaths from being as biodiverse as they are at present.

It is worth noting that Wessex Water Company in the UK has begun a trial experiment with four neighbouring farmers just to try out the economic gains of better soil management from a small part of functioning catchments. Intriguingly, the scheme may fail because the landowners need more assurance of their property freedoms so that they are not locked in by long-term agreements over which their descendants might have no authority. Hence there is an urgent need for a sensitive and careful scrutiny of the changing mix of public–private property rights.

All this will mean that credible scientific guidance must be available as to what will be needed to maintain soil, water, ecosystem services and biota in integrating wholes. That science base is not yet in place. A number of trial zones should be designated and viable; at least the first cut of science analysis should be put into place. Such zones might involve catchments, special landscapes (e.g. heath lands, wetlands and coastal margins), green zones (for community care of robust wildlife) and linking corridors and green buffers.

These should form the basis of a special designated zone for the next generation. Such a designation would be something like a *sustainable rural landscape*. To make this internationally viable, this would need the agreement of a wide number of interested parties. In the UK the Sustainable Farming and Food Commission is investigating such a concept. It would bring in functioning ecosystem services, enhanced biodiversity, the protection of heritage features, public access especially by nonmotorized means, local food sourcing for local shops and restaurants and more.

There is also a need to work with landowners and their offspring to enable all to see the scope for managing whole sustainable landscapes as an ecological, social and spiritual opportunity. This is beginning to emerge through adventurous school field units, adopt-a-landscape programme and the use of computer simulations of landscape through lenses of ecological integrity. Landscape scenarios using plausible image photography will grow in significance as ecosystem service safeguard becomes on increasing policy relevance.

In this connection, it is interesting to report that the Millennium Ecosystem Assessment has embarked on a major programme of capacity building and education to enable all manner of users to appreciate the role of sustainable rural landscapes for ecological, social, economic and spiritual purposes.

All of this hinges on three overarching conditions:

- There needs to be some agreement over what is a 'sustainable whole landscape'. This will require a blending of environmental science of water, soil and landscape care coupled with robust interpretations of integral habitats and species integration sites, to intensive new forms of biodiversity to be created to form new hybrid habitat sites alongside current protected area boundaries. This holistic science of 'total care' needs to be credible, with clear indications of what costs may be involved (soil loss; clogging of drains; culverts; loss of particular label when a landscape identity is damaged).
- Some form of public–private hybrid property right needs to be established that provides an incentive for landowners to cooperate across boundaries, and which provides a long-term financial guarantee of subsidy for a 'lower

external costs' landscape stewardship outcome. This will mean that ecologists and economists will have to combine to place gains and losses on 'good' compared to 'bad' landscape care.

- A mechanism for land owner-occupier support for such an arrangement. This could come via cross-compliance arrangements linked to EU financial farm payments. Or it may engage via special incentives for ecosystem based landscape covenants. The Austrian experience implies that this notion is beginning to become concrete (Chapter 4).

2. *Stepping stones for ecological and species pathways are also becoming better recognized on a basis for joint public–private property partnerships.* Species that have to migrate in order to tolerate climate change will need breathing space. It is likely that such corridors and patches will have to be more ubiquitous than previously imagined. This is partly because the state for 'whole landscape science' is still ill developed, and partly because nobody really knows what climate change stresses will be like for particular species and habitats. So we will have to play safe and prepare the breathing space across a range of locations, including the micro space in urban and rural settlements. All of this will require a fresh approach to public–private property rights and new forms of management agreement tried out on an experimental basis.

This is the role of a new agency in England called Natural England.[2] This body is typical of the hybrid organization discussed in the Introduction to this volume. It emerged as an amalgam of three loosely connected delivery agencies. There were the wildlife/species conservation role of English Nature, the public enjoyment landscape planning role of the Countryside Agency, and the agri-environmental payment scheme and advisory functions of the Rural Development service. Put these together and Natural England is born. Its remit is to recognize that natural ecosystem functions should be better understood and appreciated, given both economic and spiritual value, and designed into healthy living and landscape planning.

It is early days to forecast just how well Natural England will perform its functions in its new hybrid guise. The initial signs are not good. Reorganization is cumbersome and very unsettling for employees. The budget is reduced so existing commitments are cut, though there are funds for new, bright and innovative ideas. Yet the private sector is beginning to see the merits of a process that values landscape ecological and aesthetic integrity. Already the planners and road designers can see a case for protecting otherwise damaging soil erosion and wild flooding. The private water companies can see a case for reducing the costly removal of sediment and pollutants from their water sources.

There are also some mighty economic advantages. Natural England will explicitly be working with the major NGO wildlife groups to finance the establishment of large new areas of special ecological, recreational and economically advantageous areas. One example is the 'Fen Water-park' concept.

This will link eight existing and fragmented wetlands, owned and managed by different constellations of organizations, into a single fenland park in eastern England. The aim is to recreate genuine wetlands in a former fen landscape, and to link these to new housing and community developments, as well as to cycling and walking activities for residents and visitors.[3]

3. *It is likely that local food production, increasingly based on sustainability lines, will become more central in policy terms.* This will draw in the retailers and the food processors. There is an emerging discussion on the scope for identifiable local food supply and distribution chains, led by the consumer movement and being considered by the supermarkets and associated outlets. Admittedly this is still early days. The means of guaranteeing suitable food for quality and quantity from local supplies with emerging cooperative production means are variable and patchy. Much has to be done to bring sustainable and nutritious food into the retail chains. But once again the public–private property right of coherent, ecosystem service protecting landscapes will have to evolve if this kind of initiative is really going to take root. The idea is being actively considered by the UK Food and Farming Commission and can be followed up on the website of the Food Climate Research Network at the University of Surrey.[4]

The localization of food has a number of hybrid features about it. This is designated to reduce the carbon consequences of moving food around, from source to processor, to retailer to consumer. It is aimed at encouraging local enterprise and landowner initiative via the formation of cooperatives marketing identifiable food via particular 'labels'. Thus the sustainable landscape could become commoditized as a private market product that is sold on the basis of the joint public–private 'sustainability right'. There is also a commitment to sustainable rural communities[5] and to the notion of more cohesive local social and economic enterprise in small towns and villages.[6] All of this combines local food sourcing to local retailing and to the notion of sustainable whole landscapes.

OUTLOOK

Joining the public–private property right, via some sort of arrangement, for landscape sustainability is undoubtedly necessary. Such a novel legal arrangement cannot be tackled by force. It will involve the opening up of creative experiments, building upon sciences' strong sustainable landscape assessments, and bringing the landowner, land planner, land custodian and consumer and retailer all into a common endeavour. Landscapes will become social as well as ecological entities. And there should be a food-drink 'logo' for sustainable landscape sourcing and delivery. All this is being discussed. The momentum is there. But it will involve the kind of experiments that this volume of interesting and exciting essays is advocating.

In this exciting sense, the concepts discussed in the Introduction relate to decentralization, devolution, privatization, partnerships, participation and labelling all together. What is particularly pertinent is the merging of a *concept*, namely sustainable landscape care, via a *process*, namely smaller scale, participating involvement and creative choice making, with a new form of *hybrid property covenant*, namely some sort of voluntary land to land cooperative arrangement that is successful because it is socially valued, ecologically vital and commercially viable. We are not there yet, but there is undoubtedly a general sense of direction.

NOTES

1 These reports are all available on the website of the Millennium Ecosystem Assessment, www.millenniumassessment.org.
2 See www.naturalengland.org.uk.
3 For more information on the Wet Fens Partnership, see www.environment-agency.gov.uk.
4 See www.fcrn.org.uk.
5 See www.defra.org.uk.
6 See www.neweconomics.org.

REFERENCES

EC (European Commission) (2006) *Communication on Biodiversity Action Plan*, EC, Brussels
Lovelock, J (2006) *The Revenge of Gaia*, Penguin Books, London
O'Riordan T, Fairbrass, J, Welp, M and Stoll-Kleemann, S (2002) 'The politics of biodiversity in Europe' in O'Riordan, T, Stoll-Kleemann, S (eds) (2002) *Biodiversity, Sustainability and Human Communities: Protecting Beyond the Protected*, Cambridge University Press, Cambridge, pp115–141
Pretty, J (2004) *Agri-Culture: Reconnecting People, Land and Nature*, Earthscan, London
Rose, C (1994) *Property and Persuasion: Essays on the History, Theory and Rhetoric of Ownership*, Westview Press, Boulder, San Francisco, Oxford
Stoll-Kleemann, S (2001) 'Reconciling opposition to protected areas management in Europe: The German experience', *Environment*, vol 43, no 5, pp32–44

Outlook: New Publics and Property Rights

Thomas Sikor

This book is about the relations between public and private in resource governance, as elaborated in the Introduction. Insights from public and private practices in resource governance indicate that we should no longer think of the distinction between public and private as a grand dichotomy between state and market. Instead, we need to recognize that there are multiple distinctions underlying the separation between public and private. It is useful to distinguish between public and private, but we may be better off thinking in the plural: about *publics* and *privates*. We need to complement the liberal-economistic distinction between state and market with at least two further distinctions: between political community and the particular spheres of social life, and between the socially visible and the personal.

These insights challenge us to recognize the presence of multiple publics in resource governance. There is the public represented by the state, which is the kind of public that we are most familiar with. Yet the state is juxtaposed by at least two other types of publics that are less familiar to us and thus easily overlooked. There is also a type of public in the sense of the political community, going beyond the confines of the state. In addition, there are publics in the sense of the socially visible, which is different from both state and political community. Consequently, it is no longer useful to think of public in resource governance as a singular entity. Resource governance consists of many publics, including those rooted in the state and 'new' publics.

The present chapter concludes this book with some observations on contemporary property rights. The focus is on property rights because we consider them key elements in resource governance. In addition, public and private are fundamental parameters in our debates and actions as regards property rights to natural resources. Just recall the extensive discussions on the relative merits and problems of private versus public ownership in many policy fields. Should the state acquire ownership over valuable biodiversity sites or leave the management of land in protected areas under private ownership? Should the state retain direct control over forest or privatize property rights to forestland? Should irrigation water and infrastructure be in public or private ownership? Questions like these have occupied us again and again in debates about resource governance and actions in favour of sustainable resource use.

This chapter does not answer any of these questions, as it does not seek to develop policy recommendations or other normative statements about what property rights *should* be. The chapter instead offers an interpretation of ongoing changes in property rights to natural resources in practice. It seeks to develop new insights into the nature of contemporary property rights, corresponding to the main intent of this book – reflection. If there are multiple publics, the chapter argues, then there are not only states but also 'new' publics that sanction property rights to natural resources. Everyday practice in resource governance indicates that people recognize property rights endorsed by various kinds of political communities and social visibilities in addition to the state.

New publics: Overlapping, incorporeal and dynamic

Yet before we turn our attention to property rights, let us recapitulate some key insights on the nature of the new publics. A first important insight is that publics – old and new – often overlap in practice. Publics overlap because they tend to exist simultaneously. Moreover, publics may be closely interwoven in practice, as the underlying distinctions are not unrelated. As neat as the underlying distinctions between public and private are, these distinctions are diagnostic and do not translate into clear boundaries in practice. Therefore, it may be difficult for us to differentiate publics in practice. For example, members of the state are often primary actors in the political community and may even act public in all three senses at the same time: as representatives of the state, as members of the political community and in a socially visible manner.

The overlapping nature of new publics becomes evident in various contributions to this book. A particularly clear illustration emerges in the analysis of media reporting conducted in Chapter 6. Kleinschmit and Krott find that many actors cited in German and international media are from central government agencies. The government officials, therefore, may act publicly in all three dimensions simultaneously: they may speak as a representative of the state; they may participate in debates within the broader political community; and they may attain social visibility through the coverage in the media.

Second, the new publics tend to be less corporeal than the state in practice. They do not possess the physical structures and crystallized orders that make the state tangible to us. There are no 'community offices' representing political communities. Nor do we find 'visibility courts' issuing rulings on what is and is not socially visible. There are, of course, numerous organizations linked to political communities and socially visible spaces. For example, NGOs contribute to and reflect the formation of political communities. Similarly, the media are major actors that influence and determine what is socially visible. Yet, neither NGOs nor media constitute new publics on their own; rather, new publics remain incorporeal in practice.

The intangible nature of new publics becomes apparent in the discussion of food risk management in Chapter 9. Renn starts from the observation that the production, processing, distribution, consumption and disposal of food involve diverse risk situations. The risk situations call for three different types of procedures for decision making. The state and food industries can collectively deal with decisions under certainty. In contrast, other decisions call for their resolution in forums corresponding to new publics. Renn argues that decisions under risk need to include the stakeholder organizations to represent the political community affected by the particular problem. Decisions under ignorance or ambiguity need to involve quasi groups and nonorganized voices in response to the social visibility of the problem at stake. In Renn's proposal for risk management, therefore, we find reference to all three kinds of publics. In addition, we recognize the difficulty in the practice of making socially visible decisions – that is, in consideration of this type of new public. These incorporeal publics are not organized or readily identifiable, in turn calling for flexible approximations in practice.

Third, in practice the new publics are likely to be more dynamic than the state. They seldom convey the lasting presence and historical continuity that we associate with the state in many parts of this world, particularly in Europe.[1] New publics emerge and vanish in response to changes in societal concerns. In fact, much of our advocacy and everyday activism in resource governance follows the aim of promoting new publics or modifying existing ones. We call attention to new issues in resources management. We advocate new ways to deal with those issues, seeking to shift the respective roles of various actors. We demand safeguards for the protection of wider societal interests against the interests of individual resource users. In this way, we are constantly making, remaking and unmaking new publics.

The dynamic nature of new publics is evident in Chapter 7 dealing with the emergence of two bioenergy clusters in Austria and Germany. Both clusters include the classic actors in resource governance: various units of the state and market actors. Nevertheless, the cluster in the Austrian town of Güssing developed more rapidly than the cluster in the German case. In addition, bioenergy development began earlier and took a more diversified form in Güssing. Plieninger et al suggest that this was because Güssing's bioenergy cluster developed from the bottom up on the basis of the local community. The community provided the social foundations for a cooperative running a small esterification plant for rapeseed oil and for a network of state and nonstate actors to construct a CHP plant based on wood chips supplied by a local association of forest owners. Moreover, Güssing received widespread attention as 'Austria's first energy autarkic town', making Güssing's success in bioenergy development visible far beyond the confines of the state and local community. The permanence of the new publics behind Güssing's success, however, is still in question. The social visibility is likely to evaporate quickly as other bioenergy clusters vie for a spot in the social limelight.

Thus, new publics are overlapping, incorporeal and dynamic in practice. What does this imply for property rights, which are important elements in sustainable resource governance? This question occupies the remainder of the chapter. We begin our investigation with a brief review of the property concept.

Property: A simple analytical framework

We use the term *property* in many different ways. In everyday speech, we tend to employ it in reference to things. For example, we consider the house we have purchased as 'our property'. In academia, property is a concept popular in numerous disciplines, including anthropology, economics, environmental studies, law, political science and sociology. In addition, some long-standing scholarly traditions have utilized the notion of property in a normative manner, connecting property rights with economic growth, social equality, political democracy, environmental sustainability and the like. Consequently, 'property as a concept has become loaded down with a heavy freight of political and ideological baggage' (Benda-Beckmann et al, 2006a), which has often resulted in confusion, as people tend to have different notions of property.

Hence, there is a need for a simple analytical framework that helps us talk about property rights to natural resources. We can find such a framework in the work of Franz and Keebet von Benda-Beckmann; one that works in a wide variety of empirical settings and is free of cultural and ideological assumptions.[2] As the Benda-Beckmanns phrase it, property is about relationships among social actors with regard to objects of value. Property relations involve different kinds of social actors, such as people, companies and social groups. These social actors are linked by social relationships, which are often conceived in terms of property rights. The social relationships relate to different types of objects considered to be of economic or cultural value. For example, we can speak of certain people – the owners of agricultural land in this case – having property rights to the fruits of their land and establishing a relationship between themselves and others.

Another important aspect of property is that it involves 'bundles' of rights (Ciriacy-Wantrup and Bishop, 1975). The metaphor of bundles infers that there is no singular right to a thing. On the contrary, things fall under many different kinds of rights. In the example of land, there are diverse rights connected with it, such as the right to harvest its products, the right to walk on it, the right to decide about its use for agriculture or residential development, the right to sell it and so on. The metaphor also tells us that ownership, which plays such a central role in our vocabulary and thought, is a rather particular constellation of property rights, as it 'bundles' a large range of rights to a thing in the hands of a single actor. In fact, ownership has become more the exception than the rule with respect to natural resources in practice, as expanding legislation and regulation have increasingly limited the autonomy of owners (Benda-Beckmann et al, 2006a).

Third, property rights exist not only at the level of laws and regulations but also in cultural norms and social values, actual social relationships and property practices. As the Benda-Beckmanns suggest, the notion of property rights is an important element in ideologies or cultural understandings. Property rights receive extensive attention in legal systems. They also manifest themselves in actual social relationships about concrete property holders and concrete property objects. Finally, property rights are the subject of everyday practices. The distinction between these four 'layers' is an important point because it forces us to look beyond legislation when we examine property rights. We need to distinguish deeply engrained beliefs about property, such as the notion of private land ownership, from actual legislation – i.e. the many laws and regulations limiting the autonomy of 'landowners'. We also need to differentiate between legislation and actual social relationships and practices; in other words, what takes place in practice may be quite different from what the law stipulates.

This leads us to our last observation about property rights. They are highly dynamic, as property practices constantly create, strengthen, modify, weaken and obliterate property rights at the social, legal and normative levels. The practices are of two types, as the Benda-Beckmanns note. The first concern practices with abstract categories of property rights. These practices occur when people discuss categorical definitions of property holders, objects or relationships, such as when lawmakers debate on a new regulation limiting landowners' autonomy. Practices of the second type are those by which concrete actors deal with concrete property objects. These practices occur as part of everyday life, as when people use, sell or borrow a thing or dispute concrete rights to the thing. For example, a landowner may plant a new industrial crop on land previously used for grain cultivation. The point is that both practices make property very dynamic. Property as an analytical concept is thus different from how we think about property as a law separate from society. Property is an integral part of everyday practice and a part of broader economic, political and cultural changes.

The creation of property by way of legal debate and everyday practice becomes especially evident in Chapter 2 on devolution in Bulgaria's irrigation sector. Theesfeld shows that property rights to water infrastructure are rapidly changing, not only because of legislative reform but also due to new practices in Bulgaria's water sector. The legislation initially mandated a transfer of medium-scale infrastructure from the state to farmer associations and municipalities as part of the privatization process. A few years later, Bulgarian legislators provided farmers with the legal opportunity to gain 'ownership rights' to internal canal systems if they organized themselves into associations. At the same time, actual practices reconfigured property rights to water infrastructure. Some farmer associations and municipalities claimed control over internal canals, others did not. Thieves seized some valuable technical equipment in outright looting. State officials were not ready to give up their control over water infrastructure. They engaged in a variety of practices to change property relationships at concrete and categorical levels. They failed to endorse requests for the transfer of ownership rights. They also lobbied for changes in the legislation that expanded their rights over water infrastructure. The resulting property rights in practice were a far cry from what Bulgarian lawmakers had written into the law.

PROPERTY RIGHTS AS COMBINATIONS OF PUBLIC AND PRIVATE

Property rights are always combinations of public and private. Even though we tend to think in the opposite binaries of public and private ownership, property rights always include public and private elements. The reason is that the bundles include control rights and use rights. As noted by Franz von Benda-Beckmann (1995), 'in all societies there is some differentiation... between rights to control, regulate, supervise, represent in outside relations, and allocate property on the one hand, and rights to use and exploit economically property objects on the other'. This distinction between control and use rights connects with our distinction between public and private. Control rights reside with public authority, while use rights belong to the sphere of private interactions. Public authorities, such as the nationstate, perform control rights by enforcing use rights, making rules about the exercising of use rights and resolving disputes about that exercise. More broadly, public authority sanctions use rights in the sense that the application of use rights requires the (actual or potential) performance of control rights.[3]

Unfortunately there is a long tradition of ignoring public elements in property rights in our scholarship and common thought. The main concern in research on economics and related fields has been with private use rights, leading many of us believe that property rights are without public elements (Benda-Beckmann, 1995). This exclusive concern with private use rights also underlies the common distinction between private, common and state property as the major types of property rights.[4] According to this classification, all kinds of property rights fall under one of the three master categories. The value of the classification is highly dubious in general (Benda-Beckmann et al, 2006a). It is useless for our purposes because the classification suggests that property rights can be *either* public *or* private. The classification obfuscates the presence of public control rights in all bundles making up property rights.

Although all property relationships are combinations, the balance of public control rights and private use rights demonstrates significant variation. On the one end of the spectrum, we observe property constellations that grant extensive private rights. In other words, the sticks in the bundle held by private actors are significant, and the bundle held by public authority small in such property relationships. Yet even in situations that we have come to identify as real world incarnations of private ownership, public authority retains some control rights over the exercise of 'ownership rights'. Just imagine what would happen if we let our children play with the horn of our privately owned car in a quiet residential neighbourhood on a Sunday morning. Or if we decide to exercise our 'ownership rights' by testing out our car's maximum speed on an inner city street. Moreover, even in the absence of any restrictions due to control rights, the exercise of private use rights requires the (potential or actual) exercising of control rights by the public authority. How could we exercise private ownership rights if there were not even public understanding in support of private ownership, and without thieves and robbers risking the ire of public authority?

On the other end of the spectrum, we see property relationships that accord significant control rights to the public authority. In these relationships, the bundles of use rights to a particular resource are small, and the bundle of control rights held by the public authority large. Yet once again, even in situations we commonly classify as public ownership, property relationships combine public control rights with private use rights. Let us take protected areas as an example. In Chapter 5 Ring notes that the managers of protected areas in Brazil enjoy significant property rights to the land. Not only do the rights accorded to them by national legislation vary, but they also display significant variation in actual management practices. This even applies to protected areas managed by state units, as private use rights and public control rights reside with different units of the state. Even though the state holds both control and use rights, it is still useful to distinguish between control and use rights as they belong to different spheres of action – public and private. The distinction applies in the case of state managed protected areas as much as in the case of reserves managed by NGOs, companies or individual landowners.

We learn from the preceding paragraphs that all property rights combine public and private elements. Therefore, we should not be concerned with the question of whether a resource is under private or public ownership – or some joint public/private ownership. What we should be interested to know is the balance of public control rights versus private use rights. The crucial point is that property always requires the presence of a public authority to sanction private rights. It is the nature of that public authority and the scope of its control rights that matter.

PROPERTY AND MULTIPLE PUBLICS

Moreover, we learn from research on legal pluralism that multiple constructions of property rights exist in numerous situations. In plural legal situations, there is no singular system of property rights, but there are multiple overlapping rights systems. Research on legal pluralism initially focused on developing countries, as the concurrent existence of different legal systems – state law, customary law and religious law – was apparent there. Nevertheless, research now examines plural legal constellations in all kinds of settings, including industrialized countries of Europe and North America. It demonstrates that the presence of multiple overlapping legal systems is a common feature in all societies (Benda-Beckmann et al, 2006b).

In plural situations, legal constructions may duplicate, triplicate and so on the definitions of property rights (Benda-Beckmann, 1995). This multiplication affects all three components of property relations. Legal systems may possess various definitions of the actors recognized to participate in property relations. For example, indigenous groups may be considered actors entitled to hold property rights in one system but not another. Legal systems may also treat the same resources as different property objects. One legal system may define the genetic codes of food crops as property objects, while the other system may not accord that status to them. Finally, legal systems may define different kinds of property relationships. Some systems may accord the holders of private rights to land very broad, ownership like bundles of rights, while others only grant them very limited rights. Or, some systems may endow public authority with strong control rights over land, while other systems may restrict public control rights to a small set.

Yet legal systems not only display different constructions of property rights, they also tend to be connected with different bodies of public authority. As a consequence, plural legal situations tend to be associated with the presence of multiple public authorities sanctioning property rights. These typically – but not necessarily – include nationstates, which occupy themselves with the definition, enforcement and arbitration of statutory rights. In addition, we may observe the operation of transnational agreements and organizations as these sanction rights to endangered species and indigenous groups – to name just a few of the countless areas subject to transnational legal norms. Furthermore, village communities and kinship groups construct and enforce customary rights. These are mere examples of the broad spectrum of public authorities sanctioning property rights.

The presence of multiple public authorities is a key theme running through the contributions to this book. Let us take a closer look at two examples from a developing and an industrialized country. Chapter 1 looks at rights to timber in Indonesia, a country characterized by very distinct legal systems. In Indonesia, customary law has long been recognized by the colonial and independent state as coexisting with statutory law. The concurrent existence of the two legal systems also plays into the negotiation of timber rights examined by Wollenberg et al. Local residents claim rights to timber, basing such claims on statutory and customary law. Their claims not only appeal to the state in the form of the district government as the public authority sanctioning statutory law, but also seek endorsement by a variety of local communities, customary leaders and newly established ethnic associations who make up the public authority sanctioning customary law.

Portugal also has multiple bodies of public authority that sanction property rights, as discussed in Chapter 3. In the 1980s, civilians' water rights in the Algarve seemed to be endorsed by two kinds of public authority. On the one hand, local municipalities watched over the construction of the water infrastructure and distribution of available water. On the other hand, many took their rights 'into their own hands' and dug wells informally. The widespread occurrence of these wells suggests that this practice was considered legitimate, enjoying the backing of the local community. Twenty years later, in the early 21st century, the publics present in the Algarve's water sector have changed radically, as demonstrated by Thiel. The national government has gained control over water provision from the municipal governments and put regional agencies in charge. In addition, Portugal entered the EU in 1986. Accession to the EU involved the transposition of numerous European directives into Portuguese legislation. Moreover, even after formal transposition, Portuguese NGOs and a business association sued the Portuguese state with reference to European directives. There was no singular legal system and public authority defining water rights in the Algarve. Local customs, statutory law and EU norms provided different legal constructions of property rights sanctioned by multiple bodies of public authority.

PROPERTY RIGHTS AND THE NEW PUBLICS

This brief excursion into legal pluralism provides us with important clues for our interest in the implications of new publics for property regimes. We find that the publics sanctioning property rights are manifold in number. If this is true, can we also conclude that those publics may be manifold in type along the three distinctions identified above? Can the publics sanctioning property rights include not only the state but also political communities and social visibilities?

Upon initial consideration, these questions appear to call for a clear 'no' in response. We are used to thinking of property rights as being sanctioned by the state. We believe that property rights require the backing of states or state like institutions, such as the EU or international courts. Our conviction harks back to a long tradition of social thought that equates public authority sanctioning property with the state (Geisler, 2006). Early thinkers in this tradition include John Locke, Lewis Henry Morgan and Karl Marx, among many others. They portray the state as the ultimate guarantee of property rights and understand the state as deriving a major share of its legitimacy from this function. The notion of the state as the sole enforcer of property rights has continued straight into the present era, as manifested in scholarly and policy literature (e.g. de Soto, 2000). In fact, much of our own advocacy aims to modify state law as a strategy for sustainable resource governance.

Upon further consideration, given the discussion of legal pluralism in the previous section, we may answer the above questions in the positive. We recognize that the state is not the only kind of public authority sanctioning property rights in practice. Actual property rights also depend on sanctioning by political communities. Let us take the example of rights to food quality (see Chapter 8 by Roosen). Some rights are backed by the state through legislation and standards. For example, the state issues regulations on what the livestock industry can use as animal feed, or when the industry has to keep poultry inside to avoid the spread of avian flu. This legislation serves to ensure consumer rights to safe meat. Other attributes of food quality, however, do not find consideration in state law. For example, consumer rights to local produce or organic food find the necessary support in labels and accreditation schemes administered by nonstate organizations. In practice we may have a right to organic or locally produced food – not by virtue of state law but because of the political communities existing around these concerns.

The discussion of rights to landscape in Chapter 4 brings home the same point. Penker finds a large range of public authorities sanctioning rights to landscape in Austria. These logically include the state, which guarantees rights to individual landowners, such as the general rights to manage the land and harvest its products, as well as rights to greater society. In fact, the presence of 900 agri-environmental regulations at the regional, national and supra-national levels of the state speaks to major state efforts to define the property rights of different parties. Nevertheless, the public authorities sanctioning rights to landscape also include the political community beyond the state, as illustrated by the various organizations that show concern for Austria's landscapes. These include local clubs, regional associations and (inter)national NGOs. Together they form a political community concerned with the preservation of Austria's cultural landscapes. Together with the state, this political community backs up property rights to cultural landscapes.

More broadly, the analyses in this book resonate with insights from burgeoning research on common property. Many of the common property regimes analysed in the literature are rooted in political communities. Among other things, these political communities – ranging from small, local communities to global society – deliberate, decide, assign, monitor, enforce and arbitrate the property rights of their members. In turn, members' property rights include a wide range of private use rights sanctioned by the political community (Schlager and Ostrom, 1992). Common property regimes thus attest to the presence of political communities sanctioning property rights in practice (Benda-Beckmann, 2000).

The two cases discussed above even suggest that publics constituted as social visibilities endorse property rights in practice. Although the thought is daring, our actual property rights seem to depend on what is socially visible and what is not. The two cases indicate how the influence of these publics may work. In the food sector, boycott calls are an important means by which people can influence what they are able to buy. A call to boycott genetically modified food, for example, may be sponsored by a political community, yet it is only successful if it becomes socially visible – i.e. the organizations promoting the boycott have to 'go public' with their concerns. If the call achieves a sufficient degree of social visibility (i.e. reaches a public), the call may be successful and motivate the industry to change its products. We can interpret this outcome as evidence that social visibilities can sanction property rights. A similar logic applies to fair trade campaigns, retail brands and industry labels, as they seek to affect people's property rights by changing social visibilities.

Similarly, Austrians' property rights to their cultural landscapes appear to derive not only from the state and political communities but also social visibilities. As discussed for the food sector, there are a variety of food labels promoted by natural parks and trademarks exercised by regional ecotourism initiatives in Austrian landscape governance. More importantly, as pointed out in Chapter 4, Austrians generally consider their landscapes highly valuable and among those assets of which they are most proud. They view landscapes as a feature of their national identity, rating their contributions to the quality of life higher than those of material living standards. These concerns for landscape stewardship have direct implications for the distribution of property rights to Austria's cultural landscapes. Their social visibility may sanction public control rights over landscapes that restrict the use rights of individual landowners beyond those imposed by the state and environmental community. Just imagine what would happen if Austria's farmers decided to plant rapeseed throughout the country.

NEW PUBLICS IN LEGISLATION

Not only states but also new publics may sanction property rights to natural resources. In their everyday practices, people recognize a broad range of property rights endorsed by various kinds of political communities and social visibilities. Moreover, these rights have found entry into debates about state law, as this final section argues. Lawyers and legal scholars recognize rights sanctioned by political communities in their dealings on natural resources, as those find acknowledgement in constitutions, laws and regulations making up statutory legislation. In addition, state law may even recognize rights endorsed by social visibilities.

It is not difficult to identify legal traditions that attest to the significance of property rights rooted in political communities. First, the legal scholar Carol Rose (1994) argues that the common laws of the UK and US have always recognized two forms of 'public property'. One of them is owned by the state, and the other one is under the control of 'society at large, with claims independent of and indeed superior to the claims of any purported governmental manager'. The latter form has found its expression in US law in the form of doctrines on 'public trust' in waterways and 'prescription' for roadways, in addition to repeated recognition of customary rights believed to precede statutory law. More recently, Rose surmises, US courts have extended this line of reasoning to include recreation as a new use, arguing in favour of public control over access to waterfronts. In other words, Rose discusses instances in UK and US law that acknowledge rights of the political community, rights that the state merely executes on behalf of the community. These rights may be individual rights to public resources, but they relate the public nature of those to the political community and not primarily the state.

Second, we find a similar distinction between the state and the political community in the land legislation of various countries. The Vietnamese constitution, for example, states that 'the people' have ultimate control over land, and that the Vietnamese state administers this right on behalf of them. In other words, the constitution separates the rights to land from the rights to things attached to the land, such as trees, agricultural crops or buildings, and the rights to minerals and other valuables underground. In addition, the holders of property rights to land do not receive ownership rights but so-called long-term use rights. The bundles of rights they hold are not fundamentally different from those enjoyed by so-called landowners in the EU, as they can manage the land within certain limits set by the state, enjoy the fruits of the land and transfer their use rights to others. Yet the Vietnamese constitution does not call them owners because key control rights to land reside with 'the people'.[5]

Third, there is a widespread movement in postcolonial countries to recognize the authority of customary leaders over land (Fitzpatrick, 2005). One government after another in Africa, Asia and Latin America has adopted legislative reforms that reorganize authority over land and associated natural resources in a fundamental manner. The governments institute new land laws that transfer authority over land not only from central government agencies to local level state authorities but also from the state to institutions representing various kinds of political communities outside the state. The land laws grant the institutions of political communities relative autonomy, defining the boundaries between statutory and customary law along territorial or functional lines. In this way, they seek to create spaces in statutory legislation for the exercise of public control rights by customary institutions – giving statutory recognition to political communities.

Finally, land legislation in the UK has come to recognize the significance of political communities. This becomes apparent if one compares the Town and Country Planning Act of 1947 with the Countryside and Rights of Way Act of 2000. The Act of 1947 restricted the development rights of landowners in an effort to safeguard broader societal concerns in land use. It did so by expanding public control rights over development and according them to the state. The 2000 Act pursued a similar goal – restricting the rights of landowners for the sake of greater social benefits – but proceeded in a different manner. The later act referenced public control rights to specific political communities with a concern for access to the countryside (Parker and Ravenscroft, 2001). The location of public control rights changed from the 1947 Act to the 2000 Act, from the state toward political communities.

Chapter 9 suggests an idea for a subsequent act. O'Riordan calls for a reform of property rights in an effort to link public interests in sustainable landscape care to private interests in managing land. He argues that state law should oblige landowners to steward the ecosystem services of the land. O'Riordan's proposal thus builds on the tradition of adjustments in statutory land legislation in reaction to changing public concerns in land management. Just as the British state modified property rights in 1947 and 2000, it may do so once more to include a covenant for sustainable land care. In addition, in the light of the 2000 Act, it may give a prominent role to the new organization Natural England in representing public interests in landscape care, as suggested by O'Riordan. This organization brings together the major governmental and nongovernmental organizations concerned with landscape care in England. Giving it a role in the designation of sustainable rural landscapes would imply further recognition of how political communities sanction property rights to natural resources in practice.

Finally, on a more speculative note, we may argue that rights sanctioned by social visibilities are finding entry into legislation. This idea is not as farfetched as it appears if we consider the growing number of international conventions dealing with 'cultural property'. They all seek to recognize and protect cultural rights as a type of property rights that does not derive from the state and may not be backed by a political community. The Convention of Biological Diversity, for example, adopted by the United Nations in 1992, calls upon signatory nations to 'respect, preserve and maintain knowledge, innovations and practices of indigenous and local communities embodying traditional lifestyles' in their efforts to protect and use biodiversity (Article 8.j). And yet, the notion of cultural property is not only making inroads into the field of biodiversity conservation. The notion of cultural landscapes (see Chapter 4) suggests that it is also becoming more popular in other resource policy fields. In the future, lawyers and legal scholars may well debate about property rights related to traditional lifestyles, cultural landscapes, food cultures and the like – that is, rights endorsed by social visibilities.

ACKNOWLEDGEMENTS

I thank Franz von Benda-Beckmann for his highly useful comments on this chapter.

NOTES

1   Obviously, the incidence of failing states and the presence of stateless places indicates that the permanence of the state in some parts of the world is nothing natural but due to particular historical conditions. See Chapter 1 for a case in which the state has established its presence relatively recently and in a rather fragile manner.
2   See Benda-Beckmann et al (2006a) for a recent discussion of the framework.

3   Western law commonly includes a part called 'public law' and another referred to as 'private law'. This distinction is different from the analytical distinction explored here. See Benda-Beckmann (2000) for further discussion of public law and private law.
4   Private property is also referred to as individual property.
5   The same rationale applies to landholding units of the Vietnamese state. Like other nonstate actors, they can only receive long-term land use rights as the state does not hold public control rights itself but merely exercises those on the behalf of 'the people'.

REFERENCES

Benda-Beckmann, F von (1995) 'Anthropological approaches to property law and economics', *European Journal of Law and Economics*, vol 2, pp309–336

Benda-Beckmann, F von (2000) 'Relative publics and property rights: A cross-cultural perspective' in Geisler, C and Danecker, G (eds) *Property and Values: Alternatives to Public and Private Ownership*, Island Press, Washington, DC, pp151–174

Benda-Beckmann, F von, Benda-Beckmann, K von and Wiber, M (2006a) 'The properties of property' in Benda-Beckmann, F von, Benda-Beckmann, K von and Wiber, M (eds) *Changing Properties of Property*, Berghan, New York, Oxford, pp1–39

Benda-Beckmann, F von, Benda-Beckmann, K von and Wiber, M (eds) (2006b) *Changing Properties of Property*, Berghan, New York, Oxford

Ciriacy-Wantrup, S and Bishop, C (1975) '"Common property" as a concept in natural resources policy', *Natural Resources Journal*, vol 15, pp713–727

de Soto, H (2000) *The Mystery of Capital: Why Capitalism Triumphs in the West and Fails Everywhere Else*, Basic Books, New York

Fitzpatrick, D (2005) 'Best practice options for the legal recognition of customary tenure', *Development and Change*, vol 36, pp494–475

Geisler, C (2006) 'Ownership in stateless places' in Benda-Beckmann, F von, Benda-Beckmann, K von and Wiber, M (eds) *Changing Properties of Property*, Berghan, New York, Oxford, pp40–57

Parker, G and Ravenscroft, N (2001) 'Land, rights and the gift: The countryside and Rights of Way Act 2000 and the negotiation of citizenship', *Sociologia Ruralis*, vol 41, no 4, pp381–398

Rose, C (1994) *Property and Persuasion: Essays on the History, Theory and Rhetoric of Ownership*, Westview Press, Boulder, San Francisco, Oxford

Schlager, E and Ostrom, E (1992) 'Property-rights regimes and natural resources: A conceptual analysis', *Land Economics*, vol 68, no 3, pp249–262

Index